Conflicting
ALLEGIANCES

24.99

Conflicting
ALLEGIANCES

The Church-Based University in a Liberal Democratic Society

Michael L. Budde
and John Wright, eds.

BrazosPress
Grand Rapids, Michigan

Published by Brazos Press
a division of Baker Publishing Group
P.O. Box 6287, Grand Rapids, MI 49516–6287
www.brazospress.com

Printed in the United States of America

Library of Congress Cataloging-in-Publication Data
Conflicting allegiances : the church-based university in a liberal Democratic society / (edited by) Michael L. Budde and John Wright.
     p.   cm.
  Includes bibliographical references.
  ISBN 1-58743-063-0 (pbk.)
    1. Church and college—United States. 2. Universities and colleges—United States—Religion. 3. Church colleges—United States. 4. Secularization—United States. I. Budde, Michael L. II. Wright, John Wesley. III. title.
LC383.C64 2004
378'.071—dc22   2004008731

Contents

Preface

Michael L. Budde

This volume represents what is sometimes called a "thought experiment"—that is, a systematic effort to construct informed speculation focused on something that does not yet exist. For many scholars, trained by disciplines grounded in the here-and-now of existing texts, data, institutions, and actors, thought experiments are both frightening and appealing.

They frighten scholars (who, let it be admitted, are not an especially courageous lot to begin with—few crises ever prompt cries of "Quick—get me an academic!") for several reasons. Focusing attention on what doesn't exist sometimes looks unprofessional, unless you do astrophysics (in which case it seems to be a requirement). It seems like a detour from generally accepted sorts of scholarly analyses. Perhaps most important, scholars are desperately afraid of looking foolish. Get beneath the surface ego of many academics and you will find unexplored layers of insecurity—degrees and publications are the armor protecting against the terror of being shown to know far less than one claims to have mastered.

On the other hand, for some scholars a properly constructed thought experiment holds considerable appeal. It holds out the promise of imagination unleashed, freed from the restraints of "ordinary science" (Thomas Kuhn's famous term for the day-to-day research that most scholars do most of the time). It gives permission to test new assumptions in place of tired but hitherto dominant ones, and it allows scholars to take intellectual risks by venturing into potentially uncharted territory. And if the process of thinking new thoughts is appealing to its originators, the possibility exists that its products may be appealing to others who receive them. Deep down, maybe even deeper than fear and insecurity, many scholars hope that their work may help make a new thing, a good thing, in the world. A captivating vision can sometimes lead others to join together to incarnate that vision.

In March 2002, a group of Christian scholars accepted an invitation to gather in San Diego for several days of dialogue and exploration on matters relating to Christianity and higher education. These scholars came from a variety of ecclesial traditions, from various sorts of academic institutions, and from a number of different scholarly fields. What made most of them accept the invitation was not the general topic—"Christianity and higher education" is a road so heavily traveled as to be tiresome to many. Nor, I suspect, was it just the prospect of a beautiful setting in a near-perfect climate (although one participant recounted his initial discernment as "Minnesota and snow in March vs. San Diego and sun in March"). Rather, what drew most of the participants (as well as contributors unable to attend) was the unusual nature of the assignment.

Our host, Professor John Wright of Point Loma Nazarene University, asked us to imagine some of the particulars of a new sort of Christian institution of higher learning. We were all familiar with the names, the books, the arguments that have made "Christianity and higher education" a cottage industry of conferences, workshops, foundation grants, and consultancies over the past few decades. Many of us were also fairly unimpressed by the trajectory and products of that industry to date—deriving, in large measure, from a set of powerful assumptions about what the church should be and what higher education must be. Wright's invitation asked us to step outside the limits of reformism—of paring down our analyses and recommendations to fit the politics and practices of existing Christian schools, Protestant and Catholic alike.

Instead, he asked us to start first with a robust notion of the church—as a distinctive people called into being by the Holy Spirit to continue the priorities and practices of Jesus Christ in the world—and to imagine new practices of scholarship, teaching and formation appropriate to the service of this discipleship-based vision of the church.

To avoid the prospect of every person designing an entire institutional architecture *ex nihilo,* Wright established a preliminary division of labor. Some of us would consider curricular possibilities (both within traditional disciplinary categories and across disciplines), others would reflect on various aspects of student and faculty life, and a few would attempt to gauge such a hypothetical institution's hypothetical impacts on debates and constituencies within higher education, the churches, and secular society.

As you will see, most contributors took Wright's invitation at its face and wrestled with the dual processes of setting aside settled understandings of what higher education should be in a Christian context, while simultaneously struggling to express what could more faithfully serve both church and world. As you will see, a minority of contributors judged their professional locations as being sufficiently open to new ways of church-academy interaction that they focused more on possible initiatives in existing institutions rather than outlining entirely new arrangements (and John Milbank—unable to join the San Diego meeting—sent an essay focused primarily on conceptual matters rather than on current or future institutional options). Rather than impose a rigid template on these contributors, we decided to let them stand as is—they will likely be helpful to many readers no matter the readers' appraisal of thought experiments in general. And given that at least one beneficial outcome of a thought experiment done well is to inspire new and more creative incremental changes in existing institutions, we see these contributions as of a piece with the rest of the volume, surface differences notwithstanding.

The observant reader will notice these surface differences arising between the terminology of "the church-based university," as in this book's subtitle, and "the ecclesially based university," as used in many essays throughout this book. Since English-speakers typically refer to Christian institutions as "church-related," "church-based," or some similar locution, we have retained "church-based" in the subtitle for immediate ease of communication. However, many of the authors of this book's essays (the editors included) believe that the issues and challenges facing Christian higher education are so deep and radical that the entire basis of Christian higher education needs to be recast and rethought. To prevent falling back into customary, but inadequate, ways of thinking, and to signal their conviction that Christian higher education needs a new (and at the same time, older) basis, several writers resort to the Greek and refer to "ecclesially based" universities or education. Think of this locution, if you will, as an alarm bell meant to keep writer and reader awake and alive to very different possibilities than we now encounter when we typically think of "Christian colleges" or "church-related universities."

The completion of such a project has many people to thank. The editors first wish to thank each of the contributors for devoting strong commitment to the project, interrupting their own individual research agendas to think about an institution that does not yet exist. The conceptuality of the project began to be worked out within the Southwest Region of the Rhodes Consultation on the Future of Church-Related Colleges and its participants. Richard Hughes, now of Messiah College, provided an excellent dialogue partner to refine the project in discussions that took place beginning on a bus ride to dinner in Sante Fe, New Mexico. Diane Winston, Stanley Hauerwas, and Rodney Clapp shared their wisdom along the way. Of course, we are very thankful for the financial support that allowed these conversations to take place: Steven Haynes and a special grant from the Rhodes Consultation on the Future of Church-Related Colleges; Michael Beaty and the Baylor Institute for Faith and Learning; and Patrick Allen, Provost at Point Loma Nazarene University. Ms. Darlene Gresh and Mrs. Pat Veynar cared for us in the logistics of our San Diego sojourn.

Finally, we wish to thank our hosts at Point Loma Nazarene University. When we out-of-town academics arrived on campus for our discussions with one another, we found ourselves working in an oceanside conference room with floor-to-ceiling windows—quite a change from the drab enclosures within which most academic meetings occur. Even more astounding was that our discussions were to be held before an audience—not a few other faculty members, but between 70 and 100 students, most of whom were present for every session over three days. The final surprise came when we found out that not only were these students present of their own accord (they were not there to satisfy a class requirement), but that they were there *during their spring break*. If we hadn't seen it with our own eyes, we might have thought somebody had imagined it as part of a thought experiment of an entirely different sort.

I.

Introduction

How Many Masters?

From the Church-Related to an Ecclesially Based University

John W. Wright

"No slave can serve two masters; for a slave will either hate the one and love the other, or be devoted to the one and despise the other." (Luke 16:13)
"In the eyes of government, we are just one race here: It is American."

—Antonin Scalia[1]

Colleges and universities form a final passage ritual for many young people in the U.S. as they make the transition from adolescence into adulthood. Recently, an article in the *Atlantic Monthly* chronicled the lives of students at Princeton University.[2] David Brooks found the students bright, amiable, and personally involved, yet developed the impression that "something is missing" (p. 54). Brooks interprets this something as a deficiency of character and virtue: "When it comes to character and virtue, these young people have been left on their own" (p. 53).

In one sense, Brooks presents a persuasive case. He notes the discomfiture of students talking about moral issues, how they transformed questions of morality into the language of policy.[3] He is even able to quote Princeton administrators who articulate that Princeton is not in the "moral character-building" business:

> "We've taken the decision that these are adults and this is not our job," Jeffrey Herbst says. "There's a pretty self-conscious attempt not to instill character." Herbst does add that students are expected to live up to the standards that apply to academic life . . . But in general the job of the university is to supply the knowledge that students will need to prosper, and, at most, to provide a forum in which they can cultivate character on their own. "This university doesn't orchestrate students' lives outside the classroom," says Princeton dean of undergraduate students, Kathleen Deignan. "We're very conservative about how we steer. They steer themselves." (p. 53)

"Moral character-building" is not part of the task of the contemporary university; morally the university grants space for individuals to exercise their own moral autonomy. The university exists to transmit the technical expertise for the future economic success of its students within the broader horizons of the nation and the world.

Upon reflection, however, both Princeton and even Brooks seem naïve. While Princeton may consciously attempt not to instill character, such a concerted attempt across a community most certainly forms the character of its members. Princeton communally forms the character of its students to believe that they are individuals with the power of their own self-determination—i.e., students have the ability to steer themselves. The community naturalizes a political order of a morally neutral, technical, public realm of knowledge and an individual realm of values. Morality belongs to the private realm of the individual, not subject to the communal oversight of the university.[4] Such an understanding fundamentally embodies liberal political presuppositions.[5] Princeton disciplines its students into a character made to assume and perpetuate the liberal democratic political order of the U.S. In this way Brooks is absolutely correct in stating, "Princeton doesn't hate America. It reflects America" (p. 54).

Of course Princeton is not the only university to discipline its students to function obediently within and for a liberal democratic state. Such a mission is presupposed and interwoven into the very fabric of the contemporary secular and state university. Yet such a mission becomes both more interesting—and more ambiguous—when we consider the history and present reality of church-related colleges and universities, a history in which Princeton once participated. Church-related colleges and universities have, at best, a checkered history within such a context. It is the purpose of this essay to interpret the history in light of the liberal democratic society of the U.S.

The Confines of the Liberal Democratic Society

The church-related university in North America has developed and existed within the social space provided by the liberal nation-state. While various and excellent histories of such institutions have been recently told, the overdetermination of these institutions by the liberal state has been largely, if not completely, neglected. The naturalness of the liberal society seems to form an unquestionable good that the church-related university must presuppose. Such a presupposition is not surprising given that American universities, church-related or otherwise, have always understood their fundamental mission as embedded within the larger polity of the contemporary liberal democratic nation-state.[6] As a result, these various studies have understood the culprit for the demise of these institutions' Christian mission to be within the institutions themselves. Such institutions, according to these histories, lose their connection to the church either in their own movements away from "conservative" theological commitments[7] or in their "pietism"[8] or in the uncritical embrace of a "two-sphere" understanding that removed religious interests from the primary academic mission of the universities.[9] The broader political context that encourages and enables such trends remains curiously unexamined.

The neglect of the liberal democratic context in which church-related universities have lived obscures important forces within their histories. Yet the embodiment of liberal democratic theory has not remained static within the history of the U.S.—nor is it static now. By tracing the main lines of liberal political theory, and a crucial twentieth-century shift within American liberalism, it is possible to understand more deeply how liberal polity challenges the ecclesial base of church-related colleges and universities by demanding that education serve the sovereignty of the liberal nation-state.

For heuristic purposes, it is possible to sketch the political/legal theory that has governed the life of the U.S. in very broad strokes. All forms of liberal polity are constructed on a simple but far-reaching presupposition. The fundamental tenet of liberalism asserts that humanity exists as autonomous, rational individuals who seek to pursue their own self-interests. The ability to engage in this pursuit is called freedom or liberty—a formal category of the will that possesses no specific content, except as it is filled by the individual's choice. Because individuals all pursuing their own self-interests would bring about social chaos, individuals voluntarily submit themselves to a sovereign government via the consent of the people (i.e, democratic elections). The state may then protect the individual's rights to pursue his or her own self-interest within the context of the broader majority will. The state, therefore, claims sovereignty in order to maintain a social environment for liberty, especially against outside forces (i.e., other nation-states or transnational religious groups) that would infringe upon the state's ability to ensure the freedom of the individual. The individual must exhibit loyalty to the state in exchange for the freedom and peace that the state grants the individual.

This is how classical liberal theory creates two different realms of existence for the human being: a public realm and a private realm. In exchange for arrogating absolute sovereignty to the nation-state, the state grants the individual uncoerced options in the private realm, options determined by the personal choice or values of an individual. Private pluralism then masks the allegiance that the polity of the liberal state requires:

> A pluralism of conceptions of the good is protected by the liberal State, but in fact this pluralism exists only at the private level. In the public sphere, the State itself is the ultimate good whose prerogatives must be defended coercively. As Ronald Beiner has shown, the liberal State is by no means neutral. It defends and imposes a particular set of goods—e.g., the value of the market, scientific progress, the importance of choice itself—which excludes its rivals.[10]

Despite this, or possibly because of it, the state itself is not to be trusted within what has come to be called classical liberalism. The democratic will of the people protects the individual against undue encroachment of the individual's liberty from the power of the state. Within classical liberal legal theory, as described by Stephen Carter, "governmental authority itself posed a problem for the freedom of the individual, and . . . the sovereign therefore had to be constrained, its powers divided."[11]

Classical liberalism was the predominant political theory within the U.S. during the first century and a half of its existence. It came to be embraced especially among the Protestant evangelical majority that maintained a cultural hegemony over most of the U.S. in the nineteenth and early- to mid-twentieth century. Through democratic processes, Protestants established a de facto civil religion, exercising power through their majority status according to Christian morality or values. Protestants maintained their power in isolation from Catholicism until American Catholicism adopted John Courtney Murray's system of accommodation of Catholicism to the liberal order.[12] For these agendas to succeed, however, both Protestants and Catholics had to abstract Christian morality or values from their ecclesial context in order to speak in what is called the public realm. The church existed in order to produce good citizens to serve the liberal democratic nation as determined by its majority. We now typically call this type of liberalism "conservative," and it remains endemic within certain forms of evangelical American Christianity.

From within this perspective, the church serves as the chaplain of the majority of those within the society to make sure that the society functions smoothly and morally. It presupposes that

> Christianity must be "useful" in order to be a legitimate player in our contemporary world. It must help people perform their duties as defined by the secular *status quo,* not from within ecclesial traditions unless the two are identical. In addition to enabling people to work within the existing order more efficiently, Christianity must also boost people emotionally and psychologically during stressful times, and must enable them to be good citizens, employees, consumers, patriots, and family members. Indeed, for Christianity to be relevant today, it must do for the whole of society what chaplains do in the armed forces—meet spiritual needs and personal crises, provide legitimation and explanation for the way things are, and generate loyalties to the collective and its purposes.[13]

Contemporary conservative Christianity, with its private, therapeutic, individual focus, has accommodated to a conservative liberal-democratic polity by making sure that the individual remains protected from encroaching claims of the state, except in cases of national defense, when it becomes the responsibility of the church to support military activity to protect the freedoms of individuals.

A problem developed, however, within this form of liberalism. The democratic will of the people, meant to protect the individual against the state, can just as easily be employed by the electoral majority to suppress the voices—and interests—of minorities within the society of the governed.[14] The will of the people can—and historically has—democratically disenfranchised select subgroups from the ability to pursue life, liberty, and happiness. The majority can thereby ensure control of state authority for the benefit of individuals who happen to belong to the predominant social group—in the U.S., historically white Anglo-Saxon (male) Protestant land owners.

As a result, classical liberalism became contested, weakened by incoherence within its own commitments. Embraced by the Christian majority, classical liberalism repressed minorities' ability to seek their own individual self-interests by means of the will of the democratic majority. Democracy ended up looking very undemocratic. As a result, an alternative type of liberal political/legal theory arose. Stephen Carter names this position "constitutional liberalism." In constitutional liberalism, the state seeks to advocate actively for the rights of all individuals, including members of minority groups, by "enabling all citizens to enjoy a set of rights both defined and enforced by the apparatus of the national government."[15] Government must ensure the rights of historically disempowered groups to pursue their own private values in their lives, especially when these values differ from those of the majority. The government must protect the personal privacy of each individual, even of those who hold alternative private values.

This understanding of liberal theory moved toward social embodiment beginning with Roosevelt's administration.[16] Since then, constitutional liberalism has become deeply encoded in American society, especially among certain minority and élite networks in the U.S. Constitutional liberalism markedly shifts the role of the state from its position within classical liberal thought. Within constitutional liberalism, the state is not something that the individual needs to be protected from; the state takes an active role in protecting individuals via national institutions (schools, courts, etc.) from the democratic will of the majority so that minorities can pursue their own self-interests as well. To preserve democracy, therefore, the state becomes very undemocratic, overturning the will of the majority for the society by an appeal to deeper liberal commitments to personal liberty, as encoded in constitutional documents. Baldly speaking, in classical liberalism, individuals are seen to need protection *from* the state to pursue their own interests; in constitutional liberalism, individuals are seen to need the protection *of* the state in order to engage in this pursuit.

This more recent type of liberalism is commonly called "liberal." Constitutional liberalism permits élites, within their own places of privilege, to embrace the poor and dispossessed while remaining within their own places of authority and power. These élites seek to use constitutional means to ensure that others are not excluded from power by the democratic will of the majority. As a result, from the perspective of the majority, democracy again looks extremely undemocratic. Such a liberalism has now come to be embraced by mainline American Christianity, especially within its academies and the élite denominational ruling bodies. Such groups legitimate their advocacy in the name of God's preferential option for those marginalized. Chaplaincy again results, but a different type from the therapeutic individualism of evangelical Christianity. Within mainline Christianity the church seeks to exercise its influence through its legal establishment of the rights of minorities to share power within a democratic society. By exercising influence within the power of the state, the church seeks to embrace justice—equal access to power for the pursuit of individual rights—for all within the society.

Both forms of legal theory, liberal and conservative, are forms of liberal democratic polity. Yet substantial differences emerge in their resultant embodiment—witness the long-waged "culture wars." A political/moral chasm has arisen in American society from the splitting of liberal political/legal theory into classical and constitutional forms.[17] Because both are positions within the liberal polity, movements occur from one position to another within groups and within the society at large. For a given individual, socio-economic status and power appear to correlate with these positions: a high-status individual is more likely to fall in the classical liberal camp, while individuals outside the circles of power are more likely to align with the constitutional liberal camp. The exception, of course, is the élite legal and educational institutions that have formed allegiances with constitutional liberalism in order to gain power within the society.[18]

Despite the turmoil such divisions cause within American society, more serious is how these different liberal commitments have become more deter-minative for Christians than the commitments arising out of baptism. New ecclesial divisions have arisen as they mimic these tensions within liberalism. Christian positions, on both the right and the left, become basically no dif-ferent from those of non-Christians; theological traditions split down the middle according to key issues manifesting this tension in types of liberalism. Within church-related universities, the "conservative/liberal" split within liberalism can divide the university faculty from its ecclesial constituency. Formed by an élite constitutional liberal milieu, faculty, especially in the humanities, envision a polity at odds with the ideal of those in the pews, those shaped by the old hegemony of the Protestant Christian past. Tensions between church and university arise because of the different types of liberal formation that occurs in different sections of the American society.

If the above analysis of the contours of American liberal democratic society is helpful, it can highlight several aspects of the church-related university in a liberal democratic society. First, it can help describe the social space offered to the church-related university by liberal polity—the rules that the liberal polity dictates for the university. Second, it can reveal historical social processes of secularization of church-related universities as they have operated within liberal political confines. Finally, it can explain the rapid demise of church-related universities in the transition from classical to constitutional liberalism and the recent resurgence of religious colleges in the accommodation of the church-related university within a constitutional liberal environment.

■ The Church-Related University within the Confines of the Liberal Democratic Society

To understand the profound coercive role that liberal polity has imposed upon the church-related university, it is helpful to trace the emergence of the modern liberal state and the concomitant creation of religion. William Cavanaugh has persuasively argued that "religion," as a generic category of a distinctive realm of human experience, arose with the emergence of the modern nation-state:

> religion as a transhistorical phenomenon separate from "politics" is a creation of Western modernity designed to tame the Church. Religion may take different cultural and symbolic expressions, but it remains a universal essence generically distinct from political power which then must be translated into publicly acceptable "values" in order to become public currency. Religion is detached from its specific locus in disciplined ecclesial practices so that it may be compatible with the modern Christian's subjection to the discipline of the State.[19]

By creating a realm called religion isolated from other concrete, disciplined communities, the emergent nation-state attempted to assure that the state controlled ultimate allegiances. As Cavanaugh writes, "Religion is no longer a matter of certain bodily practices within the Body of Christ, but is limited to the realm of the 'soul,' and the body is handed over to the State."[20] Christianity becomes disembodied, a name of a set of beliefs or a worldview, rather than a people existing through time and exercising control over each other's bodies. The state takes the role of the sole legitimate authority that decides the fate of actual human bodies. Indeed, the modern state may be defined by the successful "claim to the monopoly of the means of violence" over bodies within a certain territory.[21]

In liberal polity, religion does not belong directly in the public economic and political realm, but is a phenomenon that occurs primarily within individuals—in the private realm of personal freedom. Religion is a consumerist option for shaping individuals (Brooks' "character and virtue") that, once abstracted from its communal origins, then may and indeed must impact the public sphere, for this is the only sphere with meaning outside of the individual. Not only does education focus on knowledge derived from and for the public sphere, the public sphere remains the ultimate arbiter of the contributions that one might make to a greater good beyond oneself. Yet it is the public sphere that the state ultimately controls—by definition.

Within such political boundaries, the church-related university had limited options if it were going to operate within and for the liberal democratic society. It could remain strictly private by focusing on the religious experience of its students; it could argue for public consequences of particular private beliefs or values that groups had transmitted to individuals. A third option, however, provided the main path for the church-related university within classical liberalism: the church-related university attempted to shape individual student's morals, values, and/or character so that the student would go into the public realm with a purpose impacted by these personal ethics.[22]

By forming the moral character of each individual student to contribute to the liberal society, the church-related university and its sponsoring congregations could achieve some manner of power within the society. Within classic liberal democratic polity, the church-related university could exercise its role as the chaplain of the society through the ethical formation of its élite. Even in state universities, Christian values were abstracted from their ecclesial context in order to shape individual students as they passed through the university.[23] By shaping individual students' moral character, the church-related university contributed to the end of the liberal society at large. University education thus helped maintain the majority Protestant control of American society.

Such a strategy came at a cost. The moral teaching of the Christian tradition had to be abstracted from the church, the community in which its practices maintain their coherence. Under the guise of neutrality toward religion, the liberal-democratic structures of U.S. society actively undercut the long-term viability of church-related colleges and universities through very particular dynamics inherent within liberal polity.

By creating the realm of the private, autonomous individual and then placing religion within this realm, liberal theory separates Christianity from the communal base that renders it viable across time. Such a cultural landscape opens the possibility of the emergence and growth of new religious groups under individual entrepreneurial leadership. As the group grows, however, it must achieve broader social legitimacy if this growth is to continue—legitimacy that only the culture can give. A community can achieve this legitimacy by assuming a mediating function in which its members, especially those marginal to the society at large, are mainstreamed into the norms, practices, and institutions of the liberal democratic society. In this way the religious organizations place the individual's religious commitments within a framework conducive to the liberal society. Religion emerges as a market choice for the private, autonomous individual, a product distinct in some way from its religious institution/provider within a competitive religious free-marketplace. The religious institution that serves the society by supporting society's ends can enhance its product, and thus its market share, through the added social-economic benefits provided by societal upward mobility that participation in the religious institution can bring.[24] In the liberal democratic setting of the U.S., therefore, a church-related university existed as a voluntary association, a mediating organization or civil society—social networks that exist "'outside' the scope of the state."[25]

Such institutions function to relate individuals to the society's practices, norms, and institutions at large. As such, they play a vital role within the liberal society in constructing social capital, a role that liberal institutions themselves, grounded in individual self-interests, cannot provide.[26] Yet from the church's perspective, a certain critical problem arises. Within such a cultural framework, the church exists as a means to a greater end—the interests of the U.S. as a nation-state. This is a difficult stance for the church to take, since its mission, by its very nature, must deal with the ultimate end, the telos, of all human life. An orthodox Christian faith requires commitments to fellow adherents that transcend the narrow confines of a particular modern nation-state.

The church-related university in the U.S. was a welcomed accomplice as long as the European Protestant élite controlled the society at large. Such universities have compliantly and uncritically adopted a role as the mediator of societal norms, practices, and institutions provided by liberal democratic polity. In one sense, however, such institutions have no choice. The cultural structures actually impose this mediating function upon them if the institutions are to maintain social legitimacy. Without such legitimacy, the church-related university will be severely handicapped in its ability to preserve and attract adherents and resources.

Yet too much legitimacy also wounds the church-related university within liberal societies. When individuals reach a certain social status, often by means of such mediating organizations as a church-related university, they no longer need the mediating function that the church provides. The cultural arrangement subtly redirects the primary commitments of its leadership and leading members from the practices, norms, and institutions of the religious group to those of the liberal society. The individuals within the group may directly benefit from the larger societal power and interests that they now embody. The commitment to the particular mediating institution wanes. The church-related university loses Christian vitality as it is not able to generate sufficient economic and personal resources to keep the institution functional and competitive—within its particularity—as a church-related university. Within the structures of a liberal democratic society, a successful church-related university may ultimately work its way out of a job—it may abandon its distinctive Christian mission so that its members might participate directly in the benefits of the society at large. In some cases, it might even do this more efficiently as a secular institution, as that is the ultimate end, even if not stated, of its mediating role.

In this way, the liberal-democratic society rewards institutions that keep religion private except to initiate their members into the norms and practices of the society at large—places like Princeton today. In the same way, it will delegitimize church-related universities that create a public realm for individuals outside the norms, practices, and institutions of the society. For instance, education degrees must conform to standards the state sets in order to provide employment opportunities for graduates of a given institution—standards that often have implications outside the education department. Universities that will not conform by requiring classes in the history of Christian martyrdom instead of histories of the U.S. for secondary education would thus lose state accreditation. At the very least, liberal-democratic polities will demand that institutions translate their Christian commitments into liberal democratic language, de-emphasizing their theological convictions and ecclesiastical commitments.[27]

The liberal democratic society thereby constructs the cultural terrain in which Christian institutions may thrive—for a time. This thriving, however, demands the eventual assimilation of the particular Christian community into the general society, and the loss of the distinctive norms, practices, and institutions that grant such communities long-term viability.

Liberal democratic societies thus place church-related universities in a quandary. Church-related colleges and universities ostensibly seek to initiate their church's young members into the society while simultaneously maintaining their loyalty to their church. Yet it is the society that measures an educational institution's quality, granting educational legitimacy by evaluating the church-related university's ability to recruit and train students who can best participate and govern within the liberal societal structures—i.e., producing those who, if they have Christian commitments and convictions, have learned to keep such convictions private and personal in service of the liberal nation-state. Ultimately, the church-relatedness of the university becomes at best a tool for personal student development within the mission of the university; at worst, a perceived obstacle to preparing its students for service within the liberal structures at large. Either a "two-sphere" system emerges and is maintained (often with difficulty) to accommodate the Christian mission of the institution within the private/public dichotomy of the liberal society[28] or the secularization of the university occurs.

In either case, the secular academy, itself formed within and to promote and protect liberal structures, provides a policing of church-related educational institutions in order to maintain a hegemony over the production of knowledge within the society. Church-relatedness either maintains its place in its subordinate, mediating role, or the institution receives little, if any, educational legitimacy from state-sponsored or élite private institutions, who often themselves have left their church-relatedness far behind.

Another wrinkle entered the story of church-related universities in the 1960s. The intellectual élite transitioned from classical to constitutional liberalism. Constitutional liberalism then presented special difficulties for church-related universities that had accommodated to their classic liberal environment. Representing an earlier majority moral tradition, the church-related university no longer served as the protector of liberal values. Suddenly, the majority's chaplaincy was not desired; it was perceived as a political threat that challenged minorities' ability to pursue their own subgroup's self-interests. No longer able to justify their social privilege within their own tradition, mainline Protestant institutions—and many Roman Catholic institutions as well—translated their particular tradition-based values into more generic religious or social values.[29] Without tradition-specificity, such quickly lost their relatedness to their founding churches except in the most marginal ways. The cycle of accommodation to liberal categories accelerated. Church-relatedness often became a historical element of a university, an element to be guarded against by the faculty lest it impose its will upon the personal freedoms of minority groups. Only "conservative" Christian institutions, those deeply embedded in the earlier accommodation to the liberal polity required by their therapeutic chaplaincy role, maintained their church-relatedness within the liberal society.

If this interpretation is useful, to blame solely the church-related colleges and universities and their leadership for their loss of church-relatedness is blaming the victim—victims who are often naïve, willing accomplices, but victims nonetheless. In fulfilling the desire of their ecclesial constituency to initiate themselves and their children into the society, all is well until, in retrospect, the shift of institutional loyalties from the church to the liberal society becomes obvious to all involved. In this naiveté, however, these institutions are no different from their interpreters who assume no structural animosity toward institutions within the political matrix of U.S. society.

Ironically, however, the situation has seemingly shifted again. As North American society drifts into a post-Christian environment, liberal constitutionalism has provided a new social space for the church-related university. A so-called pluralistic society must provide a marketplace for various communities based upon different personal beliefs. Church-related universities, or individual Christian scholars, each with their own fundamental presuppositions, may exist to compete for allegiance to their particular values as judged within the society at large. Now itself claiming protected minority status, the church-related university, or Christian scholarship, has the right to a seat at the table under the patronage of the constitutional-liberal nation state.[30] Indeed, ignoring the orthodox Christian call for catholicity, the diverse traditions of each sponsoring denomination provide different perspectives to be celebrated within the wider liberal society.

Yet the fact remains that such perspectives and values still must be abstracted from their concrete ecclesial setting in order to enter the public realm except as a consumerist option. Church-related universities may offer guidance provided by their particular traditions to the later patterns of consumption of individual students as they enter the marketplace formed by the liberal polity. Yet these can just as easily serve the spirituality of their students with no ties to future embodiment within concrete Christian communities—i.e., churches. Christian convictions are abstracted from the polity of the church so that students may serve as individual private citizens within the liberal society. Ultimately, such a university might remain church-related; however, it is liberally based because it forms its students within the general categories of liberal democratic polity that only afford Christianity social space within the private realm of individual beliefs.[31] The life of the church remains secondary—and optional—for those so formed. Such a university ultimately can only offer a value-added education supplementing the fundamental liberal polity that naturalizes the liberal political and capitalist economic tradition and produces new knowledge to extend the sovereignty of the state.

■ From the Church-Related to the Ecclesially Based University

At the root of the historical and contemporary difficulties of the church-related university, therefore, is that such universities remain liberally based—they have been and are fundamentally formed by, live within, and serve the polities of a liberal society. Liberalism, in its classic or constitutional forms, demands the creation and then privatization of religion that renders the church inconsequential as a political entity. Indeed, liberal theory offers the liberal state as an alternate doctrine of salvation, a parody of the salvation provided by the church.[32] The liberal democratic polity attempts to prevent the transmission of competing traditions and the production of alternative discourses of knowledge that might arise from, within, and for the polity and practices of the church. Liberalism thereby polices the university so that it may not challenge the power of the liberal democratic nation-state by denaturalizing liberal categories and knowledge.

Yet to so limit, to confine the university to the narrow interests of liberal polity and competing nation-states seems to belie the university's past and potential when it can serve a much broader, more numerous, interesting, and varied polity called the church. The church comprises a genuine multi-national, multiethnic, multilingual polity. It is a concrete embodiment of a polity or polities with a distinctive history, literature, practices, economics, technology, and witness. Moreover, the church has special resources within its polity to enhance the intellectual formation of its members. It has the mandate to accept the other as genuinely other, without reducing public difference to an interior sameness in the name of pluralism as liberal polity requires—the church must "show hospitality to strangers." An ecclesial base provides the practice of repentance, forgiveness, reconciliation, a sharing of common goods, and a commitment to truthfulness that does not require violence to sustain itself but, instead, draws upon the lives of the saints and the deaths of the martyrs as exemplars of its deepest convictions. As Stanley Hauerwas has recently written, "Our very ability as Christians to lead lives of witness has been compromised by our inability to sustain a Christian intellectual witness worthy of the martyrs."[33] Martyrdom cannot be reduced to a lifestyle option. Martyrdom calls forth an explication of the very nature of creation, in its created goodness, fallen sinfulness, and redeemed glory, of the most profound, honest, and penetrating kind.

If this is so, perhaps the future of the church-related university must be found in the polity it serves and into which it initiates its students, a polity not limited by the boundaries, violence, and capitalistic economics of any liberal nation-state. Perhaps the church-related university becomes most interesting—and more truthful—when it is no longer church-related and liberally based, but rather, ecclesially based and liberally related. An ecclesially based university would seek to initiate and socialize its members into the polity and practices of the church within, for, and often against the polity and practices of the liberal democratic society. In a radical reconfiguration of the university—a return to the ecclesial origins from which it came—perhaps an ecclesially based university can form its students, faculty, staff, and even administration into a witness to God the Father's peaceable kingdom that has drawn near to us in Jesus Christ through the power of the Spirit.

▨ Notes

1. Quoted in Kenji Yoshino, "Covering," *The Yale Law Journal* 111 (2002): 771. Scalia issued this statement as part of the Supreme Court majority that struck down an affirmative action program.

2. David Brooks, "The Organizational Kid," *Atlantic Monthly* (April 2001): 40–54.

3. "When I asked if Princeton builds character, they would inevitably mention the honor code again against cheating, or policies to reduce drinking. When I asked about moral questions, they would often flee such talk and start discussing legislative questions" (p. 53).

4. See Robert Bellah, et al. *Habits of the Heart: Individualism and Commitment in American Life* (Berkeley: University of California Press, 1996), pp. 44–48 for the distinction between the manager and the therapist as two separate realms in American culture. See also Dorothy Smith, *The Everyday World as Problematic: A Feminist Sociology* (Boston: Northeastern University Press, 1987). Smith describes the same cultural realms and their gendered implications as the "extralocal" and the "local."

5. Liberalism is a political philosophy arising out of "late-medieval nominalism, the protestant reformation and seventeenth-century Augustinianism, which completely privatized,

spiritualized and transcendentalized the sacred, and concurrently reimagined nature, human action and society as a sphere of autonomous, sheerly formal power" (John Milbank, *Theology and Social Theory: Beyond Secular Reason* [Oxford: Blackwell, 1993], p. 9.

6. In a liberal democratic nation-state, the state assumes sovereignty over the bodies of all those within its borders so that individuals might maintain the personal freedom to pursue their own fulfillment. In response, the citizenry are to give their allegiance and affections to a social unity (i.e., the nation) that the state manufactures. For an analysis on how this functions within the U.S., see Pierre Schlag, "The Empty Circles of Liberal Justification," *Michigan Law Review* 96 (1997): 1–46.

7. George Marsden, *The Soul of the American University. From Protestant Establishment to Established Nonbelief* (Oxford: Oxford University Press, 1994).

8. James T. Burtchaell, *The Dying of the Light: The Disengagement of Colleges and Universities from their Christian Churches* (Grand Rapids: Eerdmans, 1998).

9. Douglas Sloan, *Faith and Knowledge: Mainline Protestantism and American Higher Education* (Minneapolis: Fortress, 1994).

10. William Cavanaugh, "'A Fire Strong Enough to Consume the House': The Wars of Religion and the Rise of the State," *Modern Theology* 11 (1995): 409.

11. Stephen L. Carter, *The Dissent of the Governed* (Cambridge: Harvard University Press, 1998), p. 23.

12. See Michael Baxter, *In Service to the Nation: A Critical Analysis of the Formation of the Americanist Tradition in Catholic Social Ethics* (unpublished dissertation, Duke University; University Microfiche, 1996).

13. Michael Budde and Robert Brimlow, *Christianity Incorporated: How Big Business is Buying the Church* (Grand Rapids: Brazos, 2001), p. 10.

14. See, for instance, Alexander Keyssar, *The Right to Vote: The Contested History of Democracy in the United States* (New York: Basic Books, 2000).

15. Carter, *Dissent*, p. 19.

16. See Bruce Ackerman, *We the People: Foundations*. The *Yale Law Journal* devoted an issue to review Ackerman's work in June 1999.

17. It is entirely possible that "classical liberalism" represents an innovation as much as the "constitutional liberalism" from their historical philosophical origins in that it subtly redefines its emphasis on liberty and a limited state in light of the power of constitutional liberalism.

18. American Catholicism provides a superb test case of these dynamics. When Roman Catholics were still suspect within the Protestant culture of the mid-twentieth century in the U.S., the church deeply embraced constitutional liberalism. As Catholics, at least those of Western European descent, have risen socially and economically within American society (often due to university education), more and more Roman Catholics tend to embrace a classical liberalism—often to the dismay of Catholic academic intelligentsia.

19. Cavanaugh, "'Fire,'" p. 411; For an analysis of the concept of religion as a theological construct legitimating the colonial practices of the Western nation-state, see Timothy Fitzgerald, *The Ideology of Religious Studies* (Oxford: Oxford University Press, 2000); for a review essay of Fitzgerald's work by various scholars, see "Timothy Fitzgerald, *The Ideology of Religious Studies*," *Religious Studies Review* 27 (2001): 103–115. For another critique of the concept of religion, see Russell T. McCutcheon, *Manufacturing Religion: The Discourse on Sui Generis Religion and the Politics of Nostalgia* (Oxford: Oxford University Press, 1997).

20. Cavanaugh, "'Fire'," p. 405.

21. Anthony Giddens, *The Nation-State and Violence* (Berkeley: University of California Press), p. 18.

22. Such was the role for the class in morality that dominated the university curriculum until the early twentieth century. See Marsden, *Soul of the American University*, pp. 61–64.

23. See Marsden's treatment of the University of Michigan, *Soul*, pp. 172–78.

24. For this process within American society at large, see Roger Finke and Rodney Starke, *The Churching of America 1776–1990: Winners and Losers in our Religious Economy* (New Brunswick, New Jersey: Rutgers University Press, 1992). As a church group ascends socially, however, the process undercuts the long term viability of the ecclesial group to which they belong as clergy and leading laity seek to undermine particular "costly" commitments to the group so that they might fit in better with mainstream cultural practices.

25. Anthony Giddens, *The Nation State and Violence* (Berkeley: University of California Press, 1987), p. 20.

26. See Robert Putnam, *Bowling Alone: The Collapse and Revival of American Community* (New York: Simon & Schuster, 2000) for an analysis of the diminishing role of social capital in contemporary American society. It is not surprising that Putnam sees the "faith-based communities" as an important manufacturer of social capital necessary for the health of the liberal society (pp. 408–10). Putnam thus assumes the chaplaincy role for the church within a liberal polity, rather than understanding the church as operating with its own polity, outside the narrow confines of the contemporary liberal democratic nation-state.

27. Burtchaell shows how mission statements move from particular to more generic statements taken from language of the mainstream culture; see *Dying*, pp. 819–51.

28. For a description of universities that have maintained a connection between faith and knowledge, see Larry Lyon and Michael Beaty, "Integration, Secularization, and the Two-Spheres View at Religious Colleges: Comparing Baylor University with the University of Notre Dame and Georgetown College," *Christian Scholars Review* 29 (1999): 73–112; also Robert Benne, *Quality with Soul: How Six Premier Colleges and Universities Keep Faith with Their Religious Tradition* (Grand Rapids: Eerdmans, 2001). Yet even framing the issue in terms of faith and knowledge reflects the liberal contours of the society, with faith as the personal, private pole and knowledge as the objective, public pole. Therefore, even institutions that speak of integrating faith and knowledge have already accommodated to their liberal setting.

29. For the story of Roman Catholic institutions during this time, see Philip Gleason, *Contending with Modernity: Catholic Higher Education in the Twentieth Century* (New York: Oxford University Press, 1996).

30. See George Marsden, *The Outrageous Idea of Christian Scholarship* (New York: Oxford University Press, 1997); for a more developed form of liberal political theory that embraces a similar argument explicitly from within liberalism, see William E. Connolly, *Why I am Not a Secularist* (Minneapolis: University of Minneapolis Press, 1999).

31. Seen from this perspective, the "success stories" told by Benne (*Quality with Soul*) and by Richard T. Hughes and William B. Adrian (eds.), *Models for Christian Higher Education: Strategies for Success in the Twenty-First Century* (Grand Rapids: Eerdmans, 1997).

32. See William T. Cavanaugh, "The City: Beyond Secular Parodies" in *Radical Orthodoxy* (ed. John Milbank, Graham Ward, and Catherine Pickstock, London: Routledge, 1999), pp. 182–200.

33. Stanley Hauerwas, *With the Grain of the Universe: The Church's Witness and Natural Theology* (Grand Rapids: Brazos, 2001), p. 232.

Liberal Democratic Objections to the Ecclesially Based University and a Christian Response

Sailing Under True Colors

Academic Freedom and the Ecclesially Based University

William T. Cavanaugh

As a theologian I sometimes regard the prevailing paradigm of academic freedom the way the operator of a small family farm might regard the "Freedom to Farm" legislation passed by the U.S. Congress in 1996: if I'm so free, why does this legislation threaten to put me out of business? I have found a place to do theology in an academic context at a Catholic university, but I am unwelcome to teach at most secular universities, at which the practice of theology is *verboten*. This is because, I am told, secular universities are bastions of free inquiry. This is a problem not just for theologians, but for anyone invested in the enterprise of ecclesially based colleges and universities. Such institutions often feel pressure to be other than what they are because the prevailing paradigm of academic freedom wishes them to be more free.

In what follows I examine this paradigm and the assumptions that underlie it. I argue that the prevailing understanding of academic freedom is seriously deficient, both in its focus on the individual professor and in its understanding of freedom. I then suggest why ecclesially based universities can foster a fuller practice of academic freedom.

▓ I. The Liberal Paradigm

The American Association of University Professors has set the tone for the dominant understanding of academic freedom in the U.S. John Dewey and Arthur Lovejoy wrote a "Report on Academic Freedom" upon the founding of the AAUP in 1915. The purpose of the new organization was primarily to defend academics from being arbitrarily fired for unpopular views. Those doing the firing (there were about ten celebrated cases from 1890 to 1914) were of course college and university administrators. The AAUP was therefore anxious to establish the autonomy of the professorate from the administrations at their respective institutions. Decisions on hiring, tenure, and promotion were to be based on the quality of a professor's work as judged by those uniquely competent to do so, namely, other professors in the same field. The peer-reviewed journal was to be the primary instrument for such evaluation. The role of the administration in personnel decisions was limited in effect to giving approval for hiring. At the same time, the proliferation of peer-reviewed journals and of professional societies meant that university professors in the twentieth century came to look increasingly outside the confines of the institutions that signed their paychecks for their primary academic community.[1]

When the AAUP was formed, it represented the coming of age of a new model for American higher education, one borrowed in large part from Germany. After the Civil War, large numbers of American academics began pursuing doctorates in Germany and importing the German model back to American institutions. Johns Hopkins in 1876 was the first American university that was founded upon this model. Until the latter part of the nineteenth century, American colleges and universities had seen their fundamental task as that of passing on a tradition of learning to the next generation of students. The liberal arts dominated. In the German model, in contrast, the role of the professor was not so much the passing on of knowledge but the discovery of new knowledge. Furthermore, *Wissenschaft,* or scientific knowledge, was equated with knowledge as such. Both the "hard" sciences and the new "social sciences" began to crowd out liberal education in the traditional sense, and the empirical method reigned.[2] The great ideal became the disinterested observer, approaching his (*sic*) object free of preconceived convictions or orthodoxies that might limit where the bold pursuit of truth might take him. The AAUP's 1915 "Report on Academic Freedom" expressed serious doubts about whether such an ideal could be fostered or even permitted by a church-related institution. Such institutions do not, at least as regards one particular subject, accept the principles of freedom of inquiry, of opinion and of teaching; and their purpose is not to advance knowledge by the unrestricted research and unfettered discussion of impartial investigations, but rather to subsidize the promotion of the opinions held by persons usually not of a scholar's calling, who provide the funds for their maintenance.

The "one particular subject" is a reference to the obstinate harboring of theology at such institutions. The report then claimed, in what we might regard as an unintentionally droll parody of objectivity, "Concerning the desirability of the existence of such institutions, the committee does not desire to express any opinion." The report then warns, "But it is manifestly important that they should not be permitted to sail under false colors. Genuine boldness and thoroughness of inquiry, and freedom of speech are scarcely reconcilable with the prescribed inculcating of a particular opinion upon a controverted question."[3]

The current touchstone for academic freedom in the U.S. is the *Statement of Principles on Academic Freedom and Tenure* issued by the AAUP in 1940, along with the Interpretive Comments added in 1970. The part of the original statement dedicated to academic freedom is short. Two of the three introductory paragraphs concern academic freedom. Academic freedom is defended as essential to the "common good," which "depends upon the free search for truth and its free exposition." Indeed, the very purpose of institutions of higher education is to serve "the common good and not to further the interest of either the individual teacher or the institution as a whole."[4] The rights and duties associated with academic freedom do not attach to the institution, but academic freedom is "fundamental for the protection of the rights of the teacher in teaching and of the student to freedom in learning." This introductory section to the whole document is followed by a section entitled "Academic Freedom," which consists of three stipulations regarding the rights and duties of teachers: teachers are entitled to freedom in research and publication, to freedom in the classroom in discussing their subject, and to freedom to express their opinion as citizens, provided they do so with accuracy, restraint, and respect, and make clear that they do not speak for the academic institution by which they are employed. The second of these stipulations contains what has become known as the "limitation clause" or "lim clause": "Limitations of academic freedom because of religious or other aims of the institution should be clearly stated in writing at the time of the appointment." In 1970 the following Interpretive Comment was added here: "Most church-related institutions no longer need or desire the departure from the principle of academic freedom implied in the 1940 *Statement,* and we do not now endorse such a departure."[5]

In 1988 a subcommittee of the AAUP committee on academic freedom addressed itself again to the issue of ecclesially based institutions in an effort to further elaborate and clarify the previous statements. On the one hand, the subcommittee stepped away from the 1970 repudiation of religious "limits" on academic freedom by recognizing "the prerogative of institutions to require doctrinal fidelity." On the other hand, however, the subcommittee made clear "the necessary consequence of denying to institutions invoking this prerogative the moral right to proclaim themselves as authentic seats of higher learning." The high moral tone continues as the subcommittee claims it would be "a wrong" for "an otherwise free university" to include a school of theology "that requires creedal orthodoxy as a consequence of its singular religious mission." The subcommittee concludes, "In sum, the housing of an unfree school within a free university is a contradiction: it may be in the university but, being unfree, it is not of the university, and it has no business being there."[6] This subcommittee took up the question once again in 1996, now acknowledging that religious institutions "contribute to the pluralistic richness of the American intellectual landscape."[7] This was an important concession, but it was tempered by the recommendation that such schools not be held accountable according to the 1940 *Statement* because they are not what the *Statement* understands as proper institutions of higher education. As George Marsden comments, the view seems to be that religiously defined institutions are hopeless cases, and to hold them to standards of true academic freedom would be to dignify them beyond their station.[8]

The work of the AAUP subcommittee was published but never formally approved by the AAUP. It is, however, consonant with the guiding principles of the 1940 *Statement,* together with the Interpretive Comments. Underlying these documents are two fundamental assumptions that make life difficult for an ecclesially based university. The first such assumption is that the subject of academic freedom is the individual professor. The second is that freedom is constituted by the relative absence of limitations. I will flesh out each of these assumptions in turn, and then proceed to critique them and offer alternative suggestions for a better understanding of academic freedom. I should stress before proceeding that these assumptions are not necessarily shared by all members of the AAUP, many of whom work at ecclesially based institutions and respect and value the missions of those institutions. The point is simply that, *where and when* those who identify with the liberal model of education cast doubt upon the ability of ecclesially based institutions to foster or even tolerate academic freedom, the following two assumptions come into play.

A. The individual professor is the subject of academic freedom

The freedom of the student to learn is mentioned once in the introduction to the 1940 *Statement,* but the freedom of the individual professor is the subject of the rest of the statement. The *Statement* would appear to be informed by AAUP founder Arthur Lovejoy's judgment "that truth is more likely to emerge through the interplay and conflict of ideas resulting from the exercise of individual reason than through the imposition of uniform and standardized opinion by authority."[9] Nowhere in the documents is there contemplated the possibility that academic institutions are themselves the subjects of academic freedom—for example, the freedom from interference by government or accrediting agencies, or indeed by the AAUP itself. The statement does not explicitly deny the articulation of such a right for academic institutions as such, but it does make clear that institutions of higher education are not to promote the interests of the institution, but rather the "common good."

Given the concerns that motivated the AAUP statements, a crucial corollary to the identification of academic freedom with the individual professor is that the primary threat against which academic freedom must be defended is the professor's employing institution. It is the administrators of an institution who most frequently are in a position to override faculty decisions on hiring, firing, and granting and denying tenure. For this reason, the AAUP has been anything but a defender of institutional autonomy. The AAUP has established itself as the arbiter of disputes over academic freedom, and claims the right and competence to pass judgment on any institution of higher education. The AAUP maintains and publicizes a blacklist of institutions that have run afoul of its guidelines.

To say that the focus is on the freedom of the individual professor does not mean that the liberal model envisions the professor working in isolation, nor that she or he has no responsibilities to others. From the beginning the AAUP has stressed the advancement of knowledge through the exchange of views with others in one's field, as defined by membership in professional societies with national scope. The 1970 Interpretive Comments also state that the AAUP has long recognized not just the rights but the responsibilities of professors to their students, to their institutions, and as citizens. We should note, however, that the liberal model of education embodies a kind of cosmopolitanism that encourages the individual professor to think of her or his primary scholarly community as extending beyond the walls of the university. Ultimate judgment of the value of one's research rests with professional journals and societies and, in cases of dispute, with the AAUP itself. Responsibilities are subject to a similar cosmopolitanism. Academic freedom facilitates service to the "common good," the primary referent of which seems to be American society, and not the university or the church. Thus, the 1970 Interpretive Comments cite a 1967 Supreme Court decision to justify concern for academic freedom more broadly: "Our Nation is deeply committed to safeguarding academic freedom, which is of transcendent value to all of us and not merely to the teachers concerned. That freedom is therefore a special concern of the First Amendment, which does not tolerate laws that cast a pall of orthodoxy over the classroom."[10]

According to Marsden, the origins of this view can be traced back to the assumptions of the American Progressive Era in the early part of the twentieth century. The national consolidation and standardization of education had begun, under the banner of unifying the nation. The great enemies of economic and moral progress were seen to be parochialism and particularism. One of the functions of a university education was to bring students out of their local prejudices and into a broader and cosmopolitan worldview.[11] This view persists among many professors today, not least among those teachers of religion who believe their job is to shake students out of their dogmatic slumbers.

B. Freedom indicates the relative absence of limits

This liberation from particularity leads us directly into the second of the fundamental assumptions associated with the prevailing view of academic freedom. It is assumed that protecting academic freedom is primarily a matter of preventing individual professors from encountering external obstacles to their work. Here Isaiah Berlin's basic philosophical distinction between positive and negative freedom is helpful. Positive freedom is the ability to achieve some good purpose. Negative freedom is the absence of restraint. The AAUP definition of academic freedom is of the latter kind. It is assumed that freedom is something one simply has until it is taken away by some external force or until some obstacle is put in its path. Thus, as in the 1915 "Report" quoted above, research is meant to be *un*restricted, *un*fettered, and *im*partial; in other words, freedom is best described negatively. It is what happens in the absence of certain limiting conditions. The chief limiting conditions are orthodoxy and authority, the former imposed by the latter.

1. *Orthodoxy.* To come to the pursuit of truth already bound to some "doctrinal fidelity" is, in this view, to prejudice the search from the start. To do so, as the 1988 subcommittee says, is to be "unfree" and therefore unworthy of the higher pursuit of knowledge. One possible version of this view retains as its ideal the model of the disinterested observer. The researcher adopts a universal and cosmopolitan stand-

point, unfettered by particularity, with a God's-eye view of the data. Another possible version, chastened by historical studies emphasizing the social conditioning that even science and scientists find inescapable, will acknowledge that the researcher inevitably approaches his subject with presuppositions, but holds that the researcher must be free and willing to change those presuppositions if contrary evidence presents itself. In either case, ecclesially based higher education has an especial problem here. Christians tend to hold some beliefs that are not empirically verifiable, and they tend to hold that certain core doctrines of orthodoxy are not subject to abandonment.

2. *Authority.* Orthodoxy is accepted by Christians on the authority of revelation, either some version of *sola scriptura* or scripture together with tradition as interpreted by an authoritative church hierarchy. Revelation is authoritative, that is, not ultimately subject to acceptance or rejection by an autonomous human reason. Revelation is also heteronomous, that is, given from outside the human person, and thus constitutes a limit on the sovereignty and freedom of individual reason. Thus the "limitation clause" in the 1940 AAUP *Statement* makes clear that the religious aims of an institution often constitute limits on freedom, and that these limits should be publicly acknowledged. A negative view of freedom is clearly implied, as is the assumption that any limits on freedom constitute a departure from the norm. Nothing in the AAUP documents precludes the recognition that certain positive conditions must be present in order for freedom to flourish. But threats to academic freedom are envisioned as coming from outside the individual professor, and not from within. Ecclesially-based institutions might be valued for providing some of the positive conditions for a scholar to work—libraries, laboratories, paychecks, etc.—but the "religious aims" of the institution themselves are seen as a potential imposition on the professor's freedom. The situation is even more suspect at the colleges and universities related to those ecclesial bodies that invest a measure of the authority of revelation—that is, the power to interpret it authoritatively—in officers of the church, most commonly bishops. Here the imposition is personal, a setting of the will of one over that of another, and the potential for limits on freedom is ratcheted up a notch.

One further corollary of this view of freedom is sometimes drawn by those skeptical of the possibility of full academic freedom in ecclesially based universities: if one faith position is held as normative for an academic community, then the diversity of individual views will be limited. That a diversity of views is beneficial for the educational process follows from the necessity of truth-seeking to be unfettered; one must have access to all possible views in order to judge which is closest to the truth, or at least to judge which view is to be preferred given the current distributions of power.

▉ II. Changing the Subject

There can be no doubt that the individual professor is necessarily a subject of academic freedom, and that this concept marshals important resources in protecting professors from arbitrary treatment by university administrators. The managerial model regnant in many of our institutions of higher learning tends to mimic that of the business corporation. The administration thinks of itself as management and of the students as customers. That leaves the faculty in the position of labor, which fares increasingly poorly in today's market. The academic freedom of professors needs careful attention in such a climate. The AAUP performs a vital service in making sure that due process is followed in controversial cases and ensuring that professors are not unfairly impeded in pursuing their duties.

Nevertheless, there is no prima facie reason to suppose that the university itself cannot be a subject of academic freedom. I believe it is necessary to supplement—not replace—the emphasis on individual academic freedom with an emphasis on corporate academic freedom. These two are necessarily incompatible only if one assumes that freedom can only be a property of individuals, an assumption that depends on a strictly negative definition of freedom, that is, that other individuals are potential obstacles to one's autonomy. I will discuss that assumption below. For now, I wish to make the case that the freedom of whole communities of scholars ought to be a vital concern of anyone interested in the question of academic freedom.

Indeed, it can be argued that in its original incarnation, academic freedom was something that attached to universities, and not to individuals. Although the term "academic freedom" is modern, the medieval universities were seen as free spaces primarily because of the immunities from interference granted to the institutions themselves. The University of Paris, for example, required a new type of royal charter in 1200 because it had grown out of the cathedral school of Notre Dame, and came to be independent from the direct supervision of the cathedral. The royal charter also granted the university significant exemptions from local jurisdictions, exemptions that were to grow—at times through bloody clashes with the local citizenry—through the course of the thirteenth century. By mid-century, as recognized by king and pope, the University of Paris enjoyed, among other exemptions, immunity from the civil and criminal jurisdiction of the local magistrates, from the disciplinary ban of excommunication by the local bishop, from all tolls and taxes . . . The University had the right to make and enforce rules and regulations for its own members; to set up courses and examinations; to regulate the time, content and method of teaching.[12]

Note that the freedom from outside interference brought with it the responsibility of the university to order its own affairs and regulate the activities of its faculty. The University of Paris was typical: both the freedom from outside interference and the regulation of its internal affairs were characteristic of thirteenth-century universities. The university was seen as a corporate body, and not merely a collection of individual intellectual entrepreneurs. The university did not understand itself as standing in splendid isolation from the web of obligations that was medieval society. It did understand, however, that freedom from civil interference was necessary to achieve its purpose—the determination of the truth and the passing of that truth on to another generation of students. Freedom of higher education was understood as corporate freedom, and not primarily as the freedom of the individual.[13]

This understanding of academic freedom has not entirely disappeared from university life in a liberal democratic society, nor from jurisprudence relating to the university. In a 1957 decision, Supreme Court Justice Felix Frankfurter wrote that academic freedom consists of "the four essential freedoms of a university—to determine for itself on academic grounds who may teach, what may be taught, how it shall be taught, and who may be admitted to study."[14] This position was echoed by Justice Powell in *Regents of the University of California v. Bakke* in 1978.[15] Nevertheless, the Supreme Court has never attempted to clarify the relationship between individual and corporate academic freedom. Also left unclear by the Supreme Court is whether academic freedom should be treated legally as an extension of one's First Amendment rights of free speech, or whether it is a more specific and peculiar right that attaches to the unique office of the university professor.[16] Courts have sometimes intervened in disputes between individuals and universities based on the principle of protecting individual free speech. But as Frederick Crosson argues, "treating the academic freedom of individuals within the university simply as a first amendment right would be to ignore the specific nature of the university and to infringe or ignore the most fundamental academic freedom, that of the autonomy of the university vis-à-vis the state."[17]

In reality, court intervention is but one small example of the intrusion of the state in regulating what can and cannot happen at our universities. A partial list compiled by James Burtchaell names dozens of federal agencies—along with accrediting authorities and other institutions external to a university—that regulate every aspect of the university's life. He presents a hypothetical University of St. Dympna.

> The first outside authority to which she regularly defers is the Federal Government, incarnate in the Departments of State, Justice, Education, Agriculture, Commerce, Defense, Energy, Health and Human Services, Labor, and Veterans Affairs; also the Equal Employment Opportunity Commission, the Environmental Protection Agency, the Library of Congress, the U.S. Patent Office, the National Science Foundation, the National Endowments for the Humanities and for the Arts, the National Institutes of Health, and the Immigration and Naturalization Service. Washington forbids her to ask the race of applicants, but requires her to report the racial breakdown of her personnel and students; makes it worth her while to include in every employment notice the assurance that she is an equal opportunity employer; forbids her to save the trees on her campus by spraying DDT; determines and inspects the housing for her laboratory animals (which therefore costs roughly twice as much per square foot as faculty office space); requires protection of all human subjects of any funded research, subject to elaborate guidelines and reporting; requires a minimum number of credit hours to be taken by students receiving tuition grants or guaranteed loans; and regulates the emissions from the power plant. . . . The Comptroller of the Currency regulates the faculty credit union. The Library of Congress certifies copyrights to faculty members and sets standards for book cataloging. The U.S. Army and the U.S. Navy decide what facilities are required by their ROTC programs on campus. And obviously there is the jurisdiction of the courts.[18]

Burtchaell adds that this is only a "small and suggestive sample" of the federal authorities to which colleges and universities must defer. He then proceeds to give a similar list of activities regulated by external accrediting agencies.

In its almost exclusive concern for the freedom of the individual, the liberal democratic model of academic freedom does not seem able to take an interest in the potential infringements of freedom associated with such interference from the federal government and other external bureaucracies. Concern only seems to arise when ecclesial authorities attempt to exercise authority on campus. A recent example is the furor over the papal encyclical *Ex Corde Ecclesiae,* which recommends episcopal involvement in safeguarding the ecclesial identity of Catholic institutions of higher education. The recommendation that teachers of Catholic theology seek accreditation or *mandatum* from their local bishop was met with objections such as those of Richard McBrien that it would violate academic freedom and "institutional autonomy" by introducing an "external, non-academic agent" into the functioning of the university.[19]

The university in a liberal democratic society has in many ways suffered the same fate as other "intermediate associations" in the modern nation-state. As individual rights have become paramount, the power of the state has grown exponentially. The rise of the centralized state was necessary, as Hobbes clearly saw, to keep the myriad of atomistic individuals from interfering with each other's rights and property. The centralized state was meant not to threaten individual liberty but to permit it. In the process, the autonomy and influence of so-called intermediate associations such as the university, the church, and the family were debilitated on the one hand by the transferal of rights from corporate group to individual, and on the other hand by the state's usurpation of the power to recognize and regulate all corporate societies. In an analysis of this process written one year before the founding of the AAUP, John Neville Figgis warned that the modern reality was increasingly "that of the omnipotent State facing an equally unreal aggregate of unrelated individuals. . . . More and more it is clear that the mere individual's freedom against an omnipotent State may be no better than slavery; more and more is it evident that the real question of freedom in our day is the freedom of smaller unions to live within the whole."[20]

If we once again contrast the modern and medieval universities, we find that the medieval university was not thus subject to being squeezed between the state and the individual. Indeed, the very term *universitas* (common by the late fourteenth century) and the earlier term *studium generale* (thirteenth century) referred to the way in which the scholarly community transcended political frontiers. A *studium generale* drew scholars from all over Europe, as opposed to a *studium particulare*, which drew local students only. The mobility of teachers and students in the medieval period was extensive, as exemplified by the peripatetic career of Thomas Aquinas. This mobility was facilitated by the university degree, the *licentia ubique docendi,* a license to teach "anywhere," that is, at any of the other universities of Christendom. The idea of a national university supervised by the state was unimaginable and would have been considered a serious violation of academic freedom. According to William Hoye's study of the medieval origins of academic freedom, a student who pledged allegiance to the local civil authority would lose his membership in the university. "One could say that at the time of the origins of the university national patriotism and academic freedom were strictly incompatible with one another. Patriotism was considered a violation of academic freedom."[21]

It is not that the autonomy of the university was absolute; degrees were awarded under the authority of the Roman see. Some higher authority was necessary precisely because a degree from one university was a *licentia ubique docendi.* But this authority was more a protection for the university from civil interference than a violation of its freedom. Richard Hofstadter, author of the first extensive history of academic freedom in the U.S., writes:

> The medieval universities were ecclesiastical agencies founded at a time when the Church was still effectively guarding its institutions from the incursions of lay power. Both the church principle of ecclesiastical independence and the guild principle of corporate self-government provided the universities and society at large with dominant models of autonomy. This autonomy the Protestant Reformation had sharply circumscribed. As we have seen, the proud self-sufficiency, and with it much of the intellectual freedom, that had been characteristic of the medieval universities at their zenith went into decline.[22]

That decline is nowhere more evident than in the career of Immanuel Kant, the father of the modern German university and the great defender of the autonomy of human reason. In vindicating the hegemony of philosophy over theology in the university because of the heteronomous sources of the latter's authority, Kant admits that philosophy must recognize the authority of the state which, though heteronomous, is recognized by philosophy through its own free judgment.[23] Kant himself would give a lesson in heteronomy by his own obsequious acquiescence to Prussian King Frederick the Great's censure in 1794 of his book *On the Radical Evil in Human Nature.*[24]

Granted, then, that individual academic freedom is an important good, may we not expand the vision of academic freedom to include a consideration of the corporate freedom of the university? What this means for the ecclesially based university is the freedom to be Christian. *Ex Corde Ecclesiae* puts considerations of academic freedom in the context of the freedom of the Catholic university to be itself:

> A Catholic University possesses the autonomy necessary to develop its distinctive identity and pursue its proper mission. Freedom in research and teaching is recognized and respected according to the principles and methods of each individual discipline, so long as the rights of the individual and of the community are preserved within the confines of the truth and the common good.[25]

It is of course the case that ecclesial authority, exercised poorly, can threaten academic freedom. Nevertheless, a much greater threat to academic freedom is the threat to the autonomy of institutions of higher education. These threats apply to all colleges and universities insofar as they suffer, as we have seen, the surrender of significant powers of self-determination to the state and other external bureaucracies. Ecclesially based institutions must additionally deal with an even greater threat: secularization, a pervasive menace to the very freedom of a Christian institution to be itself. The

Christian identity of most church-related institutions has been severely eroded, as thoroughly documented in James Burtchaell's book *The Dying of the Light*.[26] The liberal democratic model's suspicion of church-based colleges and universities contributes to the pressure to secularize. The idea that church-based institutions limit academic freedom ironically is itself a limit on the academic freedom of church-based institutions of higher education.

There is one further irony of the neglect of the institution as itself a subject of academic freedom: the emphasis on a diversity of individuals within each college and university has in fact produced an increasing homogenization of institutions of higher education. Under the liberal democratic model, universities have encouraged a greater diversity of backgrounds and viewpoints within their walls. As each has sought to mirror the wider society, universities have increasingly come to mirror each other. Many Catholic universities, for example, have no more Catholic faculty than nearby state universities, and the curriculum—with the possible exception of a religion class or two—is virtually indistinguishable from its secular counterparts. Many Catholic universities today like to talk about "values" without saying which ones. The result is an increasingly bland uniformity across the educational landscape. According to Donald Kennedy, former president of Stanford University, the most significant failure of American higher education today is the unwillingness "to create sharply individualized, recognizable identities" for colleges and universities.[27] One way to redress this failure would be to allow church-based colleges and universities the academic freedom to develop their own distinctive identities.

III. Positive Freedom

To argue thus for the freedom of the ecclesially based university to be itself is a start, but cannot be the end, of a full understanding of academic freedom. For the ecclesially based university will claim more than that it should be left alone to develop its own understanding of freedom or that it deserves a place in the larger discussion so that a greater diversity of voices can be heard. The ecclesially based university will also claim that its understanding of freedom is more complete and more liberating, precisely because it is based on the truth of the Christian faith.

From the AAUP's "limitation clause" one gets the impression that the normal condition of secular universities is academic freedom, whereas the norm at church-related institutions is a limit on such freedom. If we restrict ourselves, for the moment, to talking about purely negative freedom, there are still serious problems with this view. Even when secular universities are functioning normally—that is, according to AAUP guidelines—there are still plenty of things that restrict the freedom of faculty, depending on the context. A comparison of German and American definitions of academic freedom will bear this out. The German *Lehrfreiheit* as developed in the nineteenth century gives the professor broad freedom from administrative duties, from required subjects to be taught, from prescribed syllabi, from tutorial duties, from common standards of grading. By contrast, an American professor's freedom, according the 1940 *Statement,* is "subject to the adequate performance of his other academic duties," which include teaching required courses, grading and setting syllabi according to common standards, and so on. In the 1940 *Statement,* a professor is accorded freedom "in discussing his subject," whereas German professors are free to lecture on any subject in which they are interested. American professors are also expected to be scrupulously fair in presenting all sides to an argument, whereas German professors are allowed and expected to try to win students over to their point of view.[28] These contrasts all apply to the teaching function of university professors; limits on research come in the form of orthodoxies and taboos within each field, which I will discuss below. The general point is that, even given the limits of considering negative freedom only, the contrast between limited and unlimited academic freedom is misleading. The real question in all university settings is, in what ways is negative freedom limited, and are such limitations helpful or not?

We will go deeper, however, if we see the restriction of academic freedom to negative freedom as itself a limit. If Christian views of freedom are excluded from the start in favor of the liberal view, then academic freedom is being limited by the very definition of academic freedom. For a more expansive view, we must consider the question from the point of view of positive freedom. Here what makes one free is not the mere absence of limiting conditions but the presence of the means to achieve worthwhile ends. An alcoholic over twenty-one with ten dollars in his pocket and a map to an all-night liquor store is not free but enslaved. What the alcoholic needs is not fewer restrictions but the ability to refrain from drinking. In this sense Christians see orthodox Christian doctrine not as a limit on, but as a precondition to, freedom.

1) Orthodoxy

In a footnote, *Ex Corde Ecclesiae* defines "academic freedom" in the following terms:

"academic freedom" is the guarantee given to those involved in teaching and research that, within their specific specialized branch of knowledge, and according to the methods proper to that specific area, they may search for the truth wherever analysis and evidence leads them, and may teach and publish the results of this search, keeping in mind the cited criteria, that is, safeguarding the rights of the individual and of society within the confines of the truth and the common good.[29]

Here the Pope seems to offer complete freedom of inquiry with one hand, only to rein it back into certain "confines" with the other. The translation, however, is an unhappy one; the "postulata" in "iura personae et communitatis intra veritatis bonique communis postulata" is better rendered "claims" or "requirements." The truth does not confine us but frees us (John 8:32) precisely by making certain unavoidable claims on our attention. If truth is the object of the academic search, then it is not confining to say that the search must be guided by its goal, its telos. The loss of teleology in the modern era has not liberated research but merely cast it adrift. If construed positively, freedom is that which allows us to achieve some worthwhile goal. For Christians, the goal of human life is not invented but given by a gracious God, and it is this goal that guides all human striving. Free inquiry therefore presupposes orthodoxy.

The acceptance of orthodoxy does not mean simply that one has found what one is looking for before the search begins. Faith does not end inquiry but begins it, hence Anselm's famous definition of theology as "faith seeking understanding." Orthodoxy is not static but is constantly subject to deepening critical exploration. The Chalcedonian definitions, for example, set parameters for inquiry into the nature of Christ, but those parameters are a platform for inquiry into an inexhaustible font of truth and meaning for human existence.

As Terence Nichols argues, the function of orthodoxy in a Christian context is similar to the function of paradigms in the sciences; they give the researcher a place to stand from which to conduct further inquiry. Paradigms, as originally defined by Thomas Kuhn, are the sets of theories and practices considered normative within any given scientific community at a given time. The reigning paradigm in biology, for example, is Neo-Darwinian evolutionary theory. Paradigms, however, are never reducible to theory, but depend also on a shared set of practices that require casuistic skill and practical judgment that is passed on from mentor to student. Paradigms do not limit research but set research agendas, that is, they help the researcher to limit the limitless possibilities down to those avenues of research that are likely to be fruitful.

Paradigms are not unchanging, but as long as a certain paradigm reigns, evidence that contradicts the paradigm will be treated as an anomaly and not as a falsification of the paradigm. Data and theories that do not agree with the reigning paradigm are generally ignored, and those who advocate such heterodoxies are censured and marginalized. Nichols cites several examples. At a 1997 conference at the University of Notre Dame entitled "Dissent and Orthodoxy in Quantum Mechanics," the consensus was that the Copenhagen interpretation of quantum mechanics has served as a particularly rigid orthodoxy for the past seventy years, until recently keeping the Bohm interpretation from even being discussed. Likewise, cell biologist Rupert Sheldrake's suggestion of something analogous to Aristotelian forms governing the regeneration of organisms and pediatrician Melvin Morse's work on near-death experiences have cost them jobs and research grants, with their work not refuted according to scientific method but censured or ignored. (An anonymous reviewer in the journal *Nature,* later revealed to be the journal's editor, wrote that Sheldrake's "book is the best candidate for burning there has been in many years.")[30] Nichols does not argue for the truth of these dissenters' work, but finds it significant that their work—all based on empirical data—has been rejected without anyone bothering to propose experiments to invalidate their hypotheses. This does not mean that paradigms do not usually function well, but indicates that scientific orthodoxy shares more, both good and bad, with Christian orthodoxy than is often supposed. Nichols concludes that the charge that theology

> already knows in advance what it is attempting to prove, is partly true and partly false, but to the extent that it is true, it is also true of the sciences themselves. Like theology, the sciences are based on certain core theories about the nature of reality (e.g., reality is rationally intelligible, and can be explained by natural causes) which cannot be proven beyond any doubt, but which are to a certain extent validated by the ongoing fruitfulness of their enterprises. If this is so, it means that the knowledge commanded by any discipline is but a partial view of the whole, and therefore each discipline needs the perspective of others to approximate an adequate, comprehensive view of the whole of reality.[31]

This last point is consonant with *Ex Corde Ecclesiae's* defense of the autonomy of the methods of each specialized discipline. Science must be free to use the empirical method, which is proper to it. At the same time, all inquiry must not be limited to this method. Theology in its employment of faith elevates reason to a higher order of knowledge. For free inquiry to take place, it is imperative that the autonomy of theology be respected, and that the sciences not usurp its role by trying alone to provide a comprehensive view of reality.

We need not accept the contrast between free inquiry at secular universities and inquiry limited by orthodoxy at church-related schools. What obtains in reality are simply different orthodoxies. The examples given above are taken from the natural sciences, but orthodoxies prevail across the other disciplines as well. How many Marxists teach in the business school of the typical university? Do those holding a Thomist view of human psychology get a fair hearing in the psychology department?

There is no reason to suppose that that orthodoxy that bans theological inquiry from campus and limits the educational experience to naturalistic explanation is in fact more free. Evidence suggests exactly the opposite. George Marsden writes that his students at Calvin College—a Christian Reformed school with rigorous religious requirements for its faculty—were more likely than those at the University of California at Berkeley to have higher level intellectual arguments because they could assume a higher level of agreement and did not have to begin every discussion with a debate over first principles. Students at Calvin, according to Marsden, were also more likely to be creative and intellectually curious because they were able to see some coherence in their education across disciplinary lines.[32] Gerald Graff relates the following anecdote from a secular university:

> An undergraduate tells of an art history course in which the instructor observed one day, "As we now know, the idea that knowledge can be objective is a positivist myth that has been exploded by postmodern thought." It so happens that the student is concurrently enrolled in a political science course, in which the instructor speaks confidently about the objectivity of his discipline as if objectivity had not been exploded at all. "What do you do?" the student is asked. "What else can I do?" he says, "I trash objectivity in art history and I presuppose objectivity in political science."[33]

The incoherence of a curriculum guided by little more than the orthodoxy of diversity of views can breed not freedom, but cynicism. Simply freeing a student to choose does not necessarily enable a student to choose well. Mere negative freedom in the absence of positive freedom is a trap.

2) Authority

Those who grant that orthodoxies often serve as the basis for inquiry even at secular universities might still want to claim there is a crucial difference between such orthodoxies and that of Christian faith: secular orthodoxies result from the response of autonomous reason to the buildup of convincing empirical evidence over time, whereas Christian orthodoxy is imposed on reason heteronomously by the authority of text and magisterium. The terms on which this argument is offered need careful scrutiny. On the one hand, it overstates the extent to which most disciplines rely on empirical evidence. The process of evolution, for example, is neither empirically observable nor experimentally reproducible. The plausibility of the theory of evolution depends on converging inferences gathered from many different types of evidence. As Nichols points out, this is also true of many theological claims, such as "God exists."[34] If biology sometimes operates in this way, the same may be said *a fortiori* of social sciences and humanities, which proceed not so much by the disinterested weighing of empirical evidence as through the exegesis of authoritative texts in a hermeneutical tradition. Literature and philosophy, both of which occupy comfortable homes in the secular academy, bear a closer resemblance to rabbinical midrash than to laboratory science.

On the other hand, we should also refuse to accept the fideist caricature of Christian appeals to authority. Not only is Christian truth in part supported by evidence judged at the bar of human reason, but the proper functioning of all human reasoning depends upon the acceptance of an authority from without the individual. This point is crucial to Alasdair MacIntyre's critique of Enlightenment rationality. In his *Three Rival Versions of Moral Enquiry*, MacIntyre argues the Augustinian position that the intelligence can only be rightly ordered if the will is subordinated through the virtue of humility. The problem is that one must have acquired humility and other virtues before one can understand why they are virtues and why one must acquire them, indeed, before one can reason properly at all. As MacIntyre puts it, "a prerational reordering of the self has to occur before the reader can have an adequate standard by which to judge what is a good reason and what is not."[35] Reasoning can only proceed if one initially accepts the authority of a teacher who is able to point one toward relevant and truthful texts and is able to help one learn how to read them. Acceptance of the authority of teacher and text at this stage is on the basis not of evidence but of testimony, that is, a prerational trust in the teacher by virtue of the office that he or she holds. Only later does a person learn to evaluate reasons as good or bad. A person learns the story of herself embedded in the world that the texts have opened for her. But the intelligibility of that world is never complete, and so the need for authoritative testimony to advance enquiry from where one currently stands can never in this life be completely dispensed with.[36]

The authority in question is not simply certain texts and teachers but the whole tradition of interpretation and inquiry in which the texts and teachers stand. The scholar never simply rises above this tradition and the community gathered by it. Where critical dialectical reasoning is done, it is always done in conversation with a tradition considered authoritative, even and especially where the scholar may have severe criticisms to bring against elements of the tradition. As MacIntyre makes plain, in order to bring such criticisms and have such arguments it is necessary first to be in substantial agreement on what does and does not constitute a valid reason. In this way, traditions of inquiry are not static but constantly advance, in large part because the authority of the tradition makes dialectical reasoning possible.

This very brief summary does not, of course, do justice to MacIntyre's critique of Enlightenment views of rationality, developed over three volumes beginning with *After Virtue*. MacIntyre argues that autonomous rationality is a myth, not only undesirable but empirically false and impossible, because it smuggles in one particular partisan account of the human person under the guise of universality and disinterestedness, all the while ignoring the ineluctable historicity and contextual character of all rational principles and rational persons. The Enlightenment promised a form of rational justification that would be based on principles undeniable to any rational person anywhere, regardless of the particularities of each person's history and geography. Ironically, those taken with this project have yet to agree on those principles.[37]

The point of this for our present purposes is not, of course, to argue that all authority and tradition are good, or that authority cannot be abused. The point is simply that there is no good reason to suppose that authority of itself is a hindrance to academic freedom. Indeed, Christians argue the opposite: the very exercise of rationality depends on the exercise of authority. This may seem like a counterintuitive claim, given the regularity with which students are admonished to "think for yourselves." In my experience, however, MacIntyre's account comes very close to describing what university professors and students actually do. Most scholarly articles in the social sciences and humanities—even those that incorporate fresh empirical data—build their arguments upon appeals to, and dialectical conversation with, authoritative texts in their fields. And students manifestly do not learn by becoming more autonomous. To think critically and creatively one must possess certain habits and dispositions acquired by hard experience in the context of a community in which authority has an orienting function. To ask students to make choices while attempting to strip away any basis they might have for making choices is to breed arbitrariness and cynicism, not critical reasoning. To tell students to rely on nothing but their own authority is to entrap them in the prison of the self, and they tend to resent it, not least because a professor's denial of authority is often a ploy—conscious or not—to win the students over to his or her worldview without appearing to have exercised authority over them. Students today by and large do not need to be freed from narrow dogmatism and unthinking acceptance of religious authority. They need to be freed from the confines of the self and the dreary consumerism that teaches them to regard truth as something chosen, not something received.

■ IV. Conclusion

The liberal paradigm has largely succeeded in setting the tone for discussions of academic freedom, even at church-related institutions. As a result, administrators and professors at such institutions tend to approach the subject apologetically: "Yes, we do limit academic freedom here because of our mission, but we try not to limit it very much, and the losses are offset by other gains from being church-related." This type of approach only breeds confusion and a loss of confidence in the mission of the institution. If the argument of this essay is correct, then we need not apologize, nor meekly plead for a place at the table on the basis of having a different voice. The ecclesially based university does indeed have a different understanding of academic freedom than that of secular universities, but we claim that it inscribes a more complete freedom into the life of the university. This claim is not just to be asserted but is to be argued on rational grounds. The ecclesially based university is better equipped to promote freedom precisely because it has a fuller understanding of the quest for truth. Freedom and truth are the true colors under which the ecclesially based university sails.

■ Notes

1. James Heft, "Academic Freedom and the Catholic University," in John Apczynski, ed., *Theology and the University: Annual of the College Theology Society* 33 (1987): 212–13.

2. The classic account of this shift in American higher education is Christopher Jencks and David Riesman, *The Academic Revolution* (Garden City, N.J.: Doubleday, 1969).

3. *American Association of University Professors,* "Report on Academic Freedom," quoted in *Heft,* p. 213.

4. American Association of University Professors, *1940 Statement of Principles on Academic Freedom and Tenure, with 1970 Interpretive Comments.*

5. Ibid.

6. AAUP Subcommittee on Academic Freedom, 1988, quoted in George Marsden, "Liberating Academic Freedom," *First Things* 88 (December 1998): 12.

7. AAUP Subcommittee on Academic Freedom, 1996, quoted in Marsden, "Liberating Academic Freedom," p. 12.

8. Marsden, "Liberating Academic Freedom," p. 12.

9. Arthur O. Lovejoy, "Academic Freedom," in *The Encyclopedia of the Social Sciences* (New York: Macmillan, 1930), p. 386.

10. AAUP, *1940 Statement of Principles on Academic Freedom and Tenure, with 1970 Interpretive Comments.*

11. Marsden, "Liberating Academic Freedom," p. 12.

12. "University of Paris," *New Catholic Encyclopedia,* quoted in Frederick J. Crosson, "Two Faces of Academic Freedom," in Theodore M. Hesburgh, CSC, ed., *The Challenge*

and Promise of a Catholic University, (Notre Dame, Ind.: University of Notre Dame Press, 1994), p. 46.

13. Crosson, "Two Faces," pp. 46–7. This section is greatly indebted to Crosson's argument.

14. Quoted in ibid., p. 49.

15. Crosson, "Two Faces," p. 59, n. 12.

16. David M. Rabban, "A Functional Analysis of 'Individual' and 'Institutional' Academic Freedom under the First Amendment," *Law and Contemporary Problems* 53, no.3 (Summer 1990): 227–301.

17. Crosson, "Two Faces," p. 50.

18. James T. Burtchaell, CSC, "Out of the Heartburn of the Church," *The Journal of College and University Law* 25, no. 4 (Spring 1999): 680–1.

19. Fr. Richard P. McBrien, "Why I Shall Not Seek a Mandate," *America* (Feb. 12, 2000): 14. Terrence Tilley objects to the suggestion that bishops be treated on the same footing as outside accrediting agencies. "The other agencies are academic and professional bodies, like the American Chemical Society or the Association of Business Schools. The businesses and universities see mutual benefit from an association freely chosen by each. Bishops' involvement on the *mandatum* falls into neither category"; Terrence W. Tilley, "The Misunderstood *Mandatum*," *The Council of Societies for the Study of Religion Bulletin* 30, no. 3 (September 2001): 56–7. However, it is not clear what Tilley means by "academic and professional." If it means "internal to the university," then accrediting agencies would not qualify. If it means "engaged in the scholarly practice suitable to one's field" then it is not at all clear why bishops would not or could not qualify in the area of theology, to which the *mandatum* is restricted. As for the freedom and mutual benefit of the university's relationship with accrediting agencies, in reality a university risks severe damage to its reputation if it does not maintain its accreditation, and universities are often compelled to make internal changes to avoid jeopardizing their accreditation. My own university in 2001 reorganized itself into eight separate "schools" largely in response to a request by the accrediting agency for education programs, which wanted the undergraduate and graduate programs in education united into one school.

20. John Neville Figgis, *Churches in the Modern State*, 2d ed. (London: Longmans, Green, and Co., 1914), pp. 51–2. For more analyses of this process, see Robert Nisbet, *The Quest for Community* (London: Oxford University Press, 1953) and A. J. Conyers, *The Long Truce: How Toleration Made the World Safe for Power and Profit* (Dallas: Spence Publishing, 2001).

21. William J. Hoye, "The Religious Roots of Academic Freedom," *Theological Studies* 58, no. 3 (September 1997): 415.

22. Richard Hofstadter, *Academic Freedom in the Age of the College* (New Brunswick, N.J.: Transaction Press, 1996), pp. 121–2, quoted in ibid., p. 416.

23. See Immanuel Kant, *The Conflict of the Faculties*, trans. Mary J. Gregor (Lincoln: University of Nebraska Press, 1962).

24. An account of this episode can be found in Hoye, "Religious Roots," p. 413.

25. *Ex Corde Ecclesiae: Apostolic Constitution of the Supreme Pontiff John Paul II on Catholic Universities*, Part II, art. 2, para. 5.

26. James Tunstead Burtchaell, CSC, *The Dying of the Light: The Disengagement of Colleges and Universities from their Christian Churches* (Grand Rapids: Eerdmans, 1998).

27. Donald Kennedy, "Making Choices in the Research University," *Daedalus* 122 (1993): 149, quoted in Stephen Fields, SJ, "Catholicism and Academic Freedom: Authorities in Conflict?" *Logos* 4, no. 4 (Fall 2001): 99.

28. Kenneth Kemp, "What is Academic Freedom?" in *Academic Freedom and the Catholic University*, University of St. Thomas Summer Seminar, 1997, pp. 37–8.

29. *Ex Corde Ecclesiae*, para. 12, note 15.

30. Terence L. Nichols, "Catholic Theology and Academic Freedom" in *Academic Freedom and the Catholic University*, pp. 119–21. Walker Percy tells of a visit by the eminent Australian neurobiologist Sir John Eccles to Harvard in the 1970s. Eccles concluded his lecture saying that while evolution can account for the brain, it cannot account for the mind. Some kind of transcendent cause must be responsible for the development of consciousness. Although Eccles based his conclusion on the empirical data and not on appeal to Scripture, for example, the Harvard audience began hissing. Walker Percy, *Lost in the Cosmos* (New York: Noonday Press, 1983), pp. 166–7.

31. Ibid., pp. 122–3.

32. Marsden, "Liberating Academic Freedom," p. 11.

33. Gerald Graff, *Beyond the Culture Wars: How Teaching the Conflicts Can Revitalize American Education* (New York: W. W. Norton, 1992), quoted in Francis Cardinal George, "Catholic Faith and the Secular Academy," *Logos* 4, no. 4 (Fall 2001): 74–5.

34. Nichols, "Catholic Theology," p. 122.

35. Alasdair MacIntyre, *Three Rival Versions of Moral Enquiry* (Notre Dame, Ind.: University of Notre Dame Press, 1990), 82.

36. Ibid., pp. 91–2.

37. Alasdair MacIntyre, *Whose Justice? Which Rationality?* (Notre Dame, Ind.: University of Notre Dame Press, 1988), pp. 3–6.

3

City of Carnage, City of Refuge

Accounting for the Wages of Reason in the Ecclesially Based University

Barry Harvey

Whenever the relationship between nature and grace is severed . . . then the whole of worldly being falls under the dominion of "knowledge," and the springs and force of love immanent in the world are overpowered and finally suffocated by science, technology, cybernetics.

Hans Urs von Balthasar

The main character in the popular novel and movie *The Godfather,* Vito Corleone, was, as Frank Lentricchia puts it, "a connoisseur of reason (as in 'I will reason with him'; or as in 'But no one can reason with him')." According to Lentricchia, this notorious *mafioso* knew that critical self-reflection always takes place in a context of other wills and thus in "situations that make vivid, sometimes vividly red, the consequences of taking 'unreasonable' positions."[1] In other words, rationality does not subsist in tidy conceptual worldviews, but in a world in which violence, coercion, and death are endemic to its dominant modes of operation.

Lentricchia's musings about this fictional head of a crime family as a connoisseur of reason, though admittedly made tongue-in-cheek, nonetheless draw our attention to some very serious questions as we consider the witness of an ecclesially based university. Rational reflection in its manifold forms is, after all, the proper activity of the university, not the least for one that seeks to be attentive to "the beginning and end of all things, and of reasoning creatures especially."[2] The ability to reason well about God and the world is also essential to the life and witness of the church. The stories and images of Scripture, as basic as they are to the life of discipleship, cannot by themselves sustain the body of Christ over the long term. As the members of this body seek to bear truthful witness to the Triune God, interpretive questions arise that cannot be answered simply by introducing yet more images, no matter how winsome they may be. Imagination and abstraction, metaphor and concept, figure and analogy, story and doctrine are "undivided and yet distinct," to borrow from the Chalcedonian definition of Christ's divine and human natures. In short, the faithful imagining[3] that informs Christian discipleship both gives birth to and completes itself in rational understanding.

Christians must therefore be "connoisseurs of reason," at least of a certain sort. Therein lies the opportunity and challenge before us as we consider what it would mean to institute an ecclesially based university in a social regime governed by powers and institutions whose ends are not those of the Body of Christ. As Stephen Toulmin reminds us, rationality is not an attribute of conceptual systems or worldviews as such, but of those communal practices and social projects that constitute human life and language, for which particular sets of concepts are the working cross-sections. More specifically, rationality is an attribute of the procedures that allow those who engage in these enterprises to criticize and change the concepts, judgments, and formal systems currently employed in carrying out these activities.[4]

Throughout this essay I shall consult Augustine for our bearings as we chart the path before us. In Book XIX of *The City of God*, for example, he states that though the pilgrim people of God are not to occupy themselves with differences in the customs, laws, and institutions by which earthly peace is achieved or maintained, neither are they to neglect these matters. On the contrary, they should encourage cooperation in pursuit of those things that belong to the mortal nature of human beings. Augustine does add one very important proviso. These worldly matters should "not impede the religion by which we are taught that the one supreme and true God is to be worshipped." Short of interfering with true godliness and piety, however, this society of pilgrims should prudently use earthly goods to direct them toward that alone which can truly be called peace, "a perfectly ordered and perfectly harmonious fellowship in the enjoyment of God, and of one another in God."[5]

The university is certainly among those institutions that, as Augustine puts it elsewhere, contribute to the necessary ordering of life in our time and place.[6] If Christians are to make prudent use of this institution, I would argue that we must rethink the many questionable habits of mind bequeathed to us by modern academic curricula that would impede our worship, which is to offer ourselves as part of Christ's universal sacrifice.[7] High on this list of intellectual vices is the notion that ideas and inferences are autonomous, independent of social formations and political associations. On this model, says Nicholas Lash, the life of both the church and the wider world most closely resembles a neverending academic seminar. "But," says Lash, "those who take part in the seminar, frequently unmindful of the social and economic privilege which makes their performance possible, tend to overlook the extent to which theoretical disagreement is but the abstract expression, in the order of ideas, of conflicts which, outside the seminar room or the 'salon', frequently find harsher and more concrete form."[8]

Put differently, the production and transmission of knowledge within the university are always associated with contingent social formations. The assumptions, descriptions, convictions, and procedures cultivated by connoisseurs of reason both within and outside the church are therefore inextricably connected with some network of practices. Apart from these particular practices, the various forms of knowledge that concern us are literally unimaginable. These networks are in turn vested in institutions, the majority of which, though they contribute to the necessary ordering of life, unreservedly partake of a fallen creation. They are thus implicated in the achievement and maintenance of a peace that is finally incommensurable with the practices and habits that bind us to the one supreme and true God.[9] As the principal custodian of the procedures of rational inquiry and the production of knowledge, the university has, wittingly or not, played a crucial role in their use in social contexts that make vivid, and often vividly red, the consequences of taking what "the powers that be" regard as unreasonable positions.

It behooves us, then, to consider what is at stake for the church's witness in becoming skilled in the arts of reason, and especially for a university that seeks to cultivate those arts in ways that do not divorce the love of learning from the desire for God.[10] I shall begin by recounting two stories that narrate contrasting social configurations of the arts of reason, one that is oriented to death and violence, the other oriented to the perfectly ordered and harmonious communion in the city of God. The first story is set in January of 1879 in a remote and seemingly insignificant military supply station in Natal province, South Africa, the second in a small French village during the latter half of World War II. These stories will help us see the different faiths, different hopes, and different charities[11] that crystallize at Rorke's Drift and le Chambon. It is in terms of these differences that we must account for the distinctive approach to the arts of reason within an ecclesially based university.

City of Carnage

On January 22, 1879, a small contingent of British soldiers from the 24th Regiment were encamped at Rorke's Drift, a remote missionary station in Natal Province, South Africa. They received word that a Zulu *impi*, or regiment, of 20,000 warriors had slaughtered nearly 2,000 of their comrades some six miles away in Zululand.[12] At the same time they also learned that another *impi* of 4,000 warriors was making its way toward the mission, where they were garrisoning a supply station and hospital with only 139 British soldiers, 35 of whom were bedridden, and only 80 of whom were riflemen. A number of native and European auxiliaries, together with a group of Boer militia, fled the station when news of the advance of the Zulus reached them.

In command were two lieutenants who had precious little combat experience and who, to that point in their careers, had not distinguished themselves in their duties. One, John Chard, newly arrived in South Africa, was a nearly deaf engineer assigned to supervise the construction of a ferry just below the station; the other, Gonville Bromhead, whom a superior had judged to be "hopeless," had been left behind when the bulk of his regiment had gone to their deaths across the Buffalo River. A former master sergeant, James Dalton, was also on hand and seems to have provided valuable advice to Chard and Bromhead as they prepared to defend their post in what was surely a hopeless cause. The number of men available to fight comprised only a fraction of those mustered by the British force that had just perished, and they did not occupy high ground as their fallen comrades had done.

What transpired over the next day-and-a-half has become the stuff of legend—and later of Hollywood. With detailed knowledge of Zulu tactics provided them by Boer settlers, Chard and Bromhead made good use of their few hours' warning. They ordered the construction of a series of defensive perimeters, to be built out of overturned wagons and stacks of biscuit boxes and mealie bags, with a final redoubt at the center. Armed with powerful and accurate Martini-Henry rifles (whose only drawback was that they were single shot), the small detachment successfully repulsed the *impi* of 4,000 during an engagement that lasted sixteen hours. British casualties were surprisingly light (15 killed, 12 wounded). The Zulus, who never could surmount the makeshift fortifications and thus bring to bear against the Europeans their deadly *assegais* (short, sharp stabbing spears), lost somewhere between 400 to 800 men. For those who think it important to keep track of grisly statistics, that is a kill ratio of somewhere between twenty-five and fifty to one.

How did the British triumph in the face of such overwhelming odds? According to military historian Victor Hanson, the men of the 24th Regiment

> were clearly better supplied with food, medical treatment, and ammunition; their soldiers were far better-trained shots. Most important, their system of institutionalized discipline ensured a steady curtain of fire unlike anything previously experienced in the native wars of Africa. Britain's industrialized, fully capitalist economy had the wherewithal to transport and supply thousands of such men miles from home. European science was responsible for the Martini-Henry rifle—a terrible gun whose enormous bullet and uncanny accuracy helped to destroy Zulu manhood outright. . . . On January 22, 1879, the garrison at Rorke's Drift proved to be the most dangerous hundred men in the world.[13]

According to Hanson, the reasons for the Anglo-Zulu war of 1879 are far from clear. With problems elsewhere in their empire—particularly in India, Afghanistan, and Egypt—the British did not need nor want a war in southern Africa. There were few natural resources in Zululand, only disease and a troublesome, militaristic population. And yet they did invade and, following the initial setback at Isandhlwana, subjected Zululand in relatively short order. It was incorporated into the imperial body politic of Britain, and thus into the infamous legacy that became South Africa.

The Wages of Reason

The significance of what took place at Rorke's Drift far transcends its tactical specifications. Victor Hanson argues in his provocative and controversial book *Carnage and Culture* that it is part of a larger pattern, which he characterizes as the "singular lethality" of Western civilization. This lethal pattern has consistently given its peoples a decided advantage in war against their non-Western neighbors since the fifth century B.C.E. A "cultural crystallization" occurs in this and similar clashes in which social practices and institutions whose vital contribution to Western ways of warfare had heretofore been murky and undefined become "stark and unforgiving in the finality of organized killing."[14]

Though it is doubtful that Hanson has given the definitive explanation for the military dominance of Europe and North America, he does offer a compelling account of the important role that civic habits and virtues play in the successful conduct of war.[15] He employs a historiographical approach that resembles the sort of narrative hermeneutics that theologians have sought in recent years to restore theology to its rightful place in human reasoning. He focuses on nine key battles, beginning with Salamis in 480 B.C.E., where a Greek fleet routed a much larger Persian flotilla, and concluding with the infamous Tet offensive in 1968, where the Americans won the battle, lost the war, and won the subsequent peace. His aim in this narration is not to show that the fate of civilizations hung in the balance in these particular engagements—though that was sometimes the case—or to make grandiose claims about the gallantry or nobility of war. He seeks to demonstrate instead that Western civilization is more adept at killing, often brutally and frequently with little loss of life among its own ranks, because its ways of warring are organic extensions of the customs, conventions, virtues, and practices initially cultivated by the classical Greek cities and refined by the empires, kingdoms, and nation-states that followed them.

According to Hanson, the consistent advantage in war that Western peoples have enjoyed for nearly two and a half millennia is not the result of some sort of innate genetic or moral superiority, nor can it be attributed to geography[16] or fortune. The edge is due instead to what he labels the "murderous dividend" of Hellenic civilization and its cultural offshoots. In other words, what makes for the best of the earthly city also provides the necessary conditions for its worst. He identifies and analyzes a complex network of social, economic, political, and religious practices that constitute this lethal social order. There are, first, distinctive political structures that encourage consensual government, freedom of expression, and individual initiative and innovation, all of which contribute to the tactical prosecution of war. Second, the West's agrarian-based tradition of civic militarism, with armies consisting of yeoman farmers who have a stake in political deliberations, has proved far more adept than mercenaries or slaves at maintaining the sort of lethal discipline that distinguishes effective soldiers from courageous warriors. Third, economic practices that increasingly promote unrestricted exchange and accumulation of material goods among peoples also play a crucial role in the unique capacity of the West to construct more and better weapons.[17] Fourth, a tradition of public audit and criticism of political and military leadership, though often thought in times of conflict to be detrimental to the ability of a country to deal with its enemies, actually empowers the ability and desire of a nation's population to wage war.

Of particular interest for those concerned with the ecclesially based university, however, is Hanson's contention that the traditions of rationalism, free inquiry, and dissemination of knowledge to which the Greeks gave birth contribute in substantial ways to the singular lethality of Western civilization. These practices and skills—which he classifies under the Pauline-inspired heading "the Wages of Reason"—are essential to the murderous dividend of Western civilization. To a degree unmatched by other peoples and civilizations, the West understood the conduct of war to be a rational enterprise, and its superiority in battle is directly tied to the development and refinement of procedures of rational criticism and the production and dissemination of knowledge.

The most obvious indication of the rationality of the West, of course, is its science and advanced technology. Such practices make possible the West's unparalleled ability to design and manufacture ever more sophisticated killing machines on a vast scale. As Hanson notes, "Is it not odd that Greek hoplites, Roman legionaries, medieval knights, Byzantine fleets, Renaissance foot soldiers, Mediterranean galleys, and Western harquebusiers were usually equipped with greater destructive power than their adversaries?"[18] The one-sided carnage at Rorke's Drift is but one case in point.[19]

We would be mistaken, however, if we limit the advantage of the West's traditions of rational inquiry to the obvious matter of technological progress in the design and manufacture of weapons. Most of the disciplines of study that presently exist in the modern university have made vital contributions to the achievement of peace by the earthly city through war, beginning with its traditions of literacy and literature. It is not accidental that the art of writing history, to cite one very important example, arose from the European encounter with foreign peoples and customs.[20] When the chronicles of travelers from the West, beginning in the sixth century B.C.E., described the cities and terrain of the peoples of the East, and cataloged their customs, they inscribed them within a narrative that tacitly postulated their own places and customs "as the base from which relations with an *exteriority* composed of targets or threats . . . can be managed."[21] This strategic approach to knowledge grows out of what Augustine calls the *libido dominandi*, the lust for mastery.[22] Indeed, says Hanson, the historiographical tradition that Greece and Rome bequeathed to medieval Europe was predicated on the "propensities of Herodotus, Thucydides, Livy, and Tacitus to see history largely as the story of war and politics."[23]

The widespread dissemination of this knowledge, involving the opportunity to express and exchange ideas uncensored by ruling élites—a process that the inventions of the printing press and now the Internet have extended—further contributes to the ability of these peoples to wage war. Hanson rightly points out that the so-called Dark Ages that followed the demise of the Roman Empire in Western Europe represent not so much the end of classical antiquity but its diffusion.[24] The medieval *literati* in monastic and cathedral schools kept alive and propagated the deadly military insights of classical antiquity. Arabic treatises on war, by way of contrast, tended to attribute defeat in battle to lapses of faith and dealt very little or not at all with tactical mistakes or shortcomings in strategy and logistics. Indeed, says Hanson, what we do know of the non-West in battle we learn almost exclusively from Western sources.[25]

Embedded in these modes of knowledge were the well-developed procedures of rational inquiry refined by such renowned figures as Plato and Aristotle—dialectic, deductive, and inductive modes of inference, tropes, analogy, to name just a few. These procedures enabled Greek hoplite and Frankish knight, Spanish conquistador and British rifleman, to analyze their opposition and to exploit the weaknesses they uncovered in ways that other cultures have generally only copied. When the civic heirs of the Greeks were met by the unexpected, they were not reduced to seeing their opponents as gods or magicians, as for example the Aztec ruler Montezuma did, but were able to correctly describe what was taking place, reason abstractly, and devise methods of responding effectively.

As I noted above, Hanson aptly designates the war dividend of Western civilization "the Wages of Reason." This poignant phrase not only echoes Paul's statement about the wages of sin leading to death (Rom. 6:23), but also recalls Hegel's observations about the "cunning of Reason" and Augustine's contention that the lust for mastery has mastered the activities of the earthly city. Nicholas Boyle aptly summarizes this colloquy of images for impaired natural reason as the logic of history, or to put it in a more Augustinian vein, the logic of the earthly city. Though they pursue aims that are shaped by their own passions, principles, hopes, and delusions, the great figures of this history are nonetheless instruments of historical processes that transcend their own efforts and often their own understanding.[26]

In an age of global commerce, these wages not only accrue in the war-making of nation-states, but also accumulate in the ways state and market define daily what it means to be human beings. The practices sustained by these institutions continually divest the world of the old, old stories, and reinvest its human capital more "rationally," that is, in globally extended networks of production and consumption. The logic of these networks congeals around a curious mixture of permissiveness and supervision, as people do exactly what these networks want them to do, all the while reassuring them that this is what it means to be free. The foods we choose to eat, the cars we choose to buy, the music we choose to hear, the clothes we choose to wear, in short, the lives we choose to live—these are all carefully managed by institutions that we cannot see and people we never meet face to face. As a result, says Wendell Berry, "we have been reduced almost to a state . . . in which people and all other creatures and things may be considered purely as economic 'units', or integers of production, and in which a human being may be dealt with . . . 'merely as a covetous machine'"[27]

The workings of the market stipulate not particular acts, but the range of possible acts and relationships available to us as individuals, the "rational" patterns that govern our day-to-day lives, in public *and* in private. Within the logic of the earthly city's commercial republic, the question of what we permanently are, "or what permanently is, and is permanently valuable, does not arise."[28] There is little possibility of such questions ever arising, for our age lacks the sort of imagination that would allow it even to pose them in an authoritative way. The control that this form of rationality exercises over us is therefore anonymous and indirect, but precisely for this reason all the more sweeping. It determines where we will live (and when we will move), what kind of clothes we will wear (proper business attire and uniforms with the company logo), and what sorts of food we may eat (no sack lunches at the desk, please). As Rodney Clapp observes, if a church were to impose this sort of discipline on its members it would quickly be denounced as "authoritarian," if not worse.[29]

Effectively sundered from meaningful points of reference beyond our present self-defined desires, men and women are largely reduced to the sequence of economic roles they perform. Day-to-day life is but a series of consumer choices to make and a sequence of jobs from which to be made redundant. It is therefore extremely difficult for most people most of the time to recognize the ways that the belligerence of the reasoning fostered in the earthly city rules their lives. Something more than simply being in a position to see and hear what is going on around us is needed if we are to penetrate the cunning of reason embedded in the logic of the earthly city. It requires the acquisition of new habits of life and language, new ways of assessing the world in which we live our lives. In other words, it takes a different faith, a different hope, and a different love to recognize and then to respond faithfully and courageously to what we once took as a given. To understand something of what is entailed in these new habits, I turn now to our second story.

◼ City of Refuge

On a Saturday evening in late summer of 1942 an official convoy of police cars, motorcycles, and buses pulled into le Chambon, a small village of about three thousand people in the mountainous region of southeastern France. The police chief for that district was a high official with the Vichy government, which had been set up by the Nazis following France's defeat at the hands of the dreaded German *Blitzkrieg* in 1940. He summoned the pastor of the local Protestant church to the town hall. When André Trocmé arrived, the chief told him that the authorities knew that the town was engaged in suspect activities under his leadership, and more specifically, that they were hiding a number of Jews. Trocmé was ordered to hand over a list of these persons and reveal where they were hiding, so that they could be rounded up and taken to the prefecture for "control," which, as we now know, was a chilling euphemism for deportation to the extermination camps in the east.

Trocmé refused to cooperate, telling the official (truthfully, as it so happened) that he had no such list. Even if it existed, he continued, these people had sought protection from the church in this region. This meant that he was their pastor, their shepherd, and it was not the role of a shepherd to betray the sheep committed to his keeping. The police chief warned Trocmé that failure to obey would result in his arrest and deportation. After laying down an ultimatum that set a time limit for voluntary compliance, the chief let Trocmé go. Trocmé immediately went to his office and met with a group of Boy Scouts and Bible class leaders, where they set into motion a plan that had been worked out in the weeks leading up to this fateful day. These young people went to outlying farms where the Jews were staying and warned them to flee into the woods under the cover of darkness. "Under a starlit night," writes Philip Hallie, "it was as if ghosts were purposefully making their respective ways through the square and the streets while the police waited for their ultimatum to expire, sleeping upon straw."[30]

The next morning Trocmé ascended the high pulpit in the big gray church of le Chambon and preached to the townspeople gathered there for Sunday worship. According to some accounts, he cited an ordinance in the book of Deuteronomy that established cities of refuge for safeguarding those unjustly accused in ancient Israel. Then he declared that their village must in like fashion become a city of refuge for all those sought by the Vichy government "lest innocent blood be shed" (Deut. 19:10). The Chambonnais responded to their pastor's charge. Following the admonition in the Sermon on the Mount that they were to be a city set on a hill, they continued to hide Jews (who eventually came from all parts of Europe) and smuggled them to Switzerland. Though the police remained in le Chambon for three weeks, their net snared few victims. Of the dozens of Jews whom the Chambonnais had secreted in the region, only two were arrested, and one of these was later released because it was determined that he was only "half Jewish," which at the time was sufficient to avoid deportation.

The events that occurred in le Chambon were not the actions of isolated individuals who displayed uncommon courage for brief moments of time. Employing a type of discipline not completely unlike that demonstrated by the British soldiers at Rorke's Drift, but without firing a shot, the entire village was involved to one degree or another in a complex rescue effort that took place over the span of several years. Their involvement did not come cheaply. Some in the village were imprisoned in concentration camps, including members of Trocmé's own family, and a few were executed. Nevertheless, by the end of the war the residents of this one village, led by the members of the little Protestant church and an even smaller Plymouth Brethren congregation, saved somewhere between 2,500 and 5,000 Jewish lives, most of them children.

The Logic of Incarnation

A distinctive way of assessing and responding to the world crystallized among the Christians at le Chambon that, though materially quite different, is formally analogous to what occurred at Rorke's Drift. Practices and institutions whose essential function in the pilgrimage of God's people through the present age, the significance of which has frequently been murky and undefined even for Christians, became vivid and redemptive in the process of rescuing Jews from the gas chambers. A church that seeks to live faithfully before God and the wider world around it is ordered by its own logic of history, one that runs counter to the wages of reason dispensed by the earthly city. It is a logic that, due to its figural and analogical character, takes the form of an ongoing story. The coherence and identity of a people that claims no "place" of its own from which to manage its use of the world's goods in strategic fashion depend on a critical narrative historiography. The ecclesial location of this story and of the life and language in terms of which it is narrated makes it finally unsuitable as the basis for the earthly city's strategic calculations that figure so centrally in its lust for mastery. But as the events at le Chambon also demonstrate, these practices can serve to evoke a vision of the world so persuasive and abiding that the Love that calls all things both into being and into communion is concretely manifested before the world.

The concerted action taken by the Chambonnais was cultivated by the shared life and language of a community over many generations. Trocmé's admonition that their village should transform itself into a city of refuge so that innocent blood would not be shed reveals in particular a figural imagination formed principally by the images and stories of Scripture. The communal reading and rereading of the biblical stories over the centuries by the members of this congregation decisively shaped their understanding of the world and of their place in it. When the crisis came—and no one knows beforehand when that time will come—their shared vision generated possibilities of life and action. With these arose a distinctive mode of reasoning, one that disrupted the designs of a seemingly invincible foe. And it did so during a time when the residents of countless other cities, towns, and villages claimed that they were powerless to do anything about their situation.[31]

The *lectio divina,* the sacred reading of Scripture, practiced by the Chambonnais over the years taught them how to describe the world as it is now against the backdrop of how it ought to be and—in the province, provenance, and providence of the Triune God—how it eventually will be. Indeed, according to Trocmé, those who recognize only the actual as rational, and do not have the imaginative ability to superimpose the present and the future, are seriously handicapped. Viewed separately, he writes, "Each image is flat . . . the world 'as it is' has no depth; it is a sequence of phenomena with no rhyme or reason, without origin or end. Similarly the world 'as it should be', the kingdom, is flat. Isolated from the sensible world, it remains an 'ideal' without substance, because ideas need the support of matter to become realities."[32] However, when present and future, actuality and possibility are imaginatively juxtaposed, those with eyes to see and ears to hear discern something of the true reality of the world that others cannot even imagine.

Implicit in Trocmé's theological hermeneutics is an understanding of reason that was paradigmatically articulated by Augustine in his *De Doctrina Christiana.* According to Augustine, all reality may be provisionally classified as either *res* (thing) or *signum* (sign). Each *res* that human beings encounter acts upon their willing in one of two ways. It may be something that can be enjoyed (*frui*) for its own sake and complete in itself, or it may be used (*uti*) as a means to a greater and more proper satisfaction, and thus meaning or intending more than itself. For Christians, the particular things we encounter in our comings and goings should finally be read as signs pointing us to God, who alone is to be enjoyed for his own sake.[33]

God alone, therefore, is truly *res,* yet not actually a *res* in the strict sense, not some thing or some body, but that which is beyond all naming. And yet by God's own initiative there is a *signum* in the Word made flesh that not only points to God, but that is God's own speech. Because of the embodiment of the divine utterance, God can be truly named and thus enjoyed by God's human creation as the one true end of desire. As Rowan Williams notes, Augustine contends that

> the incarnation manifests the essential quality of the world itself as "sign" or trace of its maker. It instructs us once and for all that we have our identity within the shifting, mobile realm of representation, non-finality, growing and learning, because it reveals what the spiritual eye ought to perceive

generally—that the whole creation is uttered and "meant" by God, and therefore has no meaning in itself. If we do not understand this, we seek for or invent finalities within the created order, ways of blocking off the processes of learning and desiring. Only when, by the grace of Christ, we know that we live entirely in a world of signs are we set free for the restlessness that is our destiny as rational creatures.[34]

According to this tradition of reasoning, Scripture is central to the proper formation of our understanding and desire as rational creatures whose final end is to delight in God through our prudent use of every *res* we encounter in the world. "Without sin," writes Henri de Lubac, "the symbol of the world, in its unspoiled transparency, would have sufficed." After the fall, humans need[35] the help of Scripture to decipher it. As the ninth-century theologian John Scotus Erigena puts it, "the surface of the Scriptures" and "the sensible forms of the world" form the two garments of Christ. They are like two veils that filtered the overwhelmingly brilliant light of divinity, thereby concealing the feet of the Word. But they are also signs that, through their "reason" or "spirit," allow us to catch a glimpse of the beauty of Truth itself.[36]

It is important to understand, however, that the interpretive vision and judgment displayed by the Chambonnais are not only or even primarily something that goes on in one's head. They are firmly rooted in ecclesial practices that nurture certain dispositions of character through "the structuring of common experience, and the pursuit of agreed goals and purposes in common action."[37] The practices that matter most, that is, that comprise the material sinews of this common experience and action, are baptism and Eucharist. Together they constitute the communion of the church as the earthly-historical form of Christ's body in the world,[38] and give rise to what William Cavanaugh calls "a proper 'anarchy'," not in the sense that they propose chaos, but in that they challenge the false order of the state. Through our participation in these acts of worship, Christians are united not only to God but also to each other in ways that can defuse the idolatrous usurpation of power by the state and the sorts of market exchanges and rational calculations it mandates.[39]

In addition to the sacraments, hospitality—the act of welcoming the stranger—is no doubt the most visible of the other practices that historically have distinguished the household of the church. The charity shown by the Chambonnais—which mirrored the practice of the early church, for which the outsider was in a very real sense privileged, presenting a test of its love[40]—cannot be described simply as a choice or an attitude. Love is a habit or virtue that shapes the choices we make and the attitudes we have, and is nurtured by practices such as hospitality, which in turn are sustained over time only by a truthful image of the world. In a community formed by such vision, one encounters in the stranger "a witness to the transcendence of God, one who, like God, cannot be domesticated in order to legitimate one's life, religion, or cultural-national identity—one who by his or her very . . . otherness calls one's identity into question."[41]

The charity, courage, and prudence exercised by the pilgrims in le Chambon during World War II did not generate spontaneously out of thin air. Such wisdom and clarity of judgment cannot "be acquired in a single generation . . . but [only] in the deeply rooted obligation to be guardians of a great historical heritage and intellectual tradition."[42] Nor are such traditions cultivated apart from particular social formations. Generations of French Protestants suffered through their own bloody persecutions, which forged a community that never confused being Christian with being French. This social regime enabled a handful of unarmed people to frustrate the will of a diabolical enemy that others saw as invincible. When Trocmé stood before his congregation and proclaimed that they must create a city of refuge so that innocent blood would not be shed, his summons did not fall upon deaf ears. These Christians had been trained over the centuries to heed "what the Spirit is saying to the churches" (Rev. 2:7).[43]

"In retrospect," writes G. A. Rothrock, "one is forced to the conclusion that the real 'crime' for which [French Protestants] were so often and finally so severely persecuted was neither their religious practice nor their occasionally treasonable political activity. It was, rather, their resistance to a national consciousness, emerging not just in France but across much of western Europe, that demanded conformity and submission."[44] More precisely, it was only due to their "religious" practice that these Christians resisted the idolatry of national consciousness. Laboring in quiet anonymity down through the centuries, a handful of saints cultivated a nonviolent but nevertheless disruptive tradition that nurtured habits of discernment, justice, and compassion. This tradition and its habits served their descendants in le Chambon well, allowing them to stand fast against the onslaught of the Holocaust when other Christians in Europe either stood by silently or collaborated with the criminal regime.

▨ Waiting for St. Leibowitz

What are we to conclude from the events at Rorke's Drift and le Chambon as we contemplate what the witness of an ecclesially based university might look like, particularly one that must live and work within the disciplinary sinews of liberal democratic capitalism? We are reminded above all else that the production and transmission of knowledge does not exist in some amoral sphere separate from the ebb and flow of a history that does indeed make vivid, and quite often vividly red, the consequences of taking what the earthly city regards as "unreasonable" positions. As custodian, not proprietor, of the procedures that allow human agents to critique the conceptual apparatus employed in their various projects, the university has for centuries assumed primary responsibility for developing and refining these procedures and for educating those who use them. This historically extended, socially embodied colloquy of practices, texts, and virtues has therefore served—sometimes intentionally, at other times inadvertently—as the principal accountants for the wages of reason that have been paid out in blood on battlefields down through the centuries.

We should not be surprised, then, to discover that the genealogy of the university recapitulates the story of Western civilization as a whole, beginning with the Academy in Athens and stretching through the cathedral schools and universities of the Middle Ages down to what George Grant calls the modern multiversity.[45] I single out the cathedral schools and medieval universities for special attention because they unwittingly invested in the war dividend of post-Roman Western civilization. According to de Lubac, it was in these schools, as products of the renaissances that took place in the ninth and twelfth centuries, that the liberal arts were first applied directly to the interpretation of sacred Scripture. Previously the study of the classical texts had been concerned with the preparation of students for the study of the Bible in the monastic schools. In the words of Leclercq, the reading of pagan literature was "to educate young Christians, future monks, to 'introduce' them to Sacred Scripture and guide them toward heaven by way of *grammatica*. To put them in contact with the best models would, at one and the same time, develop their taste for the beautiful, their literary subtlety, as well as their moral sense."[46] The redirection of the relationship between the study of Scripture and the liberal arts, together with the rise to prominence of scholastic disputation beginning in the eleventh century, diverted attention away from the monastic *lectio* and the maintenance of spiritual life in the company of friends, and toward more technical inquiries and secular applications involving the "literature" and "history" of the past.[47]

It was not yet a situation in which rational inquiry was completely severed from a concern for the spiritual life, as it would be in the Enlightenment. Nevertheless, says de Lubac, a gradual dissociation took place as new "masters of the divine books" and "doctors of the sacred page" began to exercise a magisterial authority over the reading of Scripture that became desacralized:

> They have become "professors of Sacred Scripture". . . "university men" before their time . . .The students who crowd around their chairs no longer resemble

the monks who come, after their work, to hear the "collatio" of their abbot within a liturgical framework. And even if they do manage to accumulate more scientific knowledge, they are also prone to a greater spirit of disquiet. How many of them seek to be taught only with a view to making a career and have already begun their drive to achieve honors! . . . It is the rising tide of "science" in the almost modern sense of the word that pushes aside humble spiritual commentary as belonging to inferior stages of growth.[48]

According to de Lubac, the seeds for the dissociation of theological convictions from the mission and practices of the church that Cavanaugh locates in the late fifteenth century[49] and Michael Buckley in the early seventeenth century[50] began to be sown as early as the ninth century.

The move from "humble spiritual commentary" to more "scientific" approaches to Scripture significantly affected the courses of study that developed in the late medieval and early modern university. Increasingly, the sort of theological hermeneutics set forth by Augustine and others no longer constituted the working cross-section of reason. As this tradition of reading Scripture and the world was replaced by more "modern" forms of exegesis in medieval academies, the close relationship between meaning and truth as narrated by the *signa* of Scripture also began to unravel, imperceptibly at first, and then more quickly as the world moved into the seventeenth and eighteenth centuries.[51] As the medieval world collapsed from its own internecine battles, people gradually looked elsewhere for the truth of the human condition. *Reason,* they were told, would satisfy their desire to learn what it meant to be a human being. This conception of reason, however, was not fashioned around the distinctions between *res* and *signum, frui* and *uti,* but around the assumption that human beings were the lords and masters of the physical world, which makes of it "something manipulable for the sake of the values we have chosen. It becomes the stock of resources on hand for the fulfillment we value."[52] The world becomes but a collection of things that exist solely for our enjoyment; the search for *signa* is abandoned.

I do not mention the role of the cathedral schools and universities in these developments to condemn them nor to suggest anachronistically that they should have known better. On the contrary, perhaps what happened at le Chambon vindicates to a certain extent schools such as the University of Paris. But, as more than one wise person has observed, if lived history is the only laboratory we have to test the social and moral consequences of human endeavors, then we dare not fail to make good use of hindsight's twenty-twenty vision. We need to reckon with the ways that Christian institutions of learning were for centuries implicated, however unwittingly, in the deadly disbursement of reason's worldly wages. The gradual dissociation of learning and inquiry from ecclesial practices within medieval academies eventually left subsequent generations at the mercy of the earthly city's cunning and utterly dependent on its wages, both real and rational. Once this process was undertaken, rational inquiry and instruction did not come to occupy some morally neutral space, but was quickly drawn into the associations of governance, exchange, and custom that constitute the earthly city. Indeed, given these developments we should not be surprised that le Chambon was the exception rather than the rule.

It serves no good purpose simply to lament the past as opposed to learning the lessons it would teach those who have eyes to see and ears to hear. On the contrary we need to ask ourselves: Where do we go from here in thinking about an ecclesially based university? If we envision as the principal aim of such a university its usefulness to the larger society in which it is located, then we will, *contra* Augustine, occupy ourselves largely with the maintenance and refinement of those customs, laws, and institutions by which earthly peace is achieved. We will do so, however, at the cost of discerning what is truly to be enjoyed for its own sake. If this is the path that is followed, I question whether it should be called a Christian institution, its philosophical "worldview" notwithstanding.

If, on the other hand, our primary concern is to investigate the use that the members of the Body of Christ should make of the goods of the earthly city in the course of responding to the Spirit's summons to become sign and foretaste of, and witness to, that perfectly ordered and perfectly harmonious fellowship in the enjoyment of God and of one another in God, then we might be on to something most extraordinary. This latter path will require that we be more rigorous and discriminating in our reasoning, not less. We do ourselves no favors when we try to safeguard claims to the truthfulness of our convictions from being examined in the unrelenting dialectic of academic inquiry. If the reasonableness of these convictions cannot be sustained there, then as Donald MacKinnon says, we had better have done with them for ever.[53]

This is not to say that Christian intellectuals must hold hat in hand and wait meekly upon the judgment of secular academics, or submit without comment to modern canons of rationality. John Milbank's contention that the pathos of modern theology has been its false humility, which transformed it into "the oracular voice of some finite idol, such as historical scholarship, humanist psychology, or transcendental philosophy," applies equally to all fields of intellectual inquiry.[54] It is to argue, rather, that the lines of interpellation must be carried out in both directions. For this to happen we must come to terms with the dissociation of erudition from the sacraments and spiritual discipline that first occurred, not in the modern university but in the medieval schools of Christendom.

This relationship between the shared life of discipleship to which God calls us and the methods of inquiry cultivated in the university will not be a simple one to negotiate. I readily admit that I have no ready formula for this task. On the contrary, the very notion of a formula is symptomatic of the managerial mindset that is characteristic of and thus perpetuates liberalism's strategic hold over our lives. I am convinced, however, that the use made of academic disciplines and procedures by Christian intellectuals will need to be more rigorous than their use made by our secular counterparts, precisely because we seek to open these matters to scrutiny by the christological reasoning that informs the church's mission. To cultivate this sort of openness, we must find ways to reconnect such inquiry to the social formation embodied in the sacramental life and spiritual disciplines of the church.

I began this reflection on the witness of the ecclesially based university by referring to a fictional character in a popular novel and movie, and thus it seems fitting that I conclude with another. Perhaps what we are waiting for, with respect to the ecclesially based university, is neither Godot nor a new St. Benedict[55] but a St. Leibowitz, the title character in Walter Miller's novel *A Canticle for Leibowitz*. Leibowitz is the founder of a Catholic religious order that emerges after a nuclear holocaust, dedicated to preserving the erudition of humankind from the "Simplification," a time of book burning and persecution by self-styled "simpletons" who blame science and technology for the destruction that had been wrought on the world. The members of the Order of the Blessed Leibowitz do not share this conviction, and so they smuggle, conceal, memorize, and copy the accumulated knowledge and wisdom of the time before the "Flame Deluge," even though what they save is largely indecipherable to them, its meaning lost in the passage of time. They are not deterred from their labors, however, for they are confident that God had not abandoned God's creation, and they believe that an "Integrator" would eventually come and fit the disjointed pieces together.[56]

In an insightful commentary on Miller's apocalyptic novel, Ralph Wood notes that the monks could wait patiently for the coming of the Integrator, for "they live not only *within* time but also *beyond* time. They live in the eschatological confidence that the God who in Jesus Christ has indwelt time has all of time to work His purposes out." Owing to their faith in the one in whom all things cohere (Col. 1:17), they go about their work, trusting that it "may eventually redound to the glory of God and the betterment of the human condition.[57] In the process they develop a rather distinctive connoisseurship of reason that refuses to respect a sharp division between the natural and the supernatural. Instead the monks have learned to recognize a vast spectrum where "things [*res*] made of mere earth, air, fire, or water tended to behave disturbingly like *Things [signa].*"[58] As Wood summarizes in a thoroughgoing Augustinian manner, "The visible and invisible worlds are woven into a seamless web of interlocking realities—divine and human, natural and supernatural. To understand the way that world works requires a radical sense of mystery that only faith can prompt, enabling reason to discern that uncertainty is built into the nature of things and thus indispensable to true knowledge."[59]

Notes

1. Frank Lentricchia, *Ariel and the Police* (Madison: University of Wisconsin Press, 1988), p. 133.

2. Thomas Aquinas, *Summa Theologiae* Ia.2.1.

3. James W. McClendon, Jr., *Systematic Theology*, vol. 3, *Witness* (Nashville, Tenn.: Abingdon, 2000), p. 351.

4. Stephen Toulmin, *Human Understanding* (Princeton, N.J.: Princeton University Press, 1972), pp. 133, 478.

5. Augustine, *The City of God Against the Pagans*, XIX.17, ed. R. W. Dyson (New York: Cambridge University Press, 1998), p. 947.

6. Augustine, *Teaching Christianity:* De Doctrina Christiana, I.25, trans. Edmund Hill, O.P. (New York: New City Press, 1996), p. 150.

7. Rom. 12:1–2; Augustine, *The City of God*, X.7, X.20; 400, 422.

8. Nicholas Lash, *Theology on the Way to Emmaus* (London: SCM, 1986), p. 22. N. T. Wright makes a similar point in connection with the life and language of the people of Israel. For Jews in the post-exilic era the ideas of "monotheism, idolatry, election, holiness, and how these interacted" were "a shorthand way of articulating the points of pressure, tension and conflict between different actual communities, specifically, Jews and pagans." N. T. Wright, *The Climax of the Covenant* (Minneapolis: Fortress, 1992), p. 122.

9. Augustine, *The City of God*, XV.4, XXII.6; 639, 1118f.

10. I take this phrase, of course, from Jean Leclercq, OSB, *The Love of Learning and the Desire for God: A Study of Monastic Culture*, trans. Catharine Misrahi (New York: Fordham University Press, 1961, 1974).

11. Augustine, *The City of God*, XVIII.54; 907.

12. This brief summary of the Battle of Rorke's Drift is taken from Victor Davis Hanson, *Carnage and Culture: Landmark Battles in the Rise of Western Power* (New York: Doubleday, 2001), pp. 279–299. Hanson references numerous accounts and analyses of this engagement, perhaps the most well known of which is Michael Glover, *Rorke's Drift: A Victorian Epic* (Hamden, Conn.: Archon, 1975)

13. Hanson, *Carnage and Culture*, p. 299.

14. Ibid., p. 9.

15. Hanson's book has obviously not gone unchallenged, both for its method and its content. Chris Bray, for example, faults Hanson in a rather pedantic review for playing fast and loose with the historical record. Unfortunately, he never manages to engage the overarching thesis of the book. Chris Bray, review of Victor Davis Hanson, *Carnage and Culture, Reason* 33 (April 2002): 56–59. For more positive reviews see Keith Windschuttle,

review of Victor Davis Hanson, *Carnage and Culture*, *The New Criterion* 20 (April 2002): 67–70; Woody West, review of Victor Davis Hanson, *Carnage and Culture*, *Policy Review* 110 (December 2001/January 2002): 73–78; and Arthur Herman, review of Victor Davis Hanson, *Carnage and Culture*, *National Review* 53 (October 15, 2001): 72–73.

16. The case for environmental geography and biogeography has most recently been made by Jerod Diamond, *Guns, Germs, and Steel: The Fates of Human Societies* (New York: W. W. Norton, 1997).

17. Hanson entitles the chapter in which he develops this theme, "The Market—or Capitalism Kills."

18. Hanson, *Carnage and Culture*, p. 230.

19. In our time, huge amounts of money are dangled before universities to entice them to do research in the lucrative areas of weapons development and procurement.

20. See Tom Conley, Translator's Introduction to *The Writing of History*, by Michel de Certeau (trans. Tom Conley; New York: Columbia University Press, 1988), pp. vii–xxiii.

21. Michel de Certeau, *The Practice of Everyday Life*, trans. Steven Rendall (Berkeley: University of California Press, 1984), 36. We have already seen how their knowledge about the Zulu served the British well at Rorke's Drift, but that is only one of many such occasions. When Xenophon and Alexander invaded Persia they knew much more about these lands than Xerxes did when he tried to conquer Greece a century earlier.

22. Augustine, *The City of God*, I.Pref; 3.

23. Hanson, *Carnage and Culture*, pp. 154f.

24. Ibid., p. 151.

25. Ibid., p. 251f.

26. Nicholas Boyle, *Who Are We Now? Christian Humanism and the Global Market from Hegel to Heaney* (Notre Dame, Ind.: University of Notre Dame Press, 1998), pp. 17, 25. The work of the scientists associated with the Manhattan Project, which designed and built the first atomic weapons during World War II, comes immediately to mind in this regard.

27. Wendell Berry, "Economy and Pleasure," in *What Are People For?* (New York: North Point, 1990), p. 130.

28. Boyle, *Who Are We Now?* pp. 78f.

29. Rodney Clapp, "At the Intersection of Eucharist and Capital," in *Border Crossings: Christian Trespasses on Popular Culture and Public Affairs* (Grand Rapids: Brazos, 2000), p. 100.

30. Philip P. Hallie, *Lest Innocent Blood Be Shed: The Story of the Village of Le Chambon and How Goodness Happened There* (New York: Harper & Row, 1979; HarperPerennial, 1994), pp. 108f.

31. Victoria J. Barnett, *Bystanders: Conscience and Complicity During the Holocaust* (Westport, Conn.: Praeger, 1999), p. 7.

32. André Trocmé, *Jesus and the Nonviolent Revolution*, trans. Michael H. Shank and Marlin E. Martin (Scottdale, Penn.: Herald Press, 1973), p. 158. The coordination of how things are and how they ought to be is one of the features that differentiates Thomas Aquinas's understanding of truth as correspondence from modern correspondence theories. See in this regard John Milbank and Catherine Pickstock, *Truth in Aquinas* (New York: Routledge, 2001), pp. 3f, 10.

33. Augustine, *Teaching Christianity*, I.1–40; 106–126.

34. Rowan Williams, "Language, Reality and Desire in Augustine's *de doctrina*," *Literature and Theology* 3 (July 1989): 141. I am deeply indebted to Williams's analysis of Augustine's theory of signs.

35. Henri de Lubac, *Medieval Exegesis: The Four Senses of Scripture*, vol. 1, trans. Mark Sebanc (Grand Rapids: Eerdmans, 1998), p. 77.

36. John Scotus Erigena, *Div. nat.*, Bk. 30, as cited in Henri de Lubac, *Medieval Exegesis*, p. 77.

37. Lash, *Theology on the Way to Emmaus*, p. 22.

38. See Karl Barth, *Church Dogmatics*, vol. 4, *The Doctrine of Reconciliation*, ed. G. W. Bromiley and T. F. Torrance (Edinburgh: T & T Clark, 1956), 1: 643ff.

39. William T. Cavanaugh, "The City: Beyond Secular Parodies," in *Radical Orthodoxy*, ed. John Milbank, Catherine Pickstock, and Graham Ward (London: Routledge, 1999), pp. 194f.

40. John Howard Yoder, *The Priestly Kingdom: Social Ethics as Gospel* (Notre Dame, Ind.: University of Notre Dame Press, 1984), p. 138. For further insight into the role of hospitality in forming a disruptive community see Scott H. Moore, *The End of Convenient Stereotypes: Extraordinary Politics at the End of Modernity* (forthcoming from InterVarsity Press), especially chapter 8, "Hospitality as an Extraordinary Practice."

41. Darrell Fasching, *Narrative Theology After Auschwitz: From Alienation to Ethics* (Minneapolis: Fortress, 1992), pp. 82f; cited in Barnett, *Bystanders*, p. 172.

42. Eberhard Bethge, *Dietrich Bonhoeffer: A Biography*, ed. Victoria J. Barnett (Minneapolis: Fortress, 2000), p. 13.

43. The Plymouth Brethren who cooperated with the Huguenots in this endeavor had their own sources of social independence in the form of a dispensationalist eschatology that led them to eschew all forms of worldly identification. See James Patrick Callahan, *Primitivist Piety: The Ecclesiology of the Early Plymouth Brethren* (Lanham, Md.: Scarecrow Press, 1996).

44. G. A. Rothrock, *The Huguenots: A Biography of a Minority* (Chicago: Nelson-Hall, 1979), pp. 189f. For a concise history of the Reformed church in France, see John T. McNeill, *The History and Character of Calvinism* (New York: Oxford University Press, 1954), pp. 237–254.

45. George Parkin Grant, "Faith and the Multiversity," in *Technology and Justice* (Notre Dame, Ind.: University of Notre Dame Press, 1986), pp. 35–77.

46. Leclercq, *The Love of Learning and the Desire for God*, p. 149.

47. De Lubac, *Medieval Exegesis*, 55. Michel de Certeau contends in this regard that modern historiography cannot escape a certain mythic character, constructing an identity through differentiation with a past that is over and done with, that is dead: "Such is history. A play of life and death is sought in the calm telling of a tale, in the resurgence and denial of the origin, the unfolding of a dead past and result of a present practice. It reiterates, under another rule, the myths built upon a murder of an originary death and fashions out of language the forever-remnant trace of a beginning that is as impossible to recover as to forget." De Certeau, *The Writing of History*, p. 47.

48. De Lubac, *Medieval Exegesis*, p. 49.

49. William T. Cavanaugh, "'A Fire Strong Enough to Consume the House': The Wars of Religion and the Rise of the State," *Modern Theology* 11 (October 1995): 403f.

50. Michael J. Buckley, SJ, *At the Origins of Modern Atheism* (New Haven: Yale University Press, 1987), p. 33.

51. Michael Gillespie has argued persuasively that modernity did not arise in opposition to the medieval world but out of its rubble. "Superior or more powerful ideas thus did not drive out or overcome medieval ideas, as it often maintained; rather, they toppled the ruins of medieval ideas that had remained standing after the internecine struggle that

brought the medieval world to an end. Modern 'reason' was thus able to overcome medieval 'superstition' and 'dogma' only because these were fatally weakened by the destruction of the world in which they made sense." In other words, modernity came into being in response to the crisis engendered by the collapse of the medieval world. Michael Allen Gillespie, "The Theological Origins of Modernity," *Critical Review* 13 (1999): 3.

52. Joseph Rouse, *Knowledge and Power* (Ithaca, N.Y.: Cornell University Press, 1987), p. 66. For a more detailed theological analysis of the rise of the modern conception of reason see my *Another City: An Ecclesiological Primer for a Post-Christian World* (Harrisburg, Penn.: Trinity Press International, 1999), especially chapter 4, "Romancing Divinity," pp. 95–134.

53. D. M. MacKinnon, "Lenin and Theology," in *Explorations in Theology* 5 (London: SCM, 1979): 21, cited by Lash, *Theology on the Way to Emmaus*, p. 116.

54. John Milbank, *Theology and Social Theory: Beyond Secular Reason* (Cambridge, Mass.: Blackwell Publishers, 1990), p. 1.

55. See Alasdair MacIntyre, *After Virtue*, 2d ed. (Notre Dame, Ind.: University of Notre Dame Press, 1984), p. 263.

56. Walter M. Miller, Jr., *A Canticle for Leibowitz* (New York: Harper & Row, 1959). It is widely assumed that the famous introduction and conclusion to MacIntyre's *After Virtue* were indebted to the plot of this novel.

57. Ralph C. Wood, "Lest the World's Amnesia Be Complete: A Reading of Walter Miller's *A Canticle for Leibowitz*," *Religion & Literature* 33 (Spring 2001): 31f.

58. Miller, *A Canticle for Leibowitz*, pp. 56f.

59. Wood, "Lest the World's Amnesia Be Complete," p. 31.

4

The House of Mirth and a Rebuke of False Wisdom

A Case for Women's Studies

Amy Laura Hall

The heart of the wise is in the house of mourning; but the heart of fools is in the house of mirth. It is better to hear the rebuke of the wise than to hear the song of fools. (Ecclesiastes 7:4–5)

Why Women's Studies?

There are various ways to narrate the importance of women's studies for a Christian academy, depending on one's operating definition of feminism. For the uninitiated reader, I will try to explain. Women's studies is less a discipline proper than an intersection, and the strands of thought that meet there differ. In a typical women's studies department, you may find a historian of women's field labor who trained in Marxist theory, a literary critic who deconstructs George Eliot by way of French philosopher Jacques Derrida, and an anthropologist who reads Western obstetrics through post-colonial theory. Each would narrate the importance of that intersection differently. But, in many colleges, the genesis of a women's studies department involved the desire to recover, uncover, and decipher the writings and lives of women. This may be a sufficiently worthy project in and of itself to warrant our attention in this volume. Inasmuch as the standard courses and discourses of the theological academy focus on a select, male, few, the very basic goal of feminism in the academy—to read neglected texts and remember ignored lives—is one that Christians should emulate.

I wish here to make a claim that goes beyond this formal goal of retrieval and recovery, however. By reading closely one recovered text, Edith Wharton's *House of Mirth,* I will suggest some material reasons for including women's studies within a Christian academy. In doing so, I am employing a method I learned in the women's studies department at Emory University, particularly in a course on Southern women's literature with Elizabeth Fox-Genovese. Professor Fox-Genovese is a Marxist historian, a feminist, and (recently) a committed Roman Catholic. Her faithful attention to class, race, and gender came together as she taught us to read closely the assigned texts, and not as a mere academic exercise. Noting carefully the twists and turns of character and gender, plot and class, Fox-Genovese encouraged this blithely oblivious undergraduate to notice the complexity of relations between African-American and white women in the South. For many women teaching in women's studies, the pedagogical is also the political. In that course we struggled not only with Southern texts but also with the intersection of race, class, and gender at an élite, overwhelmingly white university in Atlanta, Georgia.

This embodied attention to neglected texts *and* otherwise ignored contexts seems to me an imperative of truly Christian scholarship. If the Word did indeed become flesh, Christians cannot fashion an academy that is merely about words. We cannot be true to the gospel of an incarnate Messiah while simultaneously encouraging the self-deception of disembodied minds floating around a red-brick quadrangle. But we must face the fact that the gravitational pull of the modern university is indeed toward gnosticism. Many who seek "the life of the mind" are much more comfortable writing about wisdom than negotiating the tangled threads of embodied lives. The image of the absent-minded professor reading a heady tome while walking into the refectory to be served, leaving with belly full but without any idea as to how it came to be that way, is an apt metaphor for the way that the academy too often functions. We at the top of the pyramid do not cook our own meals, nor do we clean our plates. We do not take out our trash, nor do we make our copies. The college setting is often an occasion for training our protégés in such self-indulgent ignorance.

At its best, women's studies in the Christian academy may preclude this all-too-easy sequestering of texts from present context. Women's studies is an apt ally in this effort to re-embody the academy to be a place of incarnate wisdom. Attending carefully to texts created at the margins does not necessarily lead to political attention to the margins of an academic community; but it can be a start.

Given that the "service class" is populated by women, noting the embodied work that makes a school hum is inevitably women's studies. The "invisible" workers that contribute to the machinery of proper scholarship are almost always either women, or men whom the dominant culture deems extraneous. Those who do the most menial tasks are disproportionately African-American and Latino. By and large, women are the ones making copies, typing books, cleaning toilets, and making sandwiches. Gendered patterns of service crawl up the pyramid as well; statistics show that female faculty members disproportionately contribute to the daily care of students and colleagues in committee work, advising, counseling, and grading. One can gauge an individual's power at many universities thus: Is he or she able to avoid face-to-face contact with the average student? Note who has someone screening her calls, who never makes his own copies, who would not be caught dead making cookies for the Christmas party, and there you have the consummate academic power-broker. Involving a women's studies department within a Christian academy should prompt an awareness of these patterns and, hopefully, transform the hands-on work of teaching and feeding from grunt-work that the powerful can avoid into a matter of equally distributed service to Christ's body. By placing gender front and center, we may expose protestations of "different gifts" as occasions of evasion.

Attention to particular texts that scrutinize class, race, and gender, when taught alongside attention to the context in which we read, may prompt Christians to avoid another temptation of the academy: propriety that serves the powerful. I should thus make clear that I am refusing one model of feminism. Academic feminism has been in some universities largely about white women attempting to win at a white man's game. Through cleverness, charm, and wit, we have, to some extent, won. Through sought honors and meticulous publications, very carefully crafted grace and carefully administered contraception, we have made it into the ranks of the powers-that-be. Inasmuch as we have failed, we have too often written ourselves merely as victims, refusing to confess our complicity in a system that depends on the thankless, low-paid work of women much less fortunate than ourselves. Our reformations of the academy have often amounted only to tinkering, to readjusting the gauges to bring more women aboard an iniquitous ship. I commend to the Christian academy instead a women's studies that rewrites the rules. Good manners, the ways things are just simply done, the rules regarding things that shall not be noticed or named or changed, are dictated by those who have much to lose if some begin to take notice

and be rude or strange. Decent bourgeois Christians are at least as suscep-
tible to this temptation toward silence and willed ignorance as are others.
Women's studies can, when taught in a particular way, encourage students
and secretaries and cafeteria workers and faculty to take notice and to be
strategically rude.

But . . . while this vision of transformation may seem a lovely one (or
perhaps a very frightening one), it is not terribly realistic. Is it very likely
that, at our dream school, senior professors will bake cookies and listen to
the vocational woes of a B-level student? Well, perhaps, but the transformations will very likely be modest, and fragile.

I have thus chosen an appropriately disconcerting text for my task. Edith
Wharton does not write a moral prescription for communal equality, she
writes a novel. The characters are neither unambiguously good nor wholly
evil, and the book does not end with a satisfying *It's a Wonderful Life* ending.
The characters are flawed, and the ending only tentatively intimates the
possibility of a more hopeful future. A rousing, Marxist/Pelagian reading
of *House of Mirth*—as a formula for a hearty new Christian community
of resolute equality and faith—is thus not possible. But that is one of the
reasons why I have chosen it. The actors in our own proposed Christian
academy will be similarly, merely, human, and our efforts toward a truly
holy academy will be cracked with sins of pride and sloth. There will be
few easy answers as we proceed, and the task will require our willingness
not only to clean our own dishes, but to sit with the uncleanliness of
irresolution.

At least we must so sit until Christ comes in final victory, and we feast
at his heavenly banquet.

■ Why Lily Bart?

In *The House of Mirth*, Edith Wharton makes a significant advance over
the so-called (psychological) realism of her genre. She challenges that which
passes for wisdom. Into one brief scene from *The House of Mirth*, Edith
Wharton slips a subtly important prompt for this reading. The heroine of
the story, Lily Bart, is relating to her elderly aunt the details of a recent
wedding, which the aunt did not deign to attend. In the midst of their
conversation,

> Mrs. Peniston rose abruptly, and, advancing to the ormolu clock surmounted
> by a helmeted Minerva, which throned on the chimney-piece between two
> malachite vases, passed her lace handkerchief between the helmet and its
> visor. "I knew it—the parlour maid never dusts there!" she exclaimed, tri-

umphantly displaying a minute spot on the handkerchief; then, reseating herself, she went on . . . (HM, 160)

If there is a villain in this complicated story of New York society, it is Mrs. Peniston, whose simple act here signals a warning. Within the world Edith Wharton depicts, Minerva, the goddess of wisdom, has become a mere adornment, sitting "throned on the chimney piece" between two malachite vases. Mrs. Peniston rises to wipe the dust from lady wisdom's visor, but not in order that Minerva's wise vision might adjust her own perspective. Rather, the matriarch "triumphantly" displays the smallest mark, cheered that she has caught the parlour maid in an inattention. "It is better to hear the rebuke of the wise than to hear the song of fools." In this version of high society New York, also known as the house of mirth, elders neglect wisdom while rejoicing in the negligence of their servants. The inhabitants of this world little know, much less heed, the rebuke of the wise. Edith Wharton gives her readers an opportunity to see otherwise, a chance to dust the shade of Minerva's helmet and see anew the layers of parlour maids and charwomen.

The wiser, more astute vision to which Wharton calls us requires effort and a willingness to face the difficult tasks of embodied life. Reading a novel such as Wharton's is an aptly complicated way of entering that task. Wharton does not offer a rousing sermon on gender and class; she rather narrates, telling a story with an eye toward the complex interplay of man and woman, and of woman and woman, and of master and servant in a world that is treacherous. Wharton wishes to pull us into the ambiguity of blame and praise, vice and virtue, with two related aims in view. First, we are to observe the various circles of society with the blinders taken off, so to speak. As we descend with Lily through the increasingly splintered levels of society, we may begin to note the gendered and classed nuances of effort, error, risk, and peril. This vision, Wharton suggests, is necessary for wisdom. (This is but one way that Wharton improves on her predecessor, Henry James, who keeps the servants largely hidden from view.) To ignore her summons to disclose what we otherwise avoid is to participate in the one villainy that Wharton unambiguously condemns: willed self-deception. Secondly, in addition to the summons to disclose, we receive in this text a glimpse of an alternative to mirth and to mourning. Wisdom, wrought from the hard work of truly wise perception and honest disclosure, may allow for a different kind of space. As Wharton puts it, this fragile habitat has the "frail audacious permanence of a bird's nest built on the edge of a cliff—a mere wisp of leaves and straw, yet so put together that the lives entrusted to it may hang safely over the abyss" (HM, 448). This quote, from a scene at the very end of the book, hints at the tenuous hope that lies beyond Lily's purview.

I take from this "mere wisp" that "hangs safely over the abyss" a signal toward the grace that is beyond the capacity of Wharton's text and our present lives. I hope for something beyond Edith Wharton's *House of Mirth,* a text that ends with the death of our protagonist, Lily Bart. But her social demise and corrected perspective is, I believe, a crucial one for our construction of a wise, Christian academy. The disembodied pretense of Edith Wharton's New York matches well the gnostic errors toward which academics so often tend. Lily attempts to survive by playing games available to her among a willfully ignorant upper class. Only at the end does she glimpse an alternative world with changed rules. I submit that Christians who wish to fashion an academy according to rules set by Jesus Christ will do well to go behind the social tapestry with Wharton's Lily Bart, to be with those who are tying the knots and cooking the meals and carrying out the garbage and fixing the lights and binding the books and mopping the floors.

Frail Threads and Human Vanity

While material laborers lie outside the initial purview of the book, the fate of our heroine depends on her ability skillfully to arrange the attention of the men who observe her. She exists and can exist to the extent that she plays the role given her—that of beautiful, carefully crafted spectacle. We thus enter the book observing Lawrence Seldon as he observes Miss Bart. Watching him watching her, we hear that "his eyes had been refreshed by the sight of Miss Lily Bart" (HM, 17). She causes us to pause, as she causes those around her to stop and to look, "for Miss Bart was a figure to arrest even the suburban traveler rushing to his last train" (HM, 18). Wharton sets up the reader to pause, and to observe Lily. But by watching her through Seldon's eyes, we wonder already whether he will merely observe, merely be a spectator, or instead risk engagement. Observing his observation, the astute reader already finds himself hoping for the latter. Evoking our investment of interest, Wharton has accomplished something on us. For we are already set to worry over Seldon's often-detached and evaluative demeanor toward Lily's projects and plight. If we are to follow her well, we are, against our more discerning, prudent judgment, to fall rather foolishly in love. Wharton brings the reader to note that there is a person behind the portrait.

As Lily moves from the train station to the heart of high-society New York at the turn of the century, Wharton has us soon wondering: Is Lily a willful perpetrator of her troubles or an inadvertent victim of her destiny? Does she knit or is she ensnared? Seldon moves from possibility to possibility; Lily is alternatively the meticulous planner of circumstances and the "victim of the civilization which had produced her . . . the links of her bracelet seem[ing] like manacles chaining her to her fate" (HM, 23). Lily is decidedly, perpetually unwed, spoiling chance after chance for matrimony, but she is also certain that she must attach herself, given her lack of funds and her exquisite taste. Considering her predicament, Lily asks herself, "Had she lacked patience, pliancy and dissimulation? Whether she charged herself with these faults or absolved herself from them, made no difference in the sum-total of her failure" (HM, 66). This is a crucial point, which Wharton brings to bear on our own discernment. Charged or absolved, the sum-total of Lily's failure stands, and it makes little difference for her future. As Wharton words it, she attempts to "sustain the weight of human vanity" on mere "threads" (HM, 166). Always "in an attitude of uneasy alertness toward every possibility of life," Lily seeks carefully to spin and to step while also entangled in a complex web much larger than herself (HM, 145). Lily both chooses and is entrapped. Wharton denies us the satisfaction of definitive, one-sided judgment; it makes no difference in the sum-total of Lily's failure. By the end, the real reader will mourn her.

The ensnared decision that decides much of the remainder of the book involves a loan, a loan hazardously secured through means well-suited to Lily's gifts. After carefully, but inadvertently, losing her chance to marry a sanctimonious heir, Lily tallies her debts, considers her options, and hits a point of considered desperation. She cannot borrow from her female friends, for, as she puts it, "women are not generous lenders, and those among whom her lot was cast were either in the same case as herself, or else too far removed from it to understand its necessities" (HM, 121). Either above the fray through marriage, or too deeply in the fray themselves, other women render the hope of sororal assistance impossible. So, on a fateful, but planned, excursion, Lily seeks to secure her existence otherwise through her best friend's husband:

> In her inmost heart Lily knew it was not by appealing to the fraternal in-
> stinct that she was likely to move Gus Trenor; but this way of explaining the
> situation helped to drape its crudity, and she was always scrupulous about
> keeping up appearances to herself. Her personal fastidiousness had a moral
> equivalent, and when she made a tour of inspection in her own mind there
> were certain closed doors she did not open. (HM, 125)

By investing her money in Wall Street, Lily attempts to play a man's game, using the well-crafted, feminine tools at her disposal. She will fail. The closed doors Lily will not open, her willfully incomplete inspection of her own conscience, and of her dangerous context, allow her to avoid both the true nature of the game she is playing and the real stakes of her gamble.

> [S]he felt herself ready to meet any other demand which life might make. Even the immediate one of letting Trenor, as they drove homeward, lean a little nearer and rest his hand reassuringly on hers, cost her only a momentary shiver of reluctance. It was part of the game to make him feel that her appeal had been an uncalculated impulse, provoked by the liking he had inspired; and the renewed sense of power in handling men, while it consoled her wounded vanity, helped also to obscure the thought of the claim at which his manner hinted. He was a coarse dull man who, under all his show of authority, was a mere supernumerary in the costly show for which his money paid: surely, to a clever girl, it would be easy to hold him by his vanity, and so keep the obligation on his side. (HM, 129)

Lily knows that she needs money, and she perceives accurately the only possible source of such funds. But she wrongly deems herself a master at the game, underestimating, while also banking on, Gus Trenor's own mastery of a larger game on which her life depends.

Lily is, of course, wrong. Even if you have not read the book, even if you have not made her formal acquaintance, you have quite likely heard tell of Lily's demise. Becoming beholden to a man of means, a woman is expected to pay up, so to speak. Seeking not to do so is, according to Gus Trenor, "dodging the rules of the game" (HM, 211). In the scene of their confrontation, Wharton writes Mr. Trenor's power by accentuating his considerable physical presence, correcting any previous impression of his function as a supernumerary. Gus literally blocks her access to the door; no longer merely figuratively trapped, she is literally so. As one aspect of herself wishes to lash out at such treatment, she discerns that she must use again the tools dictated by her context: ". . . all the while another self was sharpening her to vigilance, whispering the terrified warning that every word and gesture must be measured" (HM, 210). Perhaps by way of such diligent attention to the finer points of the game, she triggers some recognition in Mr. Trenor: "Trenor's eye had the haggard look of the sleep-walker waked on a deathly ledge" (HM, 213). Through an undecipherable combination of her effort and his retrieved sense of decorum, she is not despoiled.

But she is ruined. The fragile threads that barely sustain human vanity require a meticulous attention to appearances. Such attention is in part what allows Lily to negotiate her role. She is the viewed, the observed, the spectacle. And, as an astoundingly graceful beauty, she is able for a time to maneuver. But this thread of the social fabric is also her undoing. The observed, in the form of a young woman, is also always the appraised. Lily's aunt, Mrs. Peniston, gives voice to this truth: "It was horrible of a young girl to let herself be talked about; however unfounded the charges against her, she must be to blame for their having been made" (HM, 186). She is seen furtively leaving Gus Trenor's abode: "as if with the turn of the stereopticon," Lily has made a scene (HM, 232). The specifics do not matter, for justice is definitely not gender-blind: "The whole truth?" Miss Bart laughed. "What is truth? Where a woman is concerned, it's the story that is easiest to believe (HM, 319). As, in the second half of the book, Lily spirals slowly but surely downward into real poverty, she becomes increasingly disillusioned with the verity of truth or the verifiability of the moral:

> She was realizing for the first time that a woman's dignity may cost more to keep up than her carriage; and that the maintenance of a moral attribute should be dependent on dollars and cents, made the world appear a more sordid place than she had conceived it. (HM, 243)

If there is to be such a thing as morals, or truth, Wharton suggests that it cannot be held up at the expense of such illusions. Disillusionment of such maintained truth, of such crafted, false wisdom, is the only route toward a truer morality. After considering the overlapping circles through which Lily travels toward death, we will return to the possibility of such a moral context.

Shaky Vehicles and Frayed Harnesses

Having been thrust into (or having brought upon herself) notoriety, Lily's hold on the generosity of others becomes ever more insecure. In her description of these others and their particular circles of influence, Wharton heightens our awareness both of the tremors that occur as such circles shift and disintegrate and the ways in which the most vulnerable inhabitants within must grasp to keep some semblance of balance. While Wharton does not offer nostalgia for an earlier age of a better, purer aristocracy, she does narrate how, as the foundation becomes ever more fixed on the flow of commerce and consumption, the circles of society whirl with only the trace remnants of a *noblesse oblige* or familial solidity. Lily puts this well while reflecting on her role as the assigned, and compensated, distraction of a wealthy woman's husband:

> There had been moments when the situation had presented itself under a homelier yet more vivid image—that of a shaky vehicle, dashed by unbroken steeds over a bumping road, while she cowered within, aware that the harness wanted mending, and wondering what would give way first. (HM, 288)

The breaking apart to take place is, as with Lily's life, an opportunity for proper disillusionment, but it is also an occasion for peril.

Lily is shaken out of the homes of aristocracy into dependence on the newly rich—whose "air of improvisation was in fact [so] strikingly present" that "one had to touch the marble columns to learn that they were not of cardboard"—to a bohemian collection of wealthy artists—whose self-generated social creed involves "less rivalry," but largely by way of the "easy promiscuity" which marks it—to the decided nadir of Wharton's time: the inhabitants of the hotel (HM, 192, 331, 388). Mrs. Hatch, a young, divorced woman from "the West," is the princess of the hotel set, whose defining quality is lack of definition. As Wharton explains:

> No definite hours were kept; no fixed obligations existed: night and day flowed into one another in a blur of confused and retarded engagements . . . [They all] swam in a haze of indeterminate enthusiasms, of aspirations culled from the stage, the newspapers, the fashion-journals, and a gaudy world of sport . . . (HM, 387)

Here, where characters have "no more real existence than the poet's shades of limbo," Wharton astutely intimates the future of a world structured solely by entertainment and commerce (HM, 386). Moving from carefully manufactured artifice, to less well-crafted lies, to the thoroughgoing absence of all structure, Wharton leads Lily, and the reader, to a place where humans can barely exist.

Behind the Social Tapestry

Here, at the edge, Lily eventually seeks a deathly darkness. But Wharton hints that our heroine, and the reader, have become privy to a perspective that may lead, alternatively, toward a fragile hope. Toward the end of the book, Lily finds herself with "the odd sense of being behind the social tapestry, on the side where the threads were knotted and the loose ends hung" (HM, 388). Here is Wharton's considerable advance over merely gendered fiction. We not only learn, from Lily's perspective, about the plight of "woman." We come to see, with Lily, a view from those who quite literally sew and fasten the knots behind the scenes. As she seeks, in a hat-factory, to attach the trifles which adorn the heads of her previous friends and family, Lily brushes harshly against a different truth. In her new "promiscuity," in the space where actual work is unconcealed, Lily becomes newly aware of the frayed underside. Wharton does not submit a romanticized coincidence of virtue and honest work. For Lily, and for others, this existence means death. Neither does she suggest that, with the fracturing of the aristocracy, society will easily readjust to accommodate the masses. Lily's fall behind what she calls the "machinery" of a "luxurious world" is not a fall into proletariat innocence (HM, 376). But, Wharton suggests, this is the only way toward wisdom.

This descent into the servicing under-layers that support the luxury of New York society begins early in the novel. On leaving Lawrence Seldon's apartment, in the first chapter, Lily finds herself disconcertingly face-to-face with a homely charwoman. Lily is conscious of the fact that she has taken a considerable risk by visiting Seldon. If anyone sees her leaving, even in broad daylight, they will suspect the worst. Wharton describes her in an encounter that becomes morally weighted:

> There was no one in sight, however, but a charwoman who was scrubbing the stairs. Her own stout person and its surrounding implements took up so much room that Lily, to pass her, had to gather up her skirts and brush against the wall . . . She had a broad sallow face, slightly pitted with small-pox, and thin straw-coloured hair through which her scalp shone unpleasantly . . . The woman, without answering, pushed her pail aside, and continued to stare as Miss Bart swept by with a murmur of silken linings. Lily felt herself flushing under the look. (HM, 31)

There is "no one" in sight, but someone sees. The charwoman's returned gaze causes Lily to flush, and Lily does not flush easily. It is this perspective, of one pitted from pain and whose scalp is exposed, that begins to inform the text.

By bringing Lily face to face with this woman who scrubs the stairs up which she climbs, Wharton inserts into the "realist" genre a new, classed, realism. As Lily slowly loses her grasp on the various privileges that come from leisure, Wharton takes the reader into the world so carefully hidden from the privileged. As Lily notes early on, "Affluence, unless stimulated by a keen imagination, forms but the vaguest notion of the practical strain of poverty" (HM, 117). In this narrative, Wharton seeks to sharpen the imagination of the reader, as Lily's imagination becomes painfully sharpened. Moving from the home of an extravagantly wealthy friend, who loses her temper when her maid must leave to care for her own family, into the neighborhood of those who provide the seamless working of the upper class, Lily comes to see differently. While she still longs for "that other luxurious world, whose machinery is so carefully concealed that one scene flows into another without perceptible agency," the machinery has been, for the reader as well as for Lily, uncovered (HM, 424). She, and we, must now note that someone does indeed scrub the floors, iron the clothes, mend the dresses, cook the food, and carefully adorn ladies' hats. As the distance between her and the charwoman lessens, their eyes meet. This is not a romanticized solidarity, but it becomes, for the reader, a truth.

The Cardinal Laws of Housekeeping

This brings us back to Mrs. Peniston, whose "dread of a scene gave her an inexorableness which the greatest strength of character could not have produced, since it was independent of all considerations of right or wrong (HM, 244). Mrs. Peniston's place of security, superiority, and willed ignorance represents the inverse of Lily's increasing peril and awareness of the concealed machinery of class. Through Mrs. Peniston, Wharton gives the book's clearest warning. This matriarch "had kept her imagination shrouded, like the drawing-room furniture," and to discover the dangerous realities of her own social world leaves her "As much aghast as if she had been accused of leaving her carpets down all summer, or of violating any of the other cardinal laws of housekeeping" (HM 181). This lady's seasonal cleaning is the full extent of her moral exploration. Determined to avoid contact with conflict, which she deems to be synonymous with "immorality," Mrs. Peniston avoids knowledge of anything that might disturb her peace: "the mere idea of immorality was as offensive to Mrs. Peniston as a smell of cooking in the drawing room." Attempting to avoid the "contagious illness" of difficulty, Mrs. Peniston remains enclosed, conveniently, tenaciously blind to the details of life around her (HM, 186). Hers is a morality of duplicity and cowardice, a song of fools.

We should note that such is, as well, the place of worship in *The House of Mirth*. Wharton depicts the banality of upper-class faith, a banality that appears increasingly malevolent through the perspective Lily eventually gains:

> The observance of Sunday at Bellomont was chiefly marked by the punctual appearance of the smart omnibus destined to convey the household to the little church at the gates. Whether any one got into the omnibus or not was a matter of secondary importance, since by standing there it not only bore witness to the orthodox intentions of the family, but made Mrs. Trenor feel, when she finally heard it drive away, that she had somehow vicariously made use of it. (HM, 82)

And again:

> The Wetheralls always went to church . . . Mr. and Mrs. Wetherall's circle was so large that God was included in their visiting-list. (HM, 84)

By referring here to the Wetheralls' visiting list, Wharton links Mrs. Peniston's conception of godliness and cleanliness. In this world, God becomes himself the guarantor of propriety and of carefully orchestrated negligence.

Christianity may become merely a matter of decorum, rather than a source for wisdom. This is brought home, literally, in a passage describing Mrs. Peniston's yearly ritual upon her return to town:

> The first two weeks after her return represented to Mrs. Peniston the domestic equivalent of a religious retreat. She "went through" the linen and blankets in the precise spirit of the penitent exploring the inner folds of conscience; she sought for moths as the stricken soul seeks for lurking infirmities. The topmost shelf of every closet was made to yield up its secret . . . and, as a final stage in the lustral rites, the entire house was swathed in penitential white and deluged with expiatory soapsuds. (HM, 147)

Wharton is clearly having fun here, but the matter is not only comic. Coming to know something about those who must scrub, and who must yield to their master's inspection, we are less able to view Mrs. Peniston merely as comic relief. She contributes a great deal to Lily's downfall, in her refusal to assist Lily with funding. By having our imaginations shaped by the very downfall of Peniston's niece, we begin to perceive the insidious underside of her master. Equating seemliness with morality, lack of conflict with truth, Mrs. Peniston personifies the very error Wharton strives to correct through the text.

Over the Abyss

Denied by circumstance the capacity any longer to ignore poverty, Lily tries to find a new way to see, and to survive. She finds the former but, tragically, not the latter. Wharton here saves a final judgment on the man with whom we began the novel. She introduces Lily through Lawrence Seldon's eye, and Lily dies in part due to his refusal to become vulnerably engaged in her plight. What Lily cannot avoid—investment in the struggles of those behind the frayed edges of the social tapestry—Lawrence cannot endure. Not able to name definitively whether Lily has erred or is wronged, Lawrence keeps himself, until it is too late, from entering into her predicament. This is the end to the story, for he is the one person Lily believes, from the start, might be a true friend:

> "Don't you see," she continued, "that there are men enough to say pleasant things to me, and that what I want is a friend who won't be afraid to say

disagreeable ones when I need them? Sometimes I have fancied you might
be that friend—I don't know why, except that you are neither a prig nor a
bounder, and that I shouldn't have to pretend with you or be on my guard
against you." (HM, 25)

In a way, Seldon remains aligned with Mrs. Peniston. Incapable of explor-
ing the inner folds of Lily's narrative, he seeks to keep her at arm's length.

Edith Wharton gives only the slightest narrative prompt toward an alternative. The penultimate scene of the book has Lily meet Nettie Struther,
a woman whom Lily has previously helped during a foray into charitable
work. Lily goes home with Nettie, and here Wharton allows the only truly
domestic scene of the book. In the "extraordinarily small" kitchen, while
feeding her baby, Nettie tells Lily that her husband "knew about" her, but
married her nonetheless. Whereas Seldon cannot engage, George does, knowing the worst there is to know about a prospective wife. As Lily later words
it, "it had taken two to build the nest; the man's faith as well as the woman's
courage" (HM, 449). After holding Nettie's baby in her arms, Lily returns
home to die. But first, she notes the significance of her encounter:

> That poor little working-girl who had found strength to gather up the frag-
> ments of her life, and build herself a shelter with them, seemed to Lily to
> have reached the central truth of existence. It was a meagre enough life, on
> the grim edge of poverty, with scant margin for possibilities of sickness or
> mischance, but it had the frail audacious permanence of a bird's nest built
> on the edge of a cliff—a mere wisp of leaves and straw, yet so put together
> that the lives entrusted to it may hang safely over the abyss.

This is the abyss over which Wharton has brought her reader, challenging us to encounter the wisdom of adjusted vision, and to have true faith
and courage. The alternative to Lily's demise, for the male as well as for
the female reader, is not the willed ignorance and safety of Mrs. Peniston,
or of Lawrence Seldon. The alternative involves real knowing, forgiveness,
and vulnerable solidarity.

Conclusion

I could have as easily chosen a different, otherwise overlooked author,
perhaps Nigerian-British novelist Buchi Emecheta or Norwegian storyteller
Sigrid Undset (both of whom I highly recommend). Writing in drastically
different contexts, many female fiction writers are unknown in the academy
because they write beneath the scope of the university. Their stories cover

the small, daily terrain of surviving, of existing within the concentric circles that revolve around the margins of dominant male culture. Stories of feeding children during times of paucity, of tending to elders in the midst of moral ambiguity, these disparately "female" narratives remain in the very niches of living that those with worldly power often seek to rise above.

As biblical scholar John Wright so helpfully reminds me, the church began in such supposedly "humble" niches, and, across time and locale, has remained statistically and formally more "female" than "male." For Christians to read such neglected stories and relate daily cultural history in women's studies is therefore quite apt, and may serve to call the ecclesial academy back down to the ground, to the incarnate practices of discipleship. As African-American theorist bell hooks suggests, listening to voices at the margin tells us much about the center, and women's studies may help a supposedly Christian academy self-assess and realign itself with those who serve.

This comes dangerously close to proposing that women's studies be the conscience, the moral heartbeat, of a university. Such a prescription has a long and dubious history, as women have sought to gain a hearing by way of a claim to inherent moral superiority. What I am suggesting is slightly different. I would contest the claim that women and women's studies are inherently more moral than are men and dominant studies. But I am persuaded by hooks, Fox-Genovese, and many others in the field of women's studies that there is a real benefit to the fact that most women in Western culture have been unable effectively to escape the work of wrapping wounds and cooking meals. Some women have strategically or genuinely narrated such as the proper, inescapable, role for women, and have advocated for votes, voices, and limited power based on such a role. Other feminists advocate for liberation from such caregiving roles. To reiterate a point I made in the introduction, it is my hope that women's studies in a Christian university will help to remap the rules for men as well as for women.

What would such a newly mapped academy look like? At the very least, it must involve a concrete revaluation of incarnational service, that is, that we pay a living wage and livable benefits to the people who feed, clean, and care for the ground on which the professors and students tread. Dreaming a bit bigger, I would suggest that the Christian academy tear down the social tapestry, not just seek better pay for those hidden behind it. This might mean that everyone, from named professor to first-year student, would rotate monthly into the refectory to assist in the preparation of meals. As in some parishes, we might propose that everyone similarly serve periodically in the onsite childcare facility. In short, a newly mapped academy would seek to distribute tasks not only according to perceived gifts (for, after all, one sometimes chooses one's "gifts" in order to avoid the less seemly tasks of discipleship) but also according to a shared life of interdependent service. Although since the founding of the University of Paris Christian scholars have often sought to live otherwise, there is a hearty tradition of incarnational Christian service and study on which the truly ecclesial academy could draw.

Short of a Maoist reeducation program, such a shared life will require an enormous amount of patience. Old dogs loathe new tricks, and old institutions move like icebergs. But Christians live our lives embedded in a story that is much larger than our mere efforts to live accordingly. We have reason to hope that God can transform even us into people ready to risk a life behind a social tapestry that cloaks false wisdom as true.

5

Hotel or Home?

Hospitality and Higher Education

Elizabeth Newman

How can an academic institution identify with a particular religious tradition and at the same time be "open to diversity"? This question has been at the forefront of numerous conversations at colleges and universities that seek to locate themselves within the Christian tradition. Is a "Catholic university," as George Bernard Shaw once said, simply a contradiction in terms? Is a college or university that identifies itself as Baptist, say, or even Christian, not inevitably excluding other points of view and thus inhibiting the unfettered quest for truth?

This essay will seek to respond to these questions by both analyzing the assumptions behind them and suggesting an alternative way to think about identity and receiving the "other." More specifically, I will argue that in the name of welcoming the other, colleges and universities have often come to function more like educational "hotels." While a college or university "hotel" may provide space for other persons, it is unable to offer genuine hospitality. Hospitality can only be fully practiced when a concrete sense of place sustains the life of an institution. Thus, Christian colleges or universities need to be rooted in a sense of place, even more in a sense of the college or university as *oikos,* in order to welcome the stranger into their midst.

What do I mean by *oikos?* In the New Testament, *oikos* can mean "household," but it can also refer to "a whole clan or tribe of people descended from a common ancestor"[1] and thus can refer to descendants or a nation. We read in Luke 1: 32–33, for example, where the angel Gabriel tells Mary she will bear a son, that "he will reign over the *house* of Jacob for ever . . ." In this latter usage, *oikos* names not so much a building as it does a people who are called to serve God. Thus *oikos* means home or household, but biblical usage indicates that *oikos* refers as well to a people who have been called into being by God and who have existed across generations, to the household or *oikos* of Jacob.[2]

At the outset, let us consider generally the difference between a hotel and a home. In many ways, a hotel is a comfortable place to be. Whether one is a guest or the host (roles that are usually clearly defined), minimal interaction is required. The host only needs to offer certain services, while the guest receives these for a set fee. And, as we know, the higher the fee, the nicer these services become. One of the central characteristics of a hotel, however, is that guest and host almost always remain anonymous to each other.

A home, on the other hand, involves much more. Homes are particular in a way that hotels are not. Since our homes are in many ways extensions of ourselves, it is very difficult to receive someone into our home for any length of time and remain strangers. Hospitality in the home is far more self-involving; it is therefore more unpredictable and risky. We do not know what we will discover about the other person or ourselves and how this will impact our lives.

While I think it is important to see how homes are concrete and particular in a way that hotels are not, it is equally important not to overlook the fact that very specific stories, and even more, that very particular *theological* assumptions inform the kind of hospitality any given place is able to offer. Later, I will return to this point and suggest that inadequate theological assumptions inform what I am referring to as "hotel" hospitality. Since Christians are called, however, to offer hospitality from the home or *oikos,* Christian colleges and universities ought to aim to offer this same kind of hospitality as well. First, however, I wish to offer a personal story.

◼ A Tale of Two Hospitalities

I am a Southern Baptist who for twelve years had the opportunity to teach at a Roman Catholic institution, Saint Mary's College in Notre Dame, Indiana. As I reflect as a "guest" (in some ways)[3] on Saint Mary's as home or hotel, I can see examples of both in my tenure at the school. "Home," as suggested above, refers to a particular place or people. Perhaps the most obvious place I received *oikos* hospitality while at Saint Mary's was through participating in the worship, particularly the baccalaureate mass. It was an odd kind of hospitality because, while all people involved in the school were invited to attend, to sit before the altar, to see the liturgical dancers, to smell the incense and hear the spoken Word, receiving and participating in the Eucharist was a more ambiguous matter. Some Catholics told me this was a matter of personal discretion, though there was some disagreement about this. All those present, however, were invited according to official Church teaching to receive a blessing from the priest or eucharistic ministers. Personally, I was always a bit hesitant to do this, since I was both unsure of the protocol and thought it would draw undue attention to myself. During the final baccalaureate mass I attended as a member of the Saint Mary's faculty, however, I decided to ask for a blessing and happened to be placed in the line where the bishop was. Looking back on this event, I interpret the bishop's blessing as a profound act of hospitality. True, I was not "welcomed" fully at the table. Nonetheless, the blessing was a *public* testimony to the brokenness of the church, while at the same time reaching across that brokenness, at once a sign of disunity and hope. I interpret this as an act of faithful hospitality because I was welcomed into the life that sustains the institution, even as our mutual identities were maintained in all their historical particularities, rooted as these are in generations of Christians from different places and times. Stated differently, the bishop (and the Catholic Church in this instance) allowed me to be both *guest*, receiving the blessing, and *host,* witnessing to the brokenness of Christ's body, the church.[4] There was, in other words, a genuine exchange flowing from our particular identities.

While I received this kind of *oikos* hospitality, I think it would also be instructive to reflect on how the institution sustained as well the kind of hospitality associated with a hotel. In writing about this, I do not wish to cast blame; indeed I too participated in this hotel hospitality. Rather, my goal is to analyze the situation in order to understand what prevents the faithful practice of Christian hospitality. One of the things that I came gradually to realize over the years was that the fact that I was Baptist, married to a United Methodist minister whose church I attended, seemed to be of little relevance to my life at the institution. In fact, I felt at times as if I were living a kind split existence. At first, I thought the split lay in the fact that I came from a deeply Protestant and Southern world and was trying to fit into a Catholic and Midwestern context. But I came to realize that the split lay rather in the privatized world of Christianity and the public world of education. So that, for example, appeals to specifically Christian or Catholic convictions in faculty assembly were rare, and when Catholic convictions were brought in, they were often met with embarrassment, or even derision.[5] It was made clear that faculty assembly was not the place to bring up specific Christian convictions, but was rather an "inclusive" space where only educational concerns ought to be addressed. Or if "Catholic" did enter into the conversation, then it was typically seen as meaning the *same* thing as "inclusive."[6] What this conviction had the effect of doing was relegating anything not "inclusive," in the sense assumed, to the private sphere. Particular convictions that could not be pitched in generic language that anyone would find acceptable were relegated to one's private room. Thus, in contrast to the blessing from the bishop where my "stranger" status was acknowledged, welcomed, and even *reversed,* the dominant assumptions that governed faculty assembly stripped everyone of the opportunity to be either guests or hosts. The common space was like the corridor of a hotel where each met the other outside of his or her particularity; governing the "common" public space were simply rules of procedure, Robert's Rules of Order.

Hotel Hospitality

This kind of hotel "hospitality" is not, of course, unique to Saint Mary's College but is rather the "atmosphere" that sustains so much of our thinking about higher education. William James perhaps captured this way of thinking about the modern university most fully in his well-known description of pragmatic liberal discourse as

> like a corridor in a hotel. Innumerable chambers open out of it. In one you may find a man writing an atheistic volume; in the next someone on his knees praying for faith and strength; in the third a chemist investigating a body's properties. In a fourth a system of idealistic metaphysics is being excogitated; in a fifth the impossibility of metaphysics is being shown. But they all own the corridor, and all must pass through it if they want a practicable way of getting into or out of their respective rooms.[7]

What are the implications of using the image of a hotel to describe the university? Even more, what assumptions sustain this kind of an image? George Marsden, who writes sympathetically about the loss of Christian identity in higher education,[8] embraces James's understanding of pragmatic liberal discourse as "quite congenial" and as really the only option available to us. Marsden elaborates: "Essentially my position is that in a pluralistic society we have little choice but to accept pragmatic standards in public life. I am not, as some might suppose, challenging pragmatic liberalism as the modus operandi for the contemporary academy. Rather I am affirming it for the limited role, but arguing that there is no adequate pragmatic basis for marginalizing all supernaturalist religious viewpoints a priori."[9] Marsden thus argues that as long as Christians share with their non-Christian colleagues "basic standards of evidence and argument," then there is no reason they ought not be able to reside in the academic "hotel," to use James's metaphor. In fact, Marsden points out that in terms of the technical, scientific side of academic inquiry, substantive Christian convictions make little difference, i.e., both Christians and non-Christians, for example, use the same technique "in determining when Washington crossed the Delaware to attack the Hessians at Trenton."[10] When particular religious commitments do impact academic scholarship, however, as long as religious persons are willing to play by the rules of the academy (i.e., use "publicly accessible" arguments and evidence), then there is no reason to exclude them. As long as one plays by these shared rules, then they may be allowed in the "hotel corridor," to use James's image, irrespective of what they are doing in their particular rooms. Marsden notes that this "game" need not be given an ultimate kind of legitimacy. For example, Christians can play basketball without abandoning their deeper commitments to God and the church.[11] Even if Christians are "alien," they nonetheless ought "to live with respect to the rules of the host culture and work to make them relatively better."[12]

This position nicely reflects what I am calling "hotel hospitality." Marsden is, of course, reflecting primarily on the presence of Christians in "secular" colleges or universities. Thus he is describing how Christians might be "guests" in the supposedly alien "host culture." His position, however, representative of our modern sensibilities on matters pertaining to education, is usually embraced even at institutions that call themselves Christian. Indeed, so accustomed are many to thinking of a division between public reason and revelation, or between public knowledge and private faith, that it is often difficult to see any alternative. Furthermore, I would say that one of the key reasons we are easily drawn to this "hotel hospitality" is that it is fired by a desire that people of widely differing ideological perspectives get along. Thus "pragmatism," as endorsed by both James and Marsden, names "how to go on when a dispute arises."[13] Yet it is important to note that the kind of hospitality Marsden and James embrace is one that ultimately erases Christian identity, just as our own identities are erased, or reduced to a credit card number, when we go to a Sheraton Hotel. For both James and Marsden, our particular religious convictions and practices remain in a private room.

■ A Theological Analysis of Hotel Hospitality

Whether Christians are primarily "guests" in a secular setting, or "hosts" in a Christian context, the hotel image that has come to dominate the way that Christians and others think about higher education is itself sustained by a particular set of convictions and practices. Stated more fully, there is no way to maintain a "corridor in a hotel" free of *theological* assumptions.

We can now turn more fully to consider what these are. What kind of theology sustains the university or college as hotel, as described above? I think the most adequate way to interpret it is as a species of gnosticism. If this is true, then I think we might legitimately ask whether or not Christians ought to be "playing" an essentially gnostic game, to use Marsden's way of putting the matter. Or, why should Christians offer and participate in a kind of gnostic hospitality when they have a much richer hospitality available to them? Or, why should we be satisfied with mass-produced fast food when we can receive and offer others a magnificent feast, such as the one Babette prepares in "Babette's Feast"?[14] Hotel hospitality fosters something akin to self-service, what Jean Vanier calls the worst of inventions:

> There we are, all with our own tray, own little bottle of wine, own little sachets of sugar, salt and pepper. It's like spending every mealtime on an aeroplane. It's terrible to assume that everyone is going to eat and drink a standard quantity, and do it alone into the bargain. How much more human to have a nice big bottle from which everyone can pour as much as they want and one nice big dish, so that everyone can make sure that the others have what they need . . .[15]

I will return to the question of "table manners" and *oikos* hospitality later in this essay.

For now, however, let us consider more fully the gnostic assumptions that sustain the image of university as hotel. First, I would say that the privatization of religious convictions and practices is essentially a gnostic move. This move inevitably locates religion in the spiritual sphere, separate from the material sphere. When the guest or host enters the fluorescent lighting of the windowless public corridor—the hall of the hotel—the religious convictions are not welcome. Thus, we can see here another gnostic feature: the material world is seen as a place that *can* be separated from the spiritual. Gerhard Lohfink notes this separation when he writes that

> one of the fundamental problems of the Church at the end of the twentieth century is that faith no longer saturates the whole of life, but only a narrow sector . . . Our employment has long since become a world in itself with its

own rules and ways of behaving. It has scarcely anything to do with Christian existence . . . In the same way leisure time has also become a world unto
itself, as have education, the economy, culture, and all the other spheres of
life. Faith is drying up. It no longer has any material that it can transform.
It has become unworldly and therefore ineffectual.[16]

As noted above, this split between the spiritual and material is fired by
the desire to sustain peace and harmony. Certain religious concerns, after
all, might well generate conflict, since not everyone will agree. I wish to
draw our attention, however, to the fact that religious convictions can
never be privatized; gnosticism sustains the whole picture that would have
us evacuate the spiritual from the material.

We might consider more fully the kind of hospitality that gnosticism is
able to offer. Is it a hospitality that offers the genuine harmony and peace
that its adherents so desperately desire? The refusal or inability to see the
material sphere as a place where God is and where God acts means it will
be difficult to see the stranger as one who is fully in the image of God and
as a gift. This will inevitably inhibit the practice of Christian hospitality.
Perhaps the gnosticized hotel university will say it desires to welcome diversity, but this welcome will always be short-circuited, not only because
of the tyranny of an abstract and gnostic rationality but even more because
it does not have the *resources* either to see and discern God's presence in
the material world or to articulate the full purpose of diversity. Thus, as
so much postmodern analysis has pointed out, unending conflict will be
inevitable as those who have "reason" and "power" will have no basis on
which to judge the "other" who does not have "reason" as fully worthy or
deserving of welcome.[17] A common response has been to say that everyone
has a right to a room in the hotel. But "rights" language too negates the
fullness of Christian hospitality. Such hospitality, which originates in God
and is displayed most fully in the gift of the Son, is freely given and received.
Hence the language of *gift* rather than "right" is central.

More Tales of Hospitality

To develop more fully this understanding of Christian *oikos* hospitality
and how it compares with gnostic hotel hospitality, let us turn to two ancient
texts: one a gnostic parable, "The Hymn of the Pearl" (also known as "The
Hymn of the Robe of Glory"), and the other, the parable of the prodigal
son (Luke 15:11–24). "The Hymn of the Pearl" powerfully captures the
gnostic sensibility that the material sphere is something entirely alien to the
spiritual. In the story, the parents of the central character, who is a prince,

send their son to Egypt to bring back a pearl guarded by a serpent. If his adventure is successful, he will become the heir along with his brother of his parent's kingdom. On his journey, in order not to attract attention, he must dress like the Egyptians and eat their food, which in due course makes him fall asleep. Eventually, he forgets who he is. His parents then send him a magical letter, which flies in the form of an eagle, alights beside him and becomes "all speech." Upon hearing the voice of the letter, the son remembers who he is, seizes the pearl, removes his unclean clothes and receives back his robe, which radiates knowledge and fits him perfectly.

In terms of our analysis of hospitality, a number of important occurrences stand out. At one point, the son observes: "in some way or other, they [those in the world] found out that I was not their countryman, and they dealt with me *treacherously*, and *gave* their food to eat."[18] The material gift of food is rejected. The same negative interpretation holds for the clothes the son wears, which he later regards as "filthy and unclean dress." The son is unable to receive gifts from the Egyptians (who represent the material world) because these are merely things that prevent him from remembering his true self. Even more significant is the fact that the son "snatched away the pearl" as he turns to go back to his father's house. Commentators suggest that the pearl can be explained as the "essential knowledge," and in the context of the story this knowledge or gnosis already resides within the son; the letter merely reminds him of what is written on his heart. In terms of the practice of hospitality, it is significant that the prince must aggressively seize, even steal, the pearl. It is not a gift, but rather represents the price that the prince must pay for discovering his identity, something entirely separate from the material world. True, the prince does receive the letter from his parents, but significantly the magical letter bypasses creation entirely; it contains words spoken from spirit to spirit.

Christians have been drawn to gnosticism for a number of powerful reasons,[19] so it is no surprise that it continues to hold sway over our imaginations. The familiar focus on the individual in our context, and on faith and values as one's private choices, continue to fan the flames of gnosticism. Isn't the spiritual life primarily about our inner journey, something separate from the material world of science and facts? Like the prince, we can easily imagine that our true identities lie within.

The parable of the prodigal son appears in some ways to be similar to "The Hymn of the Pearl." The prodigal son, too, goes into the world and forgets who he is. Like the prince, he is "lost." Luke emphasizes this fact by having the story of the prodigal son follow parables about the lost sheep and the lost coin. The prodigal son, however, is lost not because he has become trapped in a created world in which he does not belong. Rather, he is lost because he has squandered his father's gifts. His return lies not in receiving a spiritual letter reminding him of what he already knows, snatching a pearl, and abandoning the material realm; rather his return lies in acknowledging his rebellion and turning toward his father, who while "yet at a distance" sees his son and, overcome by compassion, runs to embrace him. The son's return home (*oikos*) lies ultimately in accepting and receiving again the gift of love his father desires so deeply to give. What saves the son is not a knowledge within, which he has forgotten, but the reconciliation with his father. Most significant for our analysis of hospitality, the love of the father that brings about the reconciliation is made manifest *through and within creation*. Not only does the father physically embrace the son, rather than send a "magical letter," but he says to his servants, "Bring quickly the best robe, and put it on him; and put a ring on his hand, and shoes on his feet; and bring the fatted calf and kill it, and let us eat and make merry, for this my son was dead, and is alive again; he was lost, and is found" (Luke 15: 22–23, RSV).

At this point, we can see how the story of the prodigal son is in many ways a *reversal* of "The Hymn of the Pearl": the son does not snatch a pearl, a symbol of the essential gnosis, but rather receives a ring. Both of the central characters do receive a robe, but in the "Hymn" the robe, originally worn by the son, was taken off when the son entered creation and then returned to the son when he remembers who he is and returns to his non-material home. As suggested above, the cloak, which the son leaves behind and later receives back, most likely "refers to the spirit and spiritual body with which the soul was originally united; the Egyptian clothes stand for the material body."[20] In contrast, the "best robe" that the prodigal son receives is a gift from the father in the material realm, as is also of course the festive and joyous meal celebrating the son's return. The son needs only to *receive* what the father offers: the robe, a ring, a party thrown in the son's honor and, most especially, forgiveness. The son remains in the same world, but we could say it is yet a new one. He does not have to eat what the pigs eat, but he can now feast on the best food that his father has to offer. He moves from scarcity, even starvation, to feasting and abundance. This abundance stands in stark contrast to the gnostic prince who, we are to imagine, does not need such sustenance.

A Theology of Oikos Hospitality

Irenaeus, one of the earliest theologians to argue against gnosticism, saw early on some of the deep and profound problems with the kind of gnostic sensibilities conveyed in "The Hymn of the Pearl." He recognized that those who reject the material world or place it in a separate realm will also be compelled to reject the Son, and so also the love of God. To the contrary, Irenaeus writes that ". . . God's own creation, which depends for its existence on God's power and art and wisdom, *has borne God.* In an invisible way, the creation is borne by the Father, but in a visible way, it does indeed bear the Word."[21] It is this conviction about creation and incarnation that sustains a Christian understanding of the material world. Christians are able to provide places of welcome because of the realization that God's own creation has actually borne God; therefore all places in our material world are made accessible or available to the presence of God.[22] To see that God's own creation has borne God means that God affirms the material world as the place where God is and where God acts.

In his treatise *On the Incarnation,* Athanasius notes that some may ask "why [God did] not manifest Himself by means of other and nobler parts of creation, and use some nobler instrument, such as sun or moon or stars or fire or air, instead of mere man?" He responds: "The Lord did not come to make a display. He came to heal and to teach suffering men . . . to put Himself at the disposal of those who needed Him and to be manifested according *as they could bear it, not vitiating the value of the Divine appearing by exceeding their capacity to receive it.*"[23] Thus for Athanasius, the incarnation reveals God's "divine generosity," God's superabundance, and this is precisely made manifest in the *way* in which this is given, according to our capacity to receive it. Thus, God comes in a way that we can bear it, and the way we are capable of bearing God as humans is in and through the created world, since we are ourselves creatures. We can say, even, that God has made us capable of receiving God. Here then we have at least two gifts, our own capability for God and God "matching" or "fitting" that capability through the incarnation, through coming as one who is like us. God's own hospitality, then, puts an end to any attempt to separate the material from the spiritual. The separation lies rather in the distance between the Creator and creature, when the latter refuses or squanders the gifts of God, as did the prodigal son the gifts of his father.

The *oikos* or place of Christian hospitality lies first of all, therefore, in fully receiving what God offers, just as the Son purely receives from the Father and vice versa. Such reception is precisely what enables us to give out of God's own abundance. Participation in God's own Trinitarian plenitude is the "home" of Christian hospitality, the place from which and out of which flow all hospitable gestures. Thus the invitation to others is not to walk down a hall of standard rules of evidence and procedure nor to co-exist in a hotel room, where there is minimal interaction. Rather, Christian hospitality welcomes the stranger to an overflowing banquet celebration. The only "rule" really is to come as you are, willing to participate in this endeavor at a particular place and time, a willingness that requires both courage and humility.

Table Manners in the Ecclesially Based College or University

Seeking to locate a "de-gnosticized" *oikos* hospitality in the university raises a number of questions and concerns. After all, the Christian banquet is most commonly associated with the celebration of the Eucharist or Lord's Supper. Shouldn't this practice be reserved for the church rather than the university? Even more, as my earlier personal story indicated, Christians themselves are unable fully to welcome each other to the table. What does this indicate about the welcome extended to those who are not Christian? Doesn't this seem to negate hospitality? While it is important to recognize that the standard "welcoming of diversity" privatizes "religious convictions," it is also important to state more fully how *oikos* hospitality goes about welcoming the stranger. How is this concretely displayed?

If it is true that "religious convictions" ought not to be bracketed to one sphere of the institution, then I think we can also say that the kind of "table manners" associated with the central meal of hospitality ought not to be bracketed as well, even if at the present time not all are able to join together in God's messianic banquet. In addition to the Eucharist or Lord's Supper, in fact, we can take as our cue for *oikos* hospitality in the university setting the "table manners" discussed in Jesus' parables and sayings to his disciples, particularly the parable of the marriage feast.

Gerhard Lohfink does just this in his discussion of "table manners in the reign of God." One of the first things he observes is that the disciples were not "like-minded" people, but rather a colorful mixture. Evidence indicates that Jesus selected his disciples from the most diverse groups of Judaism in his time, so that, according to Lohfink, the fascination of God's reign appears when people of "different backgrounds, different gifts, different colors, men and women sit together at a single table—and when they join their lives so that together, undivided they can serve God's cause."[24] Here diversity is not simply celebrated for its own sake nor for a non-committal aesthetic appreciation of the other."[25] Rather, diversity is the means through which God joins lives together in service, ultimately, to God. Diversity thus is the means through which the purposes and goodness of God might be more fully discerned and embodied.[26]

What are the "table manners" of *oikos* hospitality? Lohfink calls attention to several. First, there are no more classes: "all sit at the same table." Even more, as Vanier reminded us, those present are asked first to look to see that others have all that they need; only then are they to think of their own plates. Thus, the familiar saying: the greatest is the servant of all. Finally, "it is part of these manners that one does not seek the best place but rather the worst."[27] Here Lohfink refers specifically to the marriage feast parable in Luke's Gospel:

> When you are invited by any one to a marriage feast, do not sit down in a place of honor, lest a more eminent man than you be invited by him, and he who invited you both will come and say to you, "Give place to this man," and then you will begin with shame to take the lowest place. But when you are invited, go and sit in the lowest place, so that when your host comes he may say to you, "Friend, go up higher"; then you will be honored in the presence of all who sit at table with you. (Luke 14:8–10)

Lohfink notes that some have been offended by this parable because it seems to suggest a "sham humility": the guest selects the worst place only in order to receive a higher one. But Lohfink offers the following interpretation: "In God's new society people no longer have to worry about the place that is rightfully theirs. They can let other people show them the place that is right for them. What looks like a comic rule of propriety is really the reversal of all bourgeois values: no one need any longer struggle unceasingly for his or her reputation, but instead all can be concerned about God's reputation and allow their own honor to be received as a gift."[28]

Here we have a radical departure from the kind of manners that often rule the hotel university. First of all, they are decidedly noncompetitive; one does not have to elbow one's way onto the hotel corridor. Even more, they are manners that have to do with how to sit, pass, and share gifts at table where all present can see each other face to face. They are not manners about how to step onto a corridor or pass others in the hallway. Finally, these table manners call for all present to look towards each other, especially the most vulnerable or weakest. And here we come to the place of the stranger; he or she is to be treated with great honor, recognizing as does *oikos* hospitality that God is present in our giving and receiving. Part of looking out for the other and of allowing others to look out for us involves discernment and truth speaking.[29] These dimensions of Christian hospitality are often overlooked, as we frequently do not want to hear the truth about ourselves (thus the lack of humility) or we do not want to speak the truth to others (thus the lack of courage). As Reinhard Hütter notes, however, ". . .acknowledging and therefore receiving the truth of who and whose one is liberates one for genuine hospitality."[30] We become vulnerable to others in a way we are not while in the hotel university, but it is this vulnerability that enables us to open ourselves to God and others and so to practice hospitality more faithfully.

I am under no illusion: there is still a gap (if not many) in this analysis. As I have maintained, I think Christians need to practice *oikos* hospitality and the table manners that are a part of this in their educational endeavors. Yet how can we be based in the ecclesia if the ecclesia is itself broken? We can, of course, make the common eschatological observation that we live in between the time of the now and the not-yet. Even so, that our house is divided reminds us of the fact that our *oikos* hospitality itself fails to partake of all that God would offer. "The condition of Christianity at the present time," Lohfink reminds us, "is nothing like a colorful field in which wheat is growing and poppies and cornflowers are blooming; it is rather like a broken mirror that distorts the image of Christ."[31] We need to repent, then, not only of participating in gnostic hospitality (and so of corrupting our youth),[32] but also of failing to image Christ for the stranger. I think that only in a posture of repentance will we be open to perceive more fully where God is calling us in our educational efforts.

Notes

1. William F. Arndt and F. Wilbur Gingrich, *A Greek-English Lexicon of the New Testament and Other Early Christian Literature* (Chicago: University of Chicago Press, 1979), p. 561.

2. See also Acts 7:44–50.

3. I write that I was a guest "in some ways" since the role of guest and host are often very fluid. One of my Catholic colleagues who had taught at the institution for over twenty years considered himself a guest in the sense that he was a man teaching at a woman's college. He was also of course a host in important ways.

4. It might seem odd to describe an opportunity to be an "outsider," in the sense described, as a gift. But for the church to know, and reflect in its practices, that it is not yet all that it is called to be is a great good. The realization of brokenness, like the realization of sin, is itself a grace as it moves us to repent and seek more fully to discern God's own desire for his "body" in the world. What gift did I bring as I approached the table? At this particular moment, I stood as a reminder or witness to one of the deepest wounds of the church—its disunity—even as I received a blessing from the bishop. There was thus a genuine exchange.

5. In a similar vein, Stephen R. Haynes recounts a story at Rhodes College where "during the opening faculty meeting of the 1991–1992 academic year, a newly hired professor of Political Science was introduced. Following his official welcome by the Dean, he asked to address the faculty. The prestigious scholar, whom the college had lured away from a leading research university, walked to the podium and proclaimed that it had long been his dream to teach at a place like Rhodes. 'I am happy to be at a Christian college finally,' he announced, 'for my professional work is thoroughly informed by my faith.' As these words reached his audience, an awkward embarrassment became palpable," in Stephen R.

Haynes, ed., *Professing in the Postmodern Academy: Faculty and the Future of Church-Related Colleges* (Waco: Baylor University Press, 2002), p. ix–x.

6. This line of thinking is often supported or influenced by those Catholics who maintain that Catholicism is a "both/and" tradition. Michael Baxter, CSC, rightly notes that this way of thinking about identity fails to see how being inclusive or "both/and" is not only a logical contradiction (since a "both/and" position must include an "either/or" position) but that it also has no way to make discriminating judgments about convictions, ideas, or events that would clearly not be included. He asks, for example, "Do we really want to uphold the 'both/and' approach when it comes to an event such as Holocaust? Is the Catholic impulse both for anti-Semitism and against it?" in "Review Symposium" of Dennis M. Doyle's "Communion Ecclesiology," *Horizons* 29, no. 2 (Fall 2002): 331.

7. As quoted by George M. Marsden, *The Outrageous Idea of Christian Scholarship* (New York: Oxford University Press, 1997), p. 46.

8. See especially Marsden's *The Soul of the American University: From Protestant Establishment to Established Nonbelief* (New York: Oxford University Press, 1994).

9. Marsden, *Outrageous Idea*, p. 46.

10. Ibid., p. 47.

11. Marsden notes, "Literally applying the ethics of Jesus, passing the ball equally to your opponents as much as to your teammates, would not do much for the game . . . So when religious people play by the rules of the various games of society . . . they are not necessarily violating Christian principles by temporarily accommodating themselves to those rules," ibid., p. 56.

12. Ibid., p. 128.

13. This is Stanley Hauerwas's description of James's position. See his fuller analysis and criticism of James in *With the Grain of the Universe* (Grand Rapids: Brazos, 2001), pp. 43–86.

14. *Babette's Feast* is writer-director Gabriel Axel's adaptation of Isak Dinesen's short story about an expatriate French chef who prepares a sumptuous dinner for a group of devout Danish Lutherans.

15. Jean Vanier, *Community and Growth: On Pilgrimage Together* (New York: Paulist Press, 1979), p. 206.

16. Gerhard Lohfink, *Does God Need the Church? Toward a Theology of the People of God* (Collegeville, Minn.: Liturgical Press, 1999), p. 261.

17. Thus, Nicholas Boyle describes our current situation as follows, "Those who speak different idioms in the (post-)modern pluralist academy cannot talk to each other, and usually do not want to. No wonder the spokespersons in the administration building find it difficult to explain to the inquiring outsider why they are all there, and that in the most literal sense: why there windowless professional non-communicators need to be housed side by side on the same, no doubt expensive, humanities campus," in *Why Are We Now? Christian Humanism and the Global Market from Hegel to Heaney* (Notre Dame, Ind.: University of Notre Dame Press, 1998), p. 150.

18. My emphasis, "The Hymn of the Pearl," from the Gnostic Society Library, http://www.gnosis.org/library/hymnpearl.htm, p. 3.

19. See especially Philip J. Lee, *Against the Protestant Gnostics* (New York: Oxford University Press, 1987).

20. Riemer Roukema, *Gnosis and Faith in Early Christianity* (Harrisburg, Penn.: Trinity Press International, 1998), p. 147.

21. As quoted in Hans Urs von Balthasar, ed., *The Scandal of the Incarnation: Irenaeus Against the Heresies* (San Francisco: Ignatius, 1990), p. 54.

22. This is captured poetically in Brian Wren's hymn, "Christ Is Alive": "Christ is alive! No longer bound to distant years in Palestine, he comes to claim the here and now and dwell in every place and time . . . In every insult, rift, and war, where color, scorn, or wealth divide, he suffers still, yet loves the more, and lives, though ever crucified," in *The United Methodist Hymnal* (Nashville, Tenn.: U.M. Publishing House, 1989), number 318. My thanks to Jonathan Baker for this reference.

23. St. Athanasius, *On the Incarnation* (Crestwood, N.Y.: St. Vladimir's Press, 1944), p. 78.

24. Ibid., p. 174.

25. John H. Yoder observes that "respectful listening" often simply means that "one listens to the others when and because one has one's own timely reasons to think that what they say might be interesting; one listens to them on one's own terms and at one's own convenience." Yoder continues that "the price of this good-mannered ecumenical openness to hear one another at our points of distinctiveness is a pluralism that may replace the truth question with a kind of uncritical celebration of diversity," in John H. Yoder, *The Priestly Kingdom* (Notre Dame, Ind.: University of Notre Dame Press, 1984), p. 81.

26. Aquinas notes that "because the divine goodness could not be adequately represented by one creature alone, God produced many and diverse creatures, that what was wanting in one in the representation of the divine goodness might be supplied by another. For goodness, which in God is simple and uniform, in creatures is manifold and divided. Thus the whole universe together participates in the divine goodness more perfectly and represents it better than any single creature whatever" (s.Th.Ia, q. 47, ad 1), as quoted in Robert Barron, *Thomas Aquinas, Spiritual Master* (New York: Crossroad Publishing, 1998), p. 137.

27. Lohfink, *Does God Need the Church?* p. 183.

28. Ibid.

29. Reinhard Hütter, "Hospitality and Truth: The Disclosure of Practices in Worship and Doctrine," in Miroslav Volf and Dorothy C. Bass, eds. *Practicing Theology: Beliefs and Practices in Christian Life* (Grand Rapids: Eerdmans, 2002), p. 209.

30. It is interesting that Lohfink ends his analysis by saying that the "basileia . . . will not come without pure receptiveness, and that receptiveness is always a kind of suffering as well." This statement serves as a reminder that the "table manners" of *oikos* hospitality not only "turn the world on its head," but also involve a kind of suffering (Lohfink, *Does God Need the Church?* pp. 201 and 183, respectively).

31. Lohfink, p. 298.

32. See especially Stanley Hauerwas, "How Universities Contribute to the Corruption of Youth," in *Christian Existence Today: Essays on Church, World and Living In Between* (Grand Rapids: Brazos, 2001), pp. 237–252.

III.

The Curriculum of an Ecclesially Based University

6

Love Your Enemies

The Life Sciences in
the Ecclesially Based University

M. Therese Lysaught

Jesus said to his disciples: "You have heard that it was said, You shall love your neighbor and hate your enemy. But I say to you, love your enemies and pray for those who persecute you, that you may be children of your heavenly Father, for he makes his sun rise on the bad and the good, and causes rain to fall on the just and the unjust. (Matt. 5:43–45)

▧ Introduction

In 1989 one of the premier journals of the life sciences, *Nature*, ran an editorial cartoon of James Watson. With a typical mix of British wit and critique of the U.S., the cartoon pictured Watson—codiscoverer of the double helical structure of DNA, a Nobel-prize winning biologist, and then-director of the National Institutes of Health Center for Genome Research, the NIH branch of the U.S. Human Genome Project (HGP)—wrapped in an American flag.[1] Alice Domurat Dreger, a historian of science, describes the cartoon as follows:

. . . in it, the dark (usually red) stripes of the American flag were not sketched solid; instead they were drawn to be imitative of the banding of chromosomes or of an electrophoresis analysis of DNA. The result was that, in this picture, not only was a "statesman of science" wrapped in the flag of the U.S., genetics and the genome *literally formed part of the fabric of America*.[2]

Dreger uses this cartoon as a starting point from which to describe how the rhetoric and practice of science in the U.S. locates research as intrinsically aligned with and in service of American values and national goals. As she notes:

> Scientists often find themselves having to explicitly justify their public funding to nonscientists . . . [they have to show that] . . . their scientific projects are good not just for scientists, but good for the nation as a whole . . . In practice this means demonstrating that the goals of the research at issue are in some way parallel with—or at least not opposed to—national goals. Today, the more a large scientific project looks like it supports the values and goals of the nation (or at least the values and goals of the powers that be), the more likely it is to get funded. . . . Early proponents of the U.S. HGP won moral and financial support from Congress largely by aligning their professional values and goals with dominant American values and goals. . . . Project advocates garnered backing chiefly by employing metaphors which portrayed the HGP as a natural and necessary part of the American way, as an extension—indeed, as an admirable manifestation—of the traditional American value system. (pp. 157–158)

For *Nature* and Dreger, then, the field of genetics and the rhetoric of the life sciences generally tell a story in which they not only promote the ends of the nation; they are indeed an inextricable part of U.S. identity and what it means to be an American.

In an analogous way, as John Wright argues at the outset of this volume, universities in the U.S. have likewise understood their mission as serving the ends of liberal democratic culture. Universities aim to "contribute to the end of liberal society at large—the production of students to serve as 'good' leaders within the élite of the liberal democratic state and its compatriot, the capitalistic economy."[3] The stories that institutions of higher education tell about themselves—whether to prospective students and parents, at first-year convocations and commencements, or to funding and accrediting agencies—tell of students formed to serve society and to succeed within the global market.

This dynamic not only belies the myth of universities as the space of free intellectual inquiry; as Wright argues, it renders the mission of church-related universities doubly conflicted, undercutting their viability by denying their proper telos and directing their work toward alien ends. Given Dreger's analysis of the relationship between the sciences and liberal democratic polity, the practice of the life sciences within church-related or ecclesially based universities cannot but exacerbate this conflict.

In the following, I will examine the role of the life sciences within an ecclesially based university.[4] This is a multi-faceted and highly complex relationship, a thorough examination of which is well beyond the scope of this chapter. Therefore, I will not spell out specific prescriptions for how such an institution might structure its life-sciences curriculum. Rather, I would hope that this essay would serve as a starting point for reflection and discussion among administrators and faculty—especially faculty in the life sciences—who are interested in how we negotiate our professional identities in light of our call to Christian discipleship. To spur such discussion, I will focus on one main point of concern and, along the way, raise related points for consideration and discussion.

My reflections on the life sciences will focus primarily on the field of genetics, drawing supporting evidence from debates about human embryonic stem cell research and medicine generally. Genetics provides a useful entrée into these considerations for a number of reasons. As historian of science Garland Allen has argued, the development of genetics, first in the 1920s and then again under the aegis of molecular biology in the 1950s, brought together areas apparently as diverse as cytology, cell physiology, development, evolution, embryology, biochemistry, biometrics, and field natural history into a unified theory of living systems—i.e., what we could properly term "the life sciences."[5] Moreover, genetics brings together not only the varied biological and medical disciplines; it provides a window into the practice of science itself. As historian of science Phillip Sloan notes: "Intellectuals concerned with 'science studies' in the broadest sense—history, philosophy, sociology, and ethical dimensions of the sciences—can find in the HGP a dynamic field of scientific development that displays all of the issues involved in understanding of contemporary science and technology."[6]

Genetics, then, provides the main context for considering the primary concern I will address in this paper: namely, how the life sciences, as currently configured, are embedded within a context of violence. Political and military metaphors shape contemporary discourse about biomedicine and biotechnology. For many, and certainly for the media, clinical medicine through the auspices of biotechnology is engaged in a war against disease, disability, suffering, and death.[7] Drawing on the history of the field of genetics and the Human Genome Project, as well as on the rhetoric surrounding medicine and biotechnology more generally, I will first seek to show how the current practice of the life sciences cannot help but to entangle us with war and the violence of the liberal democratic state.

Moreover, the violence allied with science signals its underlying cause: a religious commitment to science as salvific. For Christians and institutions who are committed to nonviolence as a central component of discipleship and who locate salvation not in the hands of the scientific community but in the death and resurrection of Jesus Christ, these twin facets of contemporary science cannot but give pause. How then do we situate the life sciences in the ecclesially based university such that the disciplining that is part of their practice is consistent with our call to witness the Good News through lives of peaceableness? The beginning of the answer to this question lies, I will argue, in Christian attitudes toward death, attitudes necessarily formed by communal practices of the Christian life. Only within such a context might researchers and institutions find resources for resisting the paradigm of violence that informs the practice of the life sciences and hope to resituate them within a paradigm of peace.

Before turning to this main question, however, I would like to begin by raising one additional point for reflection, one concerning what many see as the inherent conflict between science and theology. One cannot get far in a conversation about religion and science without hearing the names of Copernicus, Galileo, and Darwin invoked as icons of the classic contest. While many have deconstructed this overdrawn narrative, it may be the case that contemporary universities have to deal with a different problem, namely, science as a culture of its own. Sloan, for example, believes that our contemporary situation differs from the classic battles between science and religion mentioned above. "In our present context," he notes, "a new level of conflict between theology and science is being generated not by any single issue or theory—but by the convergence of a wide range of inquiries—in a totalizing naturalistic world view that claims to give a comprehensive explanation of all aspects of existence" (p. 25). Dreger, in her analysis with which this paper opened, takes the issue beyond simply one of a worldview. She observes that scientists who try to realign their self-understanding to serve the goals of the nation (and therefore get funded) walk a tightrope:

> . . . scientists as a group have their own peculiar tradition of values and goals, a tradition which does not necessarily easily mesh with those of any other ethnicity or nation. . . . scientists form something of a sub-culture, a sort of ethnic group. . . . Like its ethnic counterparts, the scientific culture is comprised of a set of ideals, values, imperatives, a system of rewards and punishments, a hierarchy, a canonical history full of superhuman heroes and great struggles, and even an origin myth. (p. 158)

Dreger observes this dynamic from the perspective of a historian and finds a tensive fit at best between the scientist and society. If her claims about scientific culture are correct *vis à vis* the liberal democratic state, will scientists find it equally if not more difficult to mesh their own subculture with the polity of the church and the kingdom of God? Which worldview, and which identity, becomes more determinative? Will either culture allow itself to be subordinated to the other? The totalizing worldview of science, which seeks epistemological hegemony, likewise seeks total allegiance from its practitioners.

▨ I. The Life Sciences and the Violence of the State

My first task, then, is to demonstrate the relationship between the contemporary practice of the life sciences and the infrastructure of violence of the liberal democratic state. Three angles may shed light on this relationship: the genesis of the Human Genome Project and related areas in medicine; the current social location of the life sciences *vis à vis* public funding; and, most broadly, the metaphors and rhetoric surrounding new developments in the life sciences. I will begin with the story of the Human Genome Project.

The Human Genome Project (HGP) has frequently been referred to as "the Manhattan Project for biology." Even a cursory reading of the history of the HGP reveals the multiple levels on which this analogy functions. The most superficial uses of the phrase point to its character as "big science" or as working analogously at the molecular/atomic level to "unleash the awesome powers of nature." But a closer reading of that same history suggests that perhaps this is not an analogy at all, but that in fact there is a close relationship between the two projects. I will simply identify three points of contact—genealogical, conceptual, and ideological.

The HGP is in many ways rightly understood as in fact the great-grandchild of the Manhattan Project. Launched in 1989, the Human Genome Project was jointly sponsored by the National Institutes of Health and the U.S. Department of Energy. A simple genealogy notes that the Department of Energy was the successor of the Atomic Energy Commission (AEC), the postwar incarnation of the Manhattan Project.

But the relationship is more than just one of ancestry; the link is almost (dare I say?) "genetic." In other words, that the Department of Energy sponsored the HGP was not accidental, insofar as an interest in genetics traces back to the beginning. After the war (1947), the AEC created the Atomic Bomb Casualty Commission (ABCC). The ABCC had a large genetics component; it was charged with the task of evaluating the effects of radiation on the populations of Hiroshima and Nagasaki as well as on the U.S. citizens who worked in the research and development arms of weapons production. The ABCC was eventually succeeded by the Radiation Effects Research Foundation (part of the Health Effects Research Division of the DOE). It was through the RERF that the DOE sponsored the so-called "Alta Summit," a conference of geneticists and molecular biologists held in Alta, Utah, in December 1984, to review the results of the ABCC's long-term study of the effects of radiation on the Japanese population. The Alta Summit is generally marked as the place where conversations led to the genesis of the idea for the HGP.[8]

Thus, the historic roots of the Human Genome Project lie embedded within the U.S. World War II war machine. Similar sorts of genealogies can be traced for other areas in the life sciences. An equally fascinating account of the intersections between the Manhattan Project, industry, and the emerging practice of university-based research in the life sciences is the story of the development of the field of nuclear medicine. Timothy Lenoir and Marguerite Hays in their essay "The Manhattan Project for Biomedicine" demonstrate how those working for the Medical Division of the Manhattan Project began planning well before the end of the war for how they might adapt their work to the postwar world and in doing so transform contemporary medicine.[9] In this story, the AEC is again a central figure. More interestingly for our purposes, they note that a key element of the leadership's vision for attracting and retaining appropriately trained scientific personnel to the endeavor was to create faculty and research appointments at universities with provisions for tenure, an innovation that fundamentally changed the practice of scientific research at universities (p. 36).

They conclude their analysis with the observation that these efforts were successful beyond anyone's wildest imaginings. Testimony given in 1976 records the extraordinary impact of the Manhattan Project on contemporary medicine:

> The effect that nuclear medicine has had on the practice of medicine can be demonstrated in at least two ways. The first relates to the use of nuclear medicine procedures and the clinical practice of medicine. For example, in 1973, some 7.5 million Americans received in vivo nuclear medicine procedures. This represents approximately one procedure for every 4.4 hospital admissions. . . . The second area of major impact relates to the effect of nuclear medicine as a scientific discipline with regard to careers in health care. The Society of Nuclear Medicine now has some 8000 members and the American Board of Nuclear Medicine has certified 2,070 physicians as specialists in nuclear medicine since its inception on July 28, 1971. . . . That this field is well recognized as a medical discipline is shown by the establishment of the American Board of Nuclear Medicine and the recent formation of a Section on Nuclear Medicine in the American Medical Association.[10]

Some thirty years later, these figures have increased exponentially.

Thus, if one looks into the genealogy of the Human Genome Project and other areas of the life sciences, one finds an ancestry and ongoing parentage rooted in the interests and infrastructure of the U.S. military. A second link between the Manhattan Project and the HGP is conceptual. The Manhattan Project, and the military context of the 1940s and 1950s more generally, radically reshaped fundamental concepts and language of genetics. Lily Kay, in her essay "A Book of Life? How a Genetic Code Became a Language," masterfully demonstrates how, in the 1950s, the narrative of genetics was rewritten due in no small part to the influx into the field of individuals involved with World War II and the Cold War. Kay argues that the very notion of genetics as a "code" gained currency in part because of the importance of cryptology in the postwar era. As she notes: "Eminent physicists, biophysicists, chemists, mathematicians, communication engineers, and computer analysts—whose own projects situated them at the hub of weapons design, operations research, and computerized cryptology—joined in the effort to 'crack the code of life.'"[11] Information and computer metaphors now so common in genetics rhetoric came from outside the realm of molecular biology via mathematicians like Norbert Wiener and John von Neumann who, with others, were key figures in strategic military planning; Henry Quastler, the architect of the new discipline of information-based biology, was "funded through military sources" (p. 107). Kay characterizes the genetic codes of the 1950s as "'boundary objects,' migrating along the two-way traffic between molecular genetics on the one hand and the militarized world of mathematics and communication engineering on the other" (p. 120).

Thus, we can find connections between the HGP and the Manhattan Project on both the genealogical and conceptual levels. A third set of connections is more ideological. As many historians, including John Beatty, have noted, "the Human Genome Project is a post-Cold War project; and I do not just mean chronologically speaking."[12] With the ending of the Cold War and the emergence of the U.S. as an unchallenged military power, national security concerns shifted from those of military threats to that of economic competitiveness. Especially in the 1980s, the decade in which the Human Genome Project was conceived, lobbied, and funded, the U.S.'s changing economic relationships, especially relative to Japan, "led many analysts to argue for a broader notion of national security—one that emphasized economic as well as military security." As one then-Senator argued, "Trade IS defense" (p. 141).

While the HGP was not conceived specifically as an instrument of national security, Beatty notes that it very soon became promoted as such, as the NIH and DOE vied for the rights to sponsor the project. Arguments about U.S. technological competitiveness in favor of the HGP run through House and Senate authorization and appropriation hearings. Leroy Hood, a significant figure in the field of genetics, developed at length an argument that began: "As we all know, America is currently the world leader in biotechnology. This leadership is unequivocally being threatened by the Japanese. The human genome project, both through technology and the creation of a powerful infrastructure, is helping to insure this future world leadership" (p. 150). Similar arguments have been advanced with regard to many areas of science and technology, most recently by the lobby in favor of human embryonic stem cell research. Behind this threat is not simply concern about economics, however. Such rhetoric paints a specter of Americans at the mercy of others (Japanese, German, British), who, by controlling access to a valued, needed, desired technology, threaten our autonomy; more perniciously, by withholding access, they could potentially have power over our very lives.

Thus, it is clear that genetics and the Human Genome Project cannot be understood apart from their relationship with the U.S. military and notions of national security. Tracing the history of other fields in the life sciences would likely reveal similar sorts of linkages. But this is only half the story. If we turn to biotechnology and the life sciences more generally, we find rhetoric fundamentally shaped by images of war. Three examples highlight this dynamic.

First, new technologies—from genetics to regenerative medicine—are often described as "revolutionary." Although at times more benign, "revolution" is fundamentally a political word, one suggesting force, violence, and power. It traditionally refers to the overthrow of a regime, government, or social order. To locate the technologies of healing under the rubric of "revolution" suggests that they function as a means of power, that they seek to affect the social order, that they will ultimately govern the lives of individuals.[13]

Second, and more obviously, medical research is often cast in the language of war. Richard Nixon, in 1971, launched the "War on Cancer," a metaphor employed and developed extensively in a recent report on cancer research in the journal *Nature*.[14] This metaphor is employed most often when a new technology needs to be sold to political and public audiences in the U.S. The most recent example of this trend would be that of human embryonic stem cell research.

An article by Glenn McGee and Art Caplan, directors of the University of Pennsylvania Center for Bioethics and significant figures in the field of bioethics, exemplifies this dynamic.[15] In "The Ethics and Politics of Small Sacrifices in Stem Cell Research" one finds at least seven war-related images in as many pages. For McGee and Caplan, those who seek to develop therapies from human embryonic stem cells are characterized as fighting a "just war," a "war against suffering" caused by the whole gamut of diseases from Parkinson's to cancer to heart disease and more (p. 156). They compare the annual mortality of cancer, which might potentially be alleviated through human embryonic stem cell research, to the number of people killed "in both the Kosovo and Vietnam conflicts" (p. 154). They suggest that advocates of human embryonic stem cell research plan to "sacrifice embryos for a revolutionary new kind of research" (p. 152). They liken Parkinson's disease to an evil "dictator" dreaming up the most nefarious "chemical war campaign" (pp. 156, 154). Resonating with wartime rhetoric, they note that "adults and even children are sometimes forced to give life, but only in the defense or at least interest of the community's highest ideals and most pressing interests" (p. 153).

McGee and Caplan are far from alone in employing this sort of rhetoric to frame the discussion about human embryonic stem cell research. For many, and certainly for the media, clinical medicine through the auspices of biotechnology is engaged in a war against disease, disability, suffering, and death. The tools of research and the clinic are the "medical armamentarium." Those who suffer from particular illnesses are "survivors." Cures are hailed as "magic bullets." Moreover, the hyperdrive politicization of this human embryonic stem cell research points to the familiar adage that politics is but war waged by other means. As Katharine Seelye notes, on August 9, 2001, when George Bush finally revealed his decision about federal funding of human embryonic stem cell research, "They chose to have Mr. Bush announce his decision in prime time on national television, a format that presidents traditionally reserve for explaining military actions or trying to extract themselves from difficult political binds."[16]

This rhetoric of war is not accidental. A clue to its meaning comes from an article on what seems at first glance an unrelated topic—developments in American art and design in the 1940s-1960s. Commenting on the shift in American tastes from streamlined objects and architecture that celebrated the machine prior to World War II to more biomorphic images that celebrated nature, a museum curator observes that "the war didn't make the machine look like such a salvation after all. The new salvation—and the new threat—was biology and the atom."[17] Similarly, in language ubiquitous in contemporary popular literature on science and technology, Michael West, founder of Geron, the company that funded the first successful efforts to create human embryonic stem cells, and now the head of the biotech concern Advanced Cell Technology, which has been at the forefront of efforts to clone human beings, sums it up: "We're trying *to save* the lives of our fellow human beings who have *no hope* today."[18]

Threat. Hope. Salvation. These are terms associated not traditionally with scientific discourse but with religious claims, specifically with doctrines of soteriology or salvation. Therefore, to unpack these claims and examine them in relationship to the practice of the life sciences, we must turn to the discourse of theology.

▇ II. Nonviolent Science and the Enemy Death

The curator's remarks highlight an important characteristic of the soteriology of liberal democratic polity, namely, that the forces at issue are seen at one and the same time as both threat and salvation. William F. May, in an insightful reflection on the role of military metaphors in medicine, recognizes that these images are generated from the broader religious consciousness of contemporary culture and echo the duality of these powers. He notes: "The modern interpretation of disease as destructive power fits in with the religious preoccupations of our time. . . . However, the gods that enthrall modern men and women do not bless but threaten them."[19] For May, the god above all gods is death. Death and the related god of suffering are those that we fear most, those that wield the most power over us (p. 34). Perceived as absolute evil, "the *summum malum* of violent death has replaced God as the effective center of religious consciousness in the modern world" (p. 67).

These dark forces threaten us; before them we stand helpless, innocent yet powerless. Without a champion to intervene on our behalf and defend us, we have no hope. Medicine, and the biotech machine upon which it depends, is just such a champion. Noting that it is only recently that the image of the physician as fighter replaced the image of physician as parent, May observes that "the goal of medicine defines itself negatively and adversarially as being either to prevent suffering or to prevent death" (p. 69). May describes the physician as "the titan who responds to the sacred by seizing power in his or her own right and doing battle with the enemy" (p. 33). The physician is the one that wields "the retaliatory powers that modern biomedical research places at his or her disposal" (p. 34). Medicine, thus, becomes our savior.

As John Wright has noted, this account of salvation is fundamentally a parody of the soteriology offered by the Christian tradition. On one level, the account is very similar, for suffering, death, and those other forces that threaten us, and fear of which dominates our lives, are nothing other than what traditional theological language has referred to as "the principalities and powers." Even within the Christian narrative, they are rightly understood as enemies. St. Paul, in his impassioned exhortation on the essence of salvation, concludes:

> Then comes the end, when [Christ] delivers the kingdom to God the Father after destroying every rule and every authority and power. For he must reign until he has put all his enemies under his feet. The last enemy to be destroyed is death. (1 Cor. 15:25–26)

But in the liberal revision of this vision, "Christ-the-physician" becomes physician-as-Christ, the one who (with the help of biotechnology) fights relentlessly against the last enemy, death. Science is, in the words of Michael West, hope for those who have no other hope. And when the battle is won, the kingdom will be delivered. But the kingdom will not be the kingdom of God, delivered to the Father. It will be the kingdom of liberal democratic polity, delivered into the hands of America. And medicine will sit at the right hand of power.

If indeed this account of the alternative soteriology of the life sciences is convincing, how then is an ecclesially based university to proceed in structuring its curriculum? How is a life scientist, who is also committed to her Christian identity, to negotiate the conflicting worldviews operative in her work and faith? Is it possible to practice the life sciences in such a way that they do not presuppose this worldview? Is it possible to practice the life sciences in such a way that they do not aim at producing the kingdom of god in America as much as they embody what it means to live in the Kingdom of God this side of the eschaton?

May explores the image of the physician as fighter in order to draw attention to the power of images and metaphor. They tell a story, he notes, a compressed, prototypical story, a narrative in which we locate ourselves, that defines our social role and how we understand our work and vocation.[20] As such, metaphors are "demiurgic in the sense that they do not simply describe the world, they partly create and re-create the world to conform to an image" (p. 20). Which world, therefore, ought the Christian practice of the life sciences create and recreate?

I do not pretend to have a complete answer to these questions. Instead, I would like to offer three starting points for the sort of reflection and discussion on these questions that must necessarily take place within institutions of higher education that take these issues seriously.

The first question concerns how we position ourselves vis à vis death and the attendant evils against which science and medicine fight (suffering, disability, and illness). Even St. Paul clearly regards death as the enemy. As such, is it not appropriate to resist it, to war against it, to respond to it even with violent means if necessary?

At issue here is the nonviolence of the gospel. For Christians, when confronted with an enemy, even an enemy as powerful as death, are exhorted in the Sermon on the Mount to love one's enemies, to pray for those who persecute us. What would Christian nonviolence look like in the face of illness and death? Are we simply to sit back and passively accept the scourges of sickness that afflict others, to be silent in the face of threats against life? Are we to rejoice when human life, a good that reflects the very image of God, is extinguished?

Such an attitude would seem in many ways to be at odds with the Christian tradition. Even Christ, we see in the passage from 1 Corinthians above, sees death as an enemy, has triumphed over it provisionally, and will ultimately destroy it. Here, and in the Apocalypse, we have language of a great war between Christ and the principalities and powers that rule the world, the last and greatest of which is death, an enemy that has been ultimately defeated by the Cross and Resurrection. The language here is violent, even militaristic.[21] Moreover, Christian tradition has always held that part of the mandate of Christian discipleship is the call to follow Christ in his mission of healing—as we hear when Jesus, in the passage in Luke, commissions the seventy:

> After this, the Lord appointed seventy others, and sent them on ahead of him, two by two, into every town and place where he himself was about to come. And he said to them . . . "Go your way; behold, I send you out as lambs in the midst of wolves. Carry no purse, no bag, no sandals; and salute no one on the road. Whatever house you enter, first say, "Peace be to this house!" . . . Whenever you enter a town and they receive you, eat what is set before you; heal the sick in it and say to them, "The kingdom of God has come near to you." (Luke 10: 1–9)[22]

For Luke, healing is inextricably linked to the kingdom of God. It is a sign of its inbreaking, its coming near to us in Jesus. And it is a task specifically given to those sent by Jesus into the world to prepare the way for his coming.

Yet, not only does this passage from Luke point us in the direction of healing, it points us again in the direction of peace. Prior to healing, those sent are to proclaim "Peace be with you!" Like healing, the peacebearing nature of the Christian life derives squarely from the life of him who we follow. But rarely do we see those who heal—be it God, Jesus, or the disciples—locked in a violent struggle against the enemies, sickness and death. Sickness and death are clearly not adversaries to be fought at all costs. Instead, the healing witnessed in Scripture is a practice rooted in the identity and actions of the God, who is a God of peace.[23] The healing that we pursue, therefore, must be anchored in the broader context of God's work in the world and our participation therein. The healing that is part of the Christian mandate, if abstracted from this narrative context, becomes a formal claim to which any and all means might be fitted.

I would suggest that to understand what it might mean to love death as one's enemy would require that we look to analogous contexts where it is clearer what it might mean to love one's enemies. It might mean that we are to forgive death the real injuries, pain, and suffering it causes us. It might mean that we are to be reconciled to its presence, forgoing the fantasy that we will defeat death with the tools of our technology. It might mean that we are to rightly resist it, but only with the tools of love.

What are those tools? We find them highlighted in Ephesians, in the jarring military metaphors that Paul uses to describe the Christian life:

> Finally, be strong in the Lord and in the strength of his might. Put on the whole armor of God, that you may be able to stand against the wiles of the devil. For we are not contending against flesh and blood, but against the principalities, against the powers, against the world rulers of this present darkness, against the spiritual hosts of wickedness in the heavenly places. Therefore take the whole armor of God, that you may be able to withstand in the evil day, and having done all, to stand. Stand therefore, having girded your loins with truth, and having put on the breastplate of righteousness, and having shod your feet with the equipment of the gospel of peace; besides all these, taking the shield of faith, with which you can quench all the flaming darts of the evil one. And take the helmet of salvation, and the sword of the Spirit, which is the word of God. (Eph. 6:10–17)

Truth, righteousness, peace, faith, salvation, Spirit, and the word of God. These—including peace—are the weapons of the spirit. Facing death so equipped, we do not so much annihilate it but rather evaporate its power over us, its power to govern our lives with fear, to determine our actions. These tools do not eliminate its reality—we all will still die—but they can liberate us from having our lives be controlled by death (and suffering and illness).

Likewise, we need to take care in reading passages like 1 Corinthians 15 too literally. For while Christ may well consider death an enemy, it would be out of character for the risen Christ to act violently, even toward this greatest of enemies. Christ, we believe, has triumphed over death. But as his initial victory was nonviolent, so also will be his final defeat of death.

A Christ-centered understanding of discipleship sets the context for the understanding of our work, our vocations, and our very lives. One additional aspect of this reimagining relevant to the work of the life sciences concerns our relationship with nature. All too often, training in the life sciences under an overarching bellicose metaphor presumes a Baconian-cum-Manichean understanding of nature. Not only is nature understood as raw material to be exploited to ease the human condition (domination rather than dominion), certain elements of nature become cast as evil. From "bad" or "defective" or "mutant" genes to body parts that "fail," nature within this metaphor is overlaid with moral valence. It is the evil nature that must be overcome if the soteriology offered by liberal polity is to be achieved.

As Augustine reminds us, however, for Christians no aspect of nature can be deemed evil insofar as everything that exists is part of God's creation.[24] "And God saw everything that He had made, and behold, it was very good" (Gen. 1:31). In fact, Augustine acknowledges how certain aspects of creation (under which he might have included pathogens had they been known to him) might be perceived as evil in and of themselves:

> . . . [T]here are many things, such as fire, cold, wild beasts, and so forth, which are not compatible with, and which injure, the needy and frail mortality of our flesh. . . . [Those who hold them to be evil] do not notice how splendid such things are in their places and natures, and with what beautiful order they are disposed, and how much they contribute, in proportion to their own share of beauty, to the universe as a whole, as to a commonwealth. Nor do they see how these things contribute to our own wellbeing when we employ them with a knowledge of their proper uses. Thus, even poisons, which are harmful if used ill, become wholesome and curative when proper use is made of them; whereas, on the other hand, those things which delight us, such as food and drink and the sun's light, are known to be harmful if used immoderately or inopportunely. . . . For there is nothing at all which is evil by nature, and "evil" is a name for nothing other than the absence of good.[25]

For Augustine, nature in itself cannot be evil, though nature disordered as an effect of the fall will certainly be experienced as such.[26]

> For it is that which pleases us in their natures that we are displeased to see taken away by some fault. This may not be so in cases where even the natures themselves displease men, as often happens when such natures become harmful to men. For then men consider them not in themselves, but only with reference to their utility, as with those creatures whose swarms smote the pride of the Egyptians. . . . It is not with respect to our comfort or discomfort, then, but with respect to their own nature, that created things give glory to their Maker. . . . We find, then, that the same thing is hurtful when applied in one way, but most beneficial when proper use is made of it. . . . All natures, then, simply because they exist and therefore have a species of their own, a kind of their own, and a certain peace of their own, are certainly good. And when they are where they should be according to the order of their nature,

they preserve their own being according to the measure in which they have received it.[27]

In instances of illness, created things are clearly not where they should be. The result of this disordering—a consequence of the fall—is morbidity and death. But Augustine reminds us that a Christ-centered understanding of the biological world knows that all of creation is the work of God through the Word. With such an attitude, researchers in the life sciences can learn to love our common enemies, approaching viruses and mutant genes as good, simply because they exist, while joining their efforts to God's redemptive purposes by righting the order of creation.

III. Christian Practices and the Gift of Peace

In learning to love our enemies, do they necessarily remain such, namely *enemies?* The gospel does not promise that if we love our enemies, such enmity will disappear. In fact, it seems to promise that habits of loving one's enemies will most likely bring more on and may well lead to crucifixion or martyrdom.

The late Joseph Cardinal Bernardin in *The Gift of Peace,* his autobiographical account of his struggle with terminal pancreatic cancer, provides a compelling response to this question. In his narrative, we watch as he uses the tools of medicine to resist the growth of cancer in his body. We watch as he wins a short-lived remission, and then how the cancer returns with renewed virulence. The experience of his own illness leads him into a new world of ministry, being present to and praying for hundreds of others who struggle with cancer. At the end of his own journey, he comes to regard "death not as an enemy but as a friend."[28]

This transformation in his attitude toward death is clearly the fruit of the practices of the Christian life. The reorientation is first suggested to him by his friend Henri Nouwen, who learned it during his last ministry among persons with disabilities when he lived in the Daybreak Community of L'Arche. Nouwen's insight resonates with Bernardin's life, shaped as it is by practices of "letting go" and giving God Lordship over his life; of practicing forgiveness; of ministering to others who are sick and dying. Liberation from the tyranny of suffering and death, reconciliation with death, and learning to love the enemy death to the point of calling it "friend" are for Bernardin the fruits of a worshipful life lived amidst the community of the broken.

As such, Bernardin's re-reading of death is clearly Christopathic—shaped by Christ's willed self-emptying, death, and resurrection. His story strongly suggests, however, that such a rereading is only possible in a life deeply shaped by Christian practices. This is instructive for questions of pedagogy, especially for the life sciences. For unlike just about any other discipline in the university curriculum, science pedagogy is practice-based (which accounts in part for its power) and engages students in formative disciplinary activities. Science students have "lab." In most institutions, science students (and perhaps even general education students) spend more time in lab each week than in worship. How do these very embodied practices form students? In what narrative do they situate them? How to they shape the way that they see the world?

Considerations of the life sciences in the curriculum of an ecclesially based university must engage these questions. It must reflect on the spectrum of practices that complement the students' lives, giving special attention to ways in which alternative practices may be more especially necessary for students in the sciences to help them learn to resist the power that it seeks to have over their lives. To effectively help students and professors renarrate the "story" that underlies their practice of the life sciences in an ecclesial university will require not only a redescription of the world, but will also require a set of practices by which those convictions become habitually embodied. Among these practices would certainly be daily prayer and worship; service—especially with the sick and disabled; and reconciliation, insofar as these work to inculcate a habit of seeing God in all things, the virtue of compassion (suffering with), and the virtue of peaceableness. Learning to lead lives that are christologically determined may make it easier for students and practitioners of the life sciences to learn to reread the practice of their disciplines in a way that is informed by the one we follow and that, like him, points beyond ourselves, and our work, to God.

For students to be so formed, however, will require a faculty equally open to having their lives reshaped by practices of resistance. This, in many ways, is the greater challenge for an ecclesially based university. As Dreger noted at the outset, those scientists who follow the ethos of the nation may find their loyalty to the culture of science called into question. If that is the case, how much more difficult will be the challenges that face those scientists who follow the ethos of the church? As with all academics, teachers of the "life sciences" are formed by the norms and practices of their disciplines. They come to teaching positions with identities as "geneticists" or "developmental biologists." How does one maintain one's professional identity if the practice of the life sciences in an ecclesially based university requires a radical revisioning? Furthermore, funding for university research in the life sciences comes almost exclusively from two sources: the government (NIH, NSF, etc.) or private industry. Neither can help but enmesh the researcher in the aims and violence of liberal society. How ought university professors negotiate this problematic? How, if they decide to seek funding from alternative sources, do they maintain professional credibility and the academic reputation of the department and university?

Answers to these questions must be worked out within the community of those who practice the life sciences in conversation with their colleagues across the university. But in order to address the practical incorporation of the life sciences within an ecclesially based university, those who strategize must ask whether such sciences can be disentangled from the violence of the state and the idolatrous soteriology that currently hold them in thrall.

Notes

1. *Nature* 341 (1989): 679.

2. Alice Domurat Dreger, "Metaphors of Morality in the Human Genome Project," in Phillip R. Sloan, ed., *Controlling Our Destinies: Historical, Philosophical, Ethical, and Theological Perspectives on the Human Genome Project* (Notre Dame, Ind.: University of Notre Dame Press, 2000), p. 155. Emphasis added.

3. See John Wright's chapter in this volume.

4. What are "the life sciences" within a college or university context? This term might encompass such diverse educational programs as undergraduate courses in biology, wherein one's aim is basic literacy, or preprofessional education; M.A. or doctoral programs in biological subdisciplines, wherein the aim is to produce a disciplinary professional; or professional schools in health care (medical, nursing, or allied health professions). Each of these different institutional locations for "the life sciences" raises different questions for those interested in creating a university that would be ecclesially based. For our purposes, rather than specifically examining the practical issues raised by these different sorts of programs, I will raise a more global issue that is common to all.

5. Garland Allen, *Life Science in the Twentieth Century* (New York: John Wiley and Sons, 1975), p. 114.

6. Phillip R. Sloan, "Completing the Tree of Descartes," in Sloan, ed., *Controlling Our Destinies*, p. xxvi.

7. William F. May, in his book *The Physician's Covenant: Images of the Healer in Medical Ethics* (Philadelphia: Westminster, 1983), outlines how "The Fighter" serves as one of the primary images for understanding physicians and how military rhetoric shapes the practice of medicine. My comments below will focus more on how this functions within the research community, recognizing that the life sciences are not easily separated from their relationship to clinical medicine.

8. For more on this history see John Beatty, "Origins of the U.S. Human Genome Project: Changing Relationships between Genetics and National Security," in Sloan, ed., *Controlling Our Destinies*, p. 132; Robert Cook-Deegan, *The Gene Wars: Science, Politics, and the Human Genome* (New York: Norton, 1994); and Diana B. Dutton, *Worse than the Disease: Pitfalls of Medical Progress* (New York: Cambridge University Press, 1988).

9. Timothy Lenoir and Marguerite Hays, "The Manhattan Project for Biomedicine," in Sloan, ed., *Controlling Our Destinies*, p. 30.

10. Lenoir and Hays, p. 62, citing James Potchen, *Report to the Energy Research Development Agency of the Atomic Energy Commission* (1976), p. 10. Interestingly, this testimony

gives no information on how nuclear medicine has affected patient health outcomes. The interest is in usage, which one might translate as revenue, and professionalization.

11. Lily E. Kay, "A Book of Life? How a Genetic Code Became a Language," in Sloan, ed., *Controlling Our Destinies*, p. 103.

12. Beatty, "Origins," p. 132.

13. Of course, the relationship between modes of healing and social orders is not necessarily something new. As St. Luke reports:

> Jesus was driving out a demon that was mute, and when the demon had gone out, the mute man spoke and the crowds were amazed. Some of them said, "By the power of Beelzebul, the prince of demons, he drives out demons." Others, to test him, asked him for a sign from heaven. But he knew their thoughts and said to them, "Every kingdom divided against itself will be laid waste and house will fall against house. And if Satan is divided against himself, how will his kingdom stand? For you say that it is by Beelzebul that I drive out demons. If I, then, drive out demons by Beelzebul, by whom do your own people drive them out? Therefore they will be your judges. But if it is by the finger of God that I drive out demons, then the Kingdom of God has come upon you. When a strong man fully armed guards his palace, his possessions are safe. But when one stronger than he attacks and overcomes him, he takes away the armor on which he relied and distributes the spoils. Whoever is not with me is against me, and whoever does not gather with me scatters. (Luke 11:14–23)

William F. May, in fact, notes the military images used here to support his claim that military images for medicine are not entirely inappropriate from a Christian perspective.

14. Alison Abbott, "On the Offensive," *Nature* 416 (2002): 470–474.

15. Glenn McGee and Arthur Caplan, "The Ethics and Politics of Small Sacrifices in Stem Cell Research," *Kennedy Institute of Ethics Journal* 9.2 (1999): 151–157.

16. Katharine Q. Seelye, "Bush Gives His Backing for Limited Research on Existing Stem Cells," *New York Times*, August 10, 2001.

17. Doug Stewart, "Cheese Holes, Blobs, and Woggles," *Smithsonian* 32.11 (February 2002): 42. This observation reflects the cultural recognition that the tools that showed themselves most stunning and powerful in turning the tide of the war were, in different ways, the bomb and penicillin.

18. Faith Keenan, "Cloning: Huckster or Hero?" *Business Week* (July 1, 2002): 86–87. Emphasis added.

19. May, *Physician's Covenant*, p. 31.

20. Ibid., pp. 17–18.

21. For this point I am greatly indebted to Stephen Fowl.

22. This passage alone points to a number of key points. While I will develop two, others would be equally fruitful for reflection. Jesus sends the disciples out "two by two." How might this challenge the standard image of the scientist—or the academic more generally—as a solitary researcher, working alone to discover the truth? While certainly the practice of science has become increasingly collaborative over the past decades, the image of the researcher-as-individual persists. What might a more collaborative model of research mean for pedagogy, for developing alternative routes of research funding, for the process of discovery more generally, for the university community? Jesus also says "Go your way." Does this indicate a sort of freedom for the life of discipleship and likewise for the realm of intellectual inquiry? Jesus' instructions also convey a sense of the giftedness

of life—take nothing, eat whatever is put before you. How different might our work look if we understood all that comes our way—from funding to discovery, knowledge, and insight—as gifts of a gratuitous and gracious God, rather than as possessions to be translated into biotech start-up companies from which we can greatly profit?

23. A fuller account of what healing looks like in Scripture would be very helpful at this point but is beyond the scope of this essay. A first task of those engaged in conversations around the role of the life sciences in the ecclesially based university would do well to begin with a study of this question.

24. Some might observe that Augustine is an unlikely ally to invoke in an account of science as pacifist. In fact, William May supports a "just war" approach to the practice of medicine. Whether just war can rightly be construed as a form of pacifism that is appropriate for the context of healing, I will leave as a question for intrainstitutional conversations.

25. Augustine, *City of God*, trans. Gerald G. Walsh, Demetrius B. Zema, Grace Monahan, and Daniel J. Honan (New York: Doubleday, 1958), XI.22.

26. In a similar way, Augustine considers the claim that "the flesh" is to be considered evil to be fought and conquered. Insofar as the flesh is created, it is good; moreover, the very act of making an enemy, especially of part of God's creation, is an act of sin: "If a man entertains enmity, does he not entertain it in his mind? . . . so no one doubts that sins of animosity belong to the mind" (*City of God*, XIV.2), arguing in characteristic fashion that vices reside in the mind/will, not in the flesh.

27. Ibid., XXII.4–5.

27. Joseph Cardinal Bernardin, *The Gift of Peace* (Chicago: Loyola, 1997). Bernardin is not making a novel claim insofar that one finds a similar sentiment in Augustine. Augustine acknowledges the pain of death, recognizing that "there is something harsh and unnatural in the violent sundering of what, in a living person were so closely linked and interwoven," namely the soul and the body (*City of God*, XIII.6). Nonetheless, for Augustine, "Death is not to be deemed an evil when a good life precedes it; nor is death made an evil except by what follows death" (*City of God*, I.11). What is to be feared and fought is not biological death itself but spiritual death. In the Christian tradition, death is not an enemy to be feared, unless we are not prepared for it.

7

The Place of the Natural Sciences in an Ecclesially Based University

Jonathan R. Wilson

Every day I receive 5–10 messages in my e-mail box from a service that monitors news items and events that concern the relationship between "science and religion." After becoming interested in this dialogue, I began collecting books on the topic, a collection that now fills an entire bookcase. With this much activity in one area of scholarship, one might think that the issues and positions would be fairly well worked out. But that is not the case. The conversations go on separate from one another, positions are taken but seldom engaged, and the "relationship" threatens to become a prime example of incommensurability.

These discussions about "science and religion" are undisciplined and confused, for several reasons. The most obvious and frequently recognized reason is that "science" and "religion" are reifications and abstractions. There is no one thing called "science" and no one thing called "religion" except as they are created by the work of a particular scholar or set of scholars. But that bare acknowledgment is about as far as the discussion gets—if it gets to this point.

What is needed, if we are to consider "the place of the natural sciences in an ecclesially based university," is a more articulate account of this relationship, greater attention to the doctrine of creation in the church, and unremitting *local* arguments and practices about "the place." First, I turn to an articulation of this "place" rooted in Alasdair MacIntyre's presentation of institutions, practices, narratives, traditions, and virtues.[1]

Institutions

If we are to engage this question fruitfully, one of the aspects that we must recognize is that we are dealing with *institutions*. The sciences are institutions; the ecclesially based universities are institutions.

To say that the sciences are institutions is to recognize that sciences exist in networks of relationships that concern training, hiring, approving, advancing, and financing the work of the sciences. This institutionalization of sciences determines much of what goes on in particular science departments. For a college to have a "respectable" science department, say, a physics department, the faculty members in that department must have standing within the institution of physics—degrees from recognized programs, approved research projects, funding for the projects, and students to work on the projects.

This institutionalization of physics in most cases (in all that I know) overwhelms the college as an institution, so that no one would even think of the physics department as primarily identified with this or that university. The physics department is institutionally determined by physics; it happens to be located within this or that school. If it is known as the "physics department" at Wilson University, it is known as such because the institution of physics has recognized it, not because Wilson University thinks so highly of it.

Or consider the chemistry department whose curriculum is set by the American Chemical Society. According to discussions in which I have participated, the ACS curriculum sets the boundaries for a chemistry department. If a college wants to have a credible chemistry major, the other curricular requirements must not intrude on the units needed by the chemistry department. Thus, the ACS—one institutionalization of one science—sets limits for the college's curriculum.

At the same time that we recognize the institutionalization of sciences, we must also recognize that colleges are institutions—institutions of higher education. In that very identity, church-related colleges entangle themselves in other institutions—such as the sciences. For the ecclesially based university envisioned in this volume to form, survive, and thrive, must it be intertwined with other institutions? I think that it must. So what I suggest is a strategy of subversion. This strategy ultimately depends upon people, a point to which I will later turn. In the meantime, three suggestions for institutional subversion: First, accept the curricular impositions of institutionalized sciences, then work within those courses to change their character by including instruction on the aims of that science within an ecclesially based university. Second, provide required cocurricular seminars that regularly break down the disciplinary boundaries not only among the sciences but between the sciences and other disciplines. An ecclesially based university is the one place this may been done with regularity. My own college does this with an ongoing natural science seminar and with "Pascal Society" lectures on the relationship between sciences and the Christian faith. Finally, the sciences at an ecclesially based university need to be creative in seeking funding, looking beyond (but not overlooking) traditional sources, so that projects may be pursued that are integral to the school's institutional identity.

But let's take a more radical step, a thought experiment beyond subversion to re-placing the sciences. What would the sciences at an ecclesially based university look like if they thought of themselves as belonging, through the university, to the church? What if their shapes, their practices, their research programs were determined more by their place in the body of Christ than in the AAAS? I don't know the answers. I don't know whether the question can even be pondered at our present moment in history—we may be lacking the requisite ecclesiology and practices.[2]

Practices

In addition to being institutions, sciences are also practices. Among the many descriptions of the sciences as practices, I will focus on sciences as practices of apprenticeship. In our cultural moment, this seems to be an apt description.

Several summers ago I was talking to one of my colleagues who teaches science. He began telling me about the research project he was working on that summer with three students from our college. I asked what granting agency was funding his project, expecting to congratulate him on an NSF grant, or something similar. No, his funding was a regular line item in the department budget, funded by the college. "After all," he informed me, "that's the only way you can really teach science—to three or four students at a time."

This practice takes place within a Christian college that at the time required four courses in Christianity. (It has since reduced that requirement to three courses, but the description that follows remains accurate.) Those classes average between fifty-five and sixty-five students each. Of course, one can teach Christianity to that number of students, but no one would dare to think of "really" teaching science to more than a few students at a time. Sciences are practices; Christianity is . . . ?

This anecdote seems to me revelatory of the place of the natural sciences in a Christian college today. That place quite simply reflects the place of the sciences in the culture of late modernity. Sciences are entrusted with the providential care of our society and the redemption of our lives. We want to be certain that our scientists really know what they are doing.

Over against sciences as apprenticeship stands Christianity as discipleship. As the ecclesially based college pours enormous resources into science apprenticeship, does it recognize its betrayal of the call to discipleship? Apprenticeship in sciences forms students deeply. How can their formation as Christian disciples be as deep when so many more resources are poured into the sciences? Do ecclesially based universities even recognize this contrast as a problem for their mission? Or have they so accommodated to liberal democratic society that they have no resources for even recognizing this as an issue? (I can imagine raising this question at my own institution and being met with a collective "Huh?")

These practices of apprenticeship in the sciences are so deeply embedded in our Christian colleges that most administrators, professors, and students never perceive the incongruities between the practices and the propaganda. Science departments are more expensive than most other departments; the other expensive program at our college is studio and theatre arts. In the sciences we have regularly scheduled labs, so that students learn to do science. We have lab assistants alongside the professors so that our students get individual attention. And all of this is simply an accepted part of the fabric of educational excellence.

What if we actually practiced the Christianity that we profess? What if our Bible classes had discipleship sessions scheduled in the afternoon so that students learn to do Christianity? What if a doctrine class had assistants alongside the professor, so that students received individual attention in their quest to live the doctrine?

Has this rant taken us away from the sciences in an ecclesially based university? Not at all. The practices of the sciences should continue, but so also should countervailing practices in Christianity. Indeed, let's again take another step and think about reconceiving the practices of scientific apprenticeships in the ecclesially based university. What if the dominant context and purpose of such apprenticeships were training in Christian discipleship? That is, what if the practices of the sciences overcame our present fragmentation, instead of enshrining the separation of sciences and Christianity as my earlier suggestion may tend toward? On this model, professors in the sciences would then say, "After all, that's the only way to teach people to do science as Christians—just a few at a time." Such professors would also find their own identity first in the church as disciples of Jesus Christ who express that discipleship in their science.

Traditions

I must begin this section by confessing that the traditions of the sciences are so variegated that any account of the place of the natural sciences in an ecclesially based university must move very cautiously. In the next section I will consider one approach to the narratives that form these traditions. Here I will consider the traditions themselves.

With that confession and warning as a starting point, I move to a series of observations and questions. We are mistaken if we think that we can helpfully speak of "science" as if it were a clearly identifiable, coherent, clearly bounded tradition. It is certainly possible to map relationships among the "sciences," and we can find overlaps and similarities. But even those may be drawn in different ways. A theoretical physicist may share more in common with certain mathematicians than with other physicists. A biologist studying the brain may have more to talk about with some psychologists than with other biologists. Those who work in labs, whatever their "discipline," may have concerns that cross disciplines.

Therefore, when we try to think about the place of the sciences in the ecclesially based university, we must be local and particular in our concerns.[3] The first step along this path is simply to learn to talk to one another and spend time together. I learned something about this from a friend, a scientist who has taught at a Christian college for almost twenty years, has had many close friends outside his own field, and is very well read in theology. He told me recently that he has finally begun to understand what we theologians do. I congratulated him, then realized that I am not certain that I could say the same about my understanding of his work.

If traditions are "socially embodied arguments," then the traditions of the sciences are embodied by the scientist across campus or on the next floor. (Doesn't architecture reveal interesting things about our institutions and traditions?) Certainly, the traditions are not individualistic (unless the scientist in question is a "maverick"), but they are embodied by individuals. Moreover, there are similarities among the scientists at different levels and with different terms of comparison. But for us to know how these all take their places in the ecclesially based university, we must do the hard work of developing friendships across disciplines within the context of our common end.

▉ Narratives

Although it is possible to identify "traditions" common to various natural sciences, and even within one of the natural sciences, there is an identifiable "tradition" that marks the sciences in relation to the concerns of the ecclesially based university. This tradition has been narrated as one of conflict or warfare. In spite of the fine historical work that has been done to overthrow that tradition, many persist in it. One can easily imagine that those who persist in the face of a well-founded counternarrative do so because the perpetuation of the conflict tradition serves the institutional and practice dimensions of the sciences. As long as science has cultural hegemony or cultural capital, one or the other will be used to suppress and disempower those institutions that represent potential threats. Those of us who decry the state of the church may perhaps take some small comfort from the apparent danger that "sciences" still perceive in the church. Alternatively, we may regard that perception as a measure of how little understanding of the church there is within the tradition of the sciences. If they only knew how weak we really are . . .

Can the ecclesially based university narrate a different tradition that places the sciences within the church's own narrative? Possibly. Some historical work has been done, but most of it presumes a Constantinian church. What would a narrative placing of the sciences look like if they were placed within the tradition of the church as a disciple community rather than church as Christendom? Such a task is vitally important to placing the natural sciences in the ecclesially based university. Some have proposed a "theistic science," but such a proposal is still Constantinian and falls short of the narrative of good news in Jesus Christ.

It seems to me that to place the sciences properly we must develop a *cruciform* narrative for the sciences. Such a narrative would acknowledge the world as creation, but it would also recognize that to claim the world as creation is to presume also its redemption. And as followers of Jesus Christ, we recognize that the redemption of the world is accomplished by the crucifixion of Jesus. So "cruciformity" does not name some abstract principle or pattern, but the very event that gives the world its meaning.

Creation, in this view, is not a doctrine that can be separated from the cross, though Christianity has often made this mistake. If the world finds its significance, even as creation, in the cross, then creation does not provide a "Christian" or "theological" basis for sciences unless it is understood to carry with it Christ's work of redemption.

Since this will seem so contrary to much conventional Christian thinking, it is important to elaborate this view. To claim the world as "creation" is to make the claim that what we now have is not God's original creation nor is it all that ever will be. The Old Testament confession of God as creator and this world as creation is made by a people—Israel—who had come to know God's redemptive work in a chaotic, violent, unjust world. By God's redemptive work, they then came to realize that the God of the Exodus was not invading some other God's territory, nor was Israel's Redeemer come to rescue them from this world. Rather, they came to know that the God of the Exodus is the Creator and Redeemer of this world. Thus, they confess this world as "creation." Such confession makes no sense in this world as it is, but it makes cosmic, eternal sense if God is bringing God's original work to its final end: the new creation.

That redemption finds its climactic revelation and action in the cross of Christ. That sacrifice is what it took to redeem this world. Thus, we learn that the world we live in is a cruciform creation. Sciences that expect peace and orderliness in this world are mistaken. Those that seek orderliness are mistaken about our place in history. Those that use the absence of peace and orderliness to argue against God and Christ are likewise mistaken. Violence, chaos, breakdown within a particular kind of "order" are precisely what we should expect of a creation that is not yet fully redeemed.

I have struggled to say briefly here what would take at least a book to make clear. I am concerned that most attempts to make the sciences "Christian" misappropriate doctrine. The doctrine of creation, as it is typically presented, cannot provide guidance for the sciences, because, except in rare cases, creation is usually understood separate from the cross and its revelation of our sin.[4] We do not live in the world that God created. We live in the world for which and in which Christ died. More, we live in the world that put Christ to death. Thus, it is not enough to call for a "theistic" science as some general nod in the direction of "the supernatural." The God of Christianity is the God of Jesus Christ, the one who died on the cross to save the world. This is the narrative of creation that provides us with guidance for the place of the natural sciences in the ecclesially based university.

Virtues

The questions of the virtues requisite to the sciences and to the ecclesially based university are seldom addressed, but the issues should loom large in our consideration and return us to the question of persons that I noted earlier. What kind of person is drawn to the sciences and formed by them? Is that formation conducive to life in an ecclesially based university?

In his marvelous study *Exiles from Eden,* Mark Schwehn considers Max Weber's account of *Wissenschaft* and concludes that "in Weber's account, the process of knowledge formation, if conducted rationally, really does favor and cultivate the emergence of a particular personality type. And this personality type does exhibit virtues—clarity, but not charity; honesty, but not friendliness; devotion to the calling, but not loyalty to particular and local communities of learning."[5] This description embraces all *Wissenschaften,* but in so doing it includes the sciences that are our special concern here. If this list of virtues accurately reflects the "scientific character," then we can readily see the challenge presented by the ecclesially based university.

I must confess, however, to some suspicion about Weber's characterization. It may be the Weberian "ideal," and it may characterize many in the sciences. But I also know many in the sciences who are far from this ideal type. Certainly, some have been powerfully formed to value and seek clarity, honesty, and devotion, not charity, friendliness, and loyalty, as proper to the sciences. But I do know some in the sciences who value that latter list more highly. And what is true of those in the sciences is true also of those in other traditions of *Wissenschaft.*

For those formed, in spite of Weber, in charity, friendliness, and loyalty to a local and particular community, I suspect that the account of their science and character is better found in an account like Michael Polanyi's. To further shape the virtues of those in the sciences (and other traditions of scholarship), I urge that more attention be paid to Polanyi, especially the neglected question in Polanyian scholarship of the formation of the virtues requisite to "personal knowledge."[6] Such an account would have to be tied closely to a renarration of the institutions, practices, traditions of the sciences.

Such a counteraccount of the virtues and renarration is required by the identity of the ecclesially based university. That community is determinative of the virtues of its citizens. What is required, then, is a commitment to that community and its proper virtues on the part of its citizens; then, following from that commitment, a reconception of the sciences (and other scholarly traditions) that enables the pursuit of those virtues.

Telos

The telos is the goal, aim, end toward which a particular community is living. It gives coherence to the life of the community. It is expressed in and furthered by the community's narrative. The telos is extended by the tradition that is socially embodied in the community. The practices of a community are that community's attempt to participate in its telos. The virtues identify the character necessary to the proper life of the community.

Without a clear identification and continually reaffirmation of a community's telos, the life of the community loses its coherence and meaning. Without a clear telos, the way of life in a particular community becomes confused. The practices and virtues seem to have no purpose. The narrative and its tradition appear to be arbitrary. Since most of us live among many competing communities, the most coherent community or the community with the most cultural capital rules our lives in other communities.

In considering the place of the natural sciences in an ecclesially based university, we must face the reality that the sciences are typically more coherent communities with more cultural capital than ecclesially based universities. And when the differences between these two come into conflict, the university may exercise some power—in the granting of tenure, for example—but when it does so, there is seldom a coherent, persuasive account given.

In this "confrontation" between the sciences and the ecclesially based university, we are encountering a particular instance of the fragmentation of our time.[7] The world in which we live is not a pluralistic world, made of coherent, competing communities; rather, it is a fragmented world, made of incoherent, incomplete, largely incommensurable communities that live in uneasy toleration.

Thus, when two communities actually confront one another, it is a double affront: to our commitment to tolerance and to our denial of fragmentation. If this is true, it explains why the topic of this chapter is so difficult for us to untangle. Here is one of the places where we may be forced to admit our condition. The ecclesially based university, as it is imagined by most of the contributors to this volume, does not exist, though I will qualify this claim in my concluding section. The sciences, however, do exist as powerful, formative social institutions. And although the sciences take an ateleological, even antiteleological, approach to "nature," they are profoundly teleological in their social organization. As a result, the ecclesially based university finds itself relatively powerless in its "placing" of the natural sciences. In other words, it seems that the title of this chapter should question how the natural sciences "place" the ecclesially based university. Before I elucidate the meaning of "seems" in that previous sentence, I must add one more element to my account.

Nature versus Creation

One of the biggest challenges to "placing" the "natural" sciences in the ecclesially based university, rather than the opposite, is the theological abdication of the doctrine of creation. It seems to me that this abdication began shortly after the rise of modern science and became complete in the nineteenth century. This abdication took one of two forms. Either theology retreated to interiority—the pietist turn—or theology submitted to the strictures of science—the rational turn. Of course, these two turns are not mutually exclusive; we find a bit of both in Immanuel Kant.

In the first case, the pietists turn to an account of inwardness as the basis and form of theology. This is an explicit or implicit retreat from the threats of science to a place of safety. My inwardness, my experience, is immune to the challenges of science. Thus, theology becomes an elucidation of my experience of the world, not an elucidation of the shape of the world according to the gospel. In this work the doctrine of creation has little, if anything, to contribute.

In the second case, the rationalists submit their theology to screening by the sciences. Theology then says only what it is permitted to say by the sciences. The doctrine of creation reduces to a translation into religious language of the discoveries of the sciences. At this point, theology becomes redundant: we have no need for a doctrine of creation since it tells us in less precise and persuasive language what the sciences have already produced.

Given this surrender of the doctrine of creation, the tradition of the ecclesially based university lacks a robust, well-developed, highly-articulated doctrine of creation. Yes, we have the controversies over creation and evolution. Yes, we have ecological theologies. But none of these rests on highly developed, thick theological discourse about the doctrine of creation.

As a result, the ecclesially based university has only some recently developed doctrinal resources to draw upon.[8] Even the discussions of the relationship between science and religion that lurk throughout this essay are relatively immature in most of their manifestations—not because the protagonists are immature, but because the doctrinal discourse on creation is still immature. The challenge facing us is to develop this tradition in the midst of controversy and confusion. But that is where most doctrinal development takes place. What we must be careful to recognize is the relative absence of any resources in the last three hundred years and the "false humility" that has become the habit of theologians in the midst of an age of scientific reasoning.[9]

We now face the challenge of building a thick theological discourse about creation in midst of much confusion and babble. As I noted earlier, any Christian account of creation will be cruciform, because it submits to the revelation that, in Jesus Christ, the Creator became a participant in creation and died on a cross so that the world might be saved.[10] So, let the conversation begin.

Hope

My assignment for this chapter was to describe "the place of the natural sciences in the ecclesially based university." However, convinced that our present circumstances provide neither the resources nor the warrant nor a model for such a project, I have instead sought to describe some elements of a *process* by which we might form an ecclesially based university that could, with coherence and integrity, welcome the natural sciences.[11]

I am pessimistic about such formation taking place within our present civilization. Our fragmentation is too advanced, the culture of late capitalism is global, and *Techne* rules over us.[12] Therefore, I propose instead ecclesially based communities of scholars in the sciences, as well as other disciplines, who are committed to the formation that I have sketched in this chapter. These scholars would form a new kind of monasticism—after all, the monasteries were the repositories of learning for several centuries. This new scholarly monasticism would not be defined by geographical proximity. It would, rather, be spread throughout the world and be located within many kinds of institutions. These new monastics would have to be creative in finding ways within those institutions and across their geographical distances to form communities. Examples might be provided by the Society of Christian Philosophers and the Christian Theological Research Fellowship. In the sciences a model might be the Association of Christians in the Mathematical Sciences. Some of these professional associations meet along with a larger professional society (the CTRF convenes during the annual meeting of the American Academy of Religion); others are supported well enough to sponsor their own conferences. The purpose of these societies would be to "countercultivate" scholars who have been (mal)formed by their disciplines and want to be transformed by their discipleship to Jesus Christ.

This strategy seems to me to be the embodiment of hope—not an optimism rooted in a historical trajectory but a hope rooted in the knowledge of God who acts to create and redeem. This is the God in whom hope never fades. This is the God whose redemption is the telos of the world. This is the God to whom we are called to witness in all the times, tasks, and places of our lives.

Notes

1. Alasdair MacIntyre, *After Virtue: A Study in Moral Theory*, 2d ed. (Notre Dame, Ind.: University of Notre Dame Press, 1984).

2. See Jonathan R. Wilson, *Gospel Virtues: Practicing Faith, Hope and Love in Uncertain Times* (Downers Grove, Ill.: InterVarsity Press, 1998); and my forthcoming book tentatively titled *Practicing Church* (Grand Rapids: Brazos).

3. One contribution to the discussion that reflects some recognition of this differentiation is Nancey Murphy and George F. R. Ellis, *On the Moral Nature of the Universe: Theology, Cosmology and Ethics* (Minneapolis: Fortress, 1996).

4. Two notable exceptions are Jürgen Moltmann, *God in Creation: A New Theology of Creation and the Spirit of God* (San Francisco: Harper & Row, 1985); *The Way of Jesus Christ: Christology in Messianic Dimensions* (San Francisco: HarperSanFrancisco, 1990); *The Coming of God: Christian Eschatology* (Minneapolis: Fortress, 1996); and Colin E. Gunton, *Christ and Creation: The 1990 Didsbury Lectures* (Exeter, UK: Paternoster, 1993); *The One, the Three, and the Many: God, Creation and the Culture of Modernity* (Cambridge: Cambridge University Press, 1993); *The Triune Creator: A Historical and Systematic Study* (Grand Rapids: Eerdmans, 1998).

5. Mark R. Schwehn, *Exiles from Eden: Religion and the Academic Vocation in America* (New York: Oxford University Press, 1993), p. 18.

6. I refer, of course, to the seminal work by Michael Polanyi, *Personal Knowledge: Towards a Post-Critical Philosophy*, 2d ed. (London: Routledge, 1962).

7. See my argument for this fragmentation in Jonathan R. Wilson, *Living Faithfully in a Fragmented World* (Valley Forge, Penn.: Trinity Press, 1997), pp. 24–38.

8. See footnote 3 above for some suggestions.

9. In addition to the work of Gunton and Moltmann that I noted earlier, I am also intrigued by the possibilities that I discern in the work of Karl Heim, *Christian Faith and Natural Science*, trans. Neville Horton Smith (London: SCM, 1953); *Jesus the World's Perfecter: The Atonement and the Renewal of the World*, trans. D. H. van Daalen (Philadelphia: Muhlenburg Press, 1959); *The World: Its Creation and Consummation: The End of the Present Age and the Future of the World in the Light of the Resurrection*, trans. Robert Smith (Philadelphia: Muhlenburg Press, 1962).

10. For a daring account of how such a claim is the truth about this world and thus the basis for any discourse about the nature of the world, see Stanley Hauerwas, *With the Grain of the Universe* (Grand Rapids: Brazos, 2001).

11. Let me emphasize here a point that I have made earlier in this essay: the sciences present *particular* challenges to this project, but any area of scholarly inquiry does so. What is unique about the sciences is not the challenge, but the particular shape that the challenge takes.

12. In this sentence I am referring, in order, to MacIntyre's *After Virtue;* Fredric Jameson, *Postmodernism, or the Culture of Late Capitalism* (Durham, N.C.: Duke University Press, 1988); and Jacques Ellul, *The Technological Society*, trans. John Wilkinson with an introduction by Robert K. Merton (New York: Knopf, 1964).

8

The Humanities within an Ecclesially Based University

Return to Reading Greats

Scott H. Moore

How should the humanities be taught and studied in an ecclesially based university? In this essay, I will argue that the humanities are best studied and taught within a "great texts" curriculum. However, we must first recognize that the very category of the humanities is a contested one, and the confessional identity of an ecclesially based university plays an important role in defining the nature and telos of education in the humanities. Second, and most important, such a "great texts" curriculum must be done in an explicitly non-Straussian way. Such an orientation will substantially distinguish ecclesially based great texts education from the ways in which great books education has been predominantly practiced in the U.S. I call this non-Straussian approach to great texts a "hermeneutic of hospitality." In order to prosecute this thesis, I will first offer a stipulative definition of what should count as humanities studies in an ecclesially based university. Second, I will examine the Straussian tradition of great texts education and illustrate why it is inadequate for an ecclesially based university. Third, I will offer an exposition of great texts education in such a university. I will do this by briefly illustrating the hermeneutic of hospitality with respect to a great text which is usually considered to be outside of the Christian tradition, namely, William Wordsworth's poem "Ode" [Intimations of Immortality].

What Are the "Humanities?"

The modern university is subdivided in a variety of ways. Perhaps the most important of the "unofficial" divisions in this country is the distinction among humanities, social sciences, and natural sciences. Traditionally, the humanities have been represented by the study of arts and letters, namely, research and teaching in the areas of language and literature, fine arts, philosophy, history, and religion. Of course, one encounters immediate difficulties here; in many institutions, philosophy, history, and religious studies are pursued with and through the current methodologies of the social sciences and in some cases are officially located in the social sciences.

An ecclesially based university should consider the humanities in a broad but carefully defined sense. I want to point to two models, drawing on two disparate but related traditions. Rather than distinguishing along the lines of humanities, natural sciences, and social sciences, one should distinguish between the *artes liberales* and the *artes serviles*—the liberal arts and the servile, or applied, arts. Originally these two terms served to distinguish those arts that served some extrinsic purpose (that which by itself is dependent upon something else) and those liberating arts that do not have a purpose outside of themselves because they are meaningful in and of themselves. A humanities education (*artes liberales*) is not useful *for* anything; it is useful *in and of itself*.[1] Why would such humanities education be useful in and of itself?

In the contemporary university, it is increasingly difficult to give a persuasive account of why the *artes liberales* should be the focus of one's study (let alone part of core requirements for all students) if it is "not useful for anything." If, however, these are the arts wherein one comes to understand the human condition and understand what it means to flourish as a human being, then it is not at all difficult to see how these arts are meaningful in and of themselves. The difficulty for the contemporary university lies in its inability to speak coherently or persuasively about what it means to flourish as a human being.

An ecclesially based institution has a chance of approaching the humanities as the locus of these *artes liberales* by virtue of its abiding recognition that human beings are created in the *imago Dei* and thus are intrinsically valuable. Those great texts and master works that address the human predicament and human condition contribute substantially to this inquiry. Such texts might be predominantly literary in their character, but many of the more recent texts will have "social scientific" origins (Freud, Weber, Marx, Durkheim, etc.). This means that "humanities" should reflect the more comprehensive European tradition of the "*Geisteswissenschaften*," often translated "human or moral sciences." On the continent, the *Geisteswissenschaften* are juxtaposed to the *Naturwissenschaften* and refer roughly to both the humanities and the social sciences, as we call them in this country. These "spiritual sciences" constitute inquiry into the human predicament and, in an ecclesially based university, should represent the "humanities," broadly understood.

What then is the relationship between the *artes liberales* and the *Geisteswissenschaften?* Is there a danger of an essential confusion between arts and sciences here? There is certainly no necessary confusion. Rather, within the *Geisteswissenschaften,* one finds both the *artes liberales* and the *artes serviles.* Within the "spiritual sciences" one finds the liberating arts and the applied arts. In the framework of the Aristotelian intellectual virtues, the *artes liberales* produce *phronesis* and *episteme* (as concerns human subjects) and the *artes serviles* produce the necessary *techne.* Humanities education is not education toward some *techne*—art understood as skill—though it will of necessity need to provide students with certain skills required for other endeavors. A university education should be an education that attempts to foster (in varying degrees of totality) all of the intellectual virtues. Virtues, intellectual and moral, seem to be meaningless without an organizing telos.[2]

Many students and parents (and not a few faculty) have difficulty imagining any role for higher education other than the cultivation of techne. Moreover, as noted above, most universities have no organizing telos other than some vague attempt to produce good citizens and critical thinkers. The categories of "good citizens" and "critical thinkers" invite equivocation on the grandest of scales. This state of affairs is in many ways understandable. Students come to the university in order to acquire skills and useful knowledge which will enable them to pursue a career upon graduation, and while faculties are concerned with development of particular competencies arising from a knowledge base, university administrators must devote the lion's share of their time to keeping the institution's doors open and interesting to students while being uninteresting to local lawyers. All of these factors discourage explicit reflection on a coherent telos for the university.

I believe that an ecclesially based university has resources to avoid the "lure of *techne.*"[3] No resource has more potential in this regard than the cultivation and development of sustained, cross-disciplinary inquiry into the great texts that question, address, explore, lament, ridicule, and celebrate the human predicament. These texts may be of Eastern, Western, or neocolonial origin. Reflection and study in these texts and on these topics presents again and again the contested nature of the telos of human flourishing. Because a contemporary ecclesially based university must live and work within the tradition of democratic liberalism, such a university has a unique opportunity to present a genuinely countercultural alternative and thereby become a place for the cultivation of subversive friendships.[4] Aristotle would be proud.

It will not be sufficient, however, for an ecclesially based university merely to establish a great books program and assume that the reading of these timeless and timely texts will accomplish the goals stated above. In this country, no single thinker has influenced the development of the great books tradition more than Leo Strauss. An ecclesially based university, however, must intentionally cultivate a non-Straussian approach to the study of great texts while emulating the many things that Strauss and his students do well.

Leo Strauss and the Great Books Tradition

Leo Strauss (1899–1973) was born and educated in Germany. There he studied with Edmund Husserl and Martin Heidegger before emigrating to the U.S. in 1938 to avoid persecution at the hands of German National Socialism. Teaching first at the New School for Social Research, in 1949 he joined the faculty of the University of Chicago, where he remained for almost the entirety of his career. A prolific author and a persuasive teacher, Strauss wrote fifteen books, primarily in the field of political philosophy.

At the University of Chicago, Strauss was named the Robert Maynard Hutchins Distinguished Professor. It is appropriate that this honor would go to Strauss, whose passion for liberal education mirrored that of Hutchins. Despite the fact that great books education is most often identified with Hutchins and fellow Chicagoan Mortimer Adler, Strauss's influence in the turn toward the classic texts of Western civilization is unparalleled. For Strauss, the turn toward the history of political philosophy and, by implication, those classic texts of Western civilization was motivated by several driving factors. Four of those factors can be briefly mentioned here. They are (a) the crisis of the West, (b) the threat of Communism, (c) the essential disjunction of faith and reason, and (d) the necessity of an atraditional hermeneutic for the apprehension of the truth. It is important to bear in mind that this interpretation of Strauss is also an instance of tradition-constituted hospitality that I describe in greater detail below.

(a) *Crisis of the West.* For Strauss, no issue necessitated the return to classic texts more than the crisis of the West. Strauss begins his 1964 *The City and Man* with these words: "It is not self-forgetting and pain-loving antiquarianism nor self-forgetting and intoxicating romanticism which induces us to turn with passionate interest, with unqualified willingness to learn, toward the political thought of classical antiquity. We are impelled to do so by the crisis of our time, the crisis of the West."[5] For Strauss, this crisis "consists in the West's having become uncertain of its purpose." What, according to Strauss, is that purpose? It is "the universal prosperous society of free and equal men and women."[6] Strauss describes it as "a purpose in which all men could be united, . . . [with] a clear vision of its future as the future of mankind."[7]

Strauss clearly endorses an imperial perspective for the West. The future of the West is the future of humankind. However, the crisis of confidence produces despair among those who would instantiate the vision. Strauss's call for a return to classic texts is designed to redress the crisis and overcome the despair. For Strauss, "the despair explains many forms of contemporary Western degradation."

(b) *Threat of Communism.* For Strauss, the crisis of the West is most clearly seen in the threat that Communism posed to the democratic West. Strauss believed that while the West's universalism distinguished it from most rival perspectives, Communism espoused a universal thesis as well. According to Strauss, "while the Western movement agrees with Communism regarding the goal—the universal prosperous society of free and equal men and women—it disagrees with it regarding the means: for Communism, the end, the common good of the whole human race, being the most sacred thing, justifies any means."[8] The difference for Strauss was one of "morality—the choice of means."

(c) *Essential disjunction of Faith and Reason.* Strauss not only believed that the dialectic between faith and reason was the central narrative of the Western intellectual tradition but also that the tension between Jerusalem and Athens can never and should never be resolved. For Strauss, the disjunction between Athens and Jerusalem was closely related to the "crisis of the West." According to G. B. Smith, for Strauss "the viability of Western civilization—with Western liberal democracy being one of its central components—rested on the ever-renewed reinvigoration of the West's distinctive tension between Reason and Revelation."[9]

But the question of the disjunction between faith and reason is a far more complicated one for Strauss. While he certainly believed that this "distinctive tension" between reason and revelation is the central narrative of the West, it is certainly not the case that Strauss failed to affirm one of these disjuncts. For Strauss, the tension between Jerusalem and Athens effectively demonstrates the necessity for a distinction between the exoteric and the esoteric teachings of the philosophers. The exoteric teachings are those public, prudential political teachings that must be maintained to secure a certain sort of order. The esoteric teachings are guarded (and hidden) teachings of what is true always and everywhere but may not be said openly. Strauss not only found this distinction throughout the history of philosophy, he utilized it in his own writings. Much ink has been spilt on this question, and I shall not rehearse those arguments here, but it is important to note that while Strauss taught publicly (exoterically) that the tension between Jerusalem and Athens was irrevocable and must be maintained as a tension, he believed and taught (esoterically) that Athens definitively trumps Jerusalem.

(d) *Atraditional hermeneutic.* Strauss not only insisted *that* one return to the classic texts but also taught one *how* to return to these texts. For Strauss, this meant employing an atraditional hermeneutic. According to Strauss, a "genuine understanding" is only made possible "by the shaking of all traditions; the crisis of our time may have the accidental advantage of enabling us to understand in an untraditional or fresh manner what was hitherto understood only in a traditional or derivative manner."[10] For Strauss, understanding these texts means one must "understand an earlier author exactly as he understood himself."[11]

Why Strauss Is Inadequate for a Great Texts Education

There is much that is good and helpful in the work of Leo Strauss, and these insights should be neither ignored nor forgotten. He was a vigorous defender of the priority of the primary text and of the necessity of reading that text closely and carefully. He recognized that an adequate understanding of ancient and medieval philosophy requires a "certain emancipation from the influence of modern philosophy,"[12] which in turn disabuses one of the inclination to think of the history of thought merely as intellectual progress. Though I disagree with some of his conclusions, his reflection on the quarrels between the ancients and the moderns, between poetry and philosophy, and between reason and revelation stands as an exceedingly important contribution to political philosophy in the twentieth century.

Despite these insights, however, I believe that a Straussian approach is inadequate for a Great Texts education in an ecclesially based university. It is necessary to make this distinction only because so much great books education is done (by either design or default) from implicitly Straussian assumptions. The second and third generations of Strauss's students have played enormously important roles at leading institutions that affirm the great books approach (Chicago, St. John's, Program of Liberal Studies at Notre Dame, and others). My argument is that humanities education in an ecclesially based university should be based on a great texts curriculum, and yet it is important that this curriculum not be beholden to Straussian assumptions. Perhaps it will be useful to make this case by examining each of the points presented above.

Crisis of the West and Threat of Communism? Obviously, the threat of "Communism" must be considered in a different light after the fall of the Soviet bloc countries. Though there are, no doubt, many who still believe that communism is a threat and danger to the U.S., this threat is not, and should not be, a pressing concern for the ecclesially based university. The material threat of communism is all but nonexistent.

However, the experience of the "threat of Communism" should be considered as formally analogous to other "threats" and "dangers." In our own day, the "threat of terrorism" occupies a similar place in the collective imagination of many Americans. Strauss saw the return to the great texts as instructive in democracy's response to communism, and many Americans today see a similar value in the appeal of timeless texts to the newly-experienced fear of terror. Bruce Cole, chairman of the National Endowment for the Humanities, has even suggested that reading great books is an essential dimension to "homeland security."[13]

Ecclesially based education must reject these sorts of speculation. Christian education does not arise out of the "crisis of the West" at all; it is the attempt at formation—intellectual, spiritual, physical, and political. That Christian education is necessarily political has always tempted both its interlocutors and itself to choose among the various contemporary political alternatives. Christian education in the great texts must always reject this temptation. Some have attempted to avoid this dilemma by pretending, even believing, that Christian faith is not political. Nothing could be further from the truth. Since Christian faith is always already political, formation in Christian faith (i.e., Christian education) must be as well. But it must never lose sight of its telos. When the telos is lost, Christian education becomes mere clamoring.

Moreover, while the Christian formation of persons does affirm that the future of the church will be the future of humankind, Christian formation explicitly denies both Strauss's "clear vision of its future" and its "despair of the future." The Christian perspective is one of hope, a virtue unknown to Aristotle but determinatively tied to faith and love in Aquinas. As such, there is no place for despair.

The practical problem for the church (and by implication for the ecclesially based university, which is not a church) is that we have assumed that the well-being of the West was necessary for the flourishing of authentic Christianity. This conclusion was part of the "Constantinian" or "Carolingian" inheritance of the church. But the end of Constantinian Christianity frees Christians from the debilitating belief that the Christians and the church must (or even have the capacity to) underwrite the moral well-being of the modern nation-state. An ecclesially based university offers a competing account of human flourishing that stands against the one offered by the modern nation-state and thus by the "West."

In order to make this argument, such a university can employ a much wider spectrum of resources. Thus a hermeneutic of hospitality overcomes one of the most oft-repeated criticisms of a great books curriculum, namely that great books education is only education of the West and into the minds of "dead white European males." This point requires clarification. The hospitable approach does not value diversity or multiculturalism merely for diversity's sake. Diversity for diversity's sake is recognized as incoherent and ultimately self-defeating. However, any education of the West for the West's sake is unchristian.

For an ecclesially based university, the prosperity, poverty, and travails of the West simply are not the primary issues. The status of the intellectual heritage of the West is not even the issue. Consequently, it can employ a much wider spectrum of resources—both from within and outside of the "West."

Necessary disjunction of Faith and Reason? A great texts curriculum would agree with Strauss that the dialectic of faith and reason is one of the major themes of Western thought. Indeed, many of the central disputes and questions that have animated Western and Eastern intellectual history can be understood as having their roots in this tension. However, an orientation toward hospitality in teaching great texts education denies that the tension is irresolvable. In fact, it is important to recognize that the confessional, hospitable orientation affirms that faith and reason complement, rather than contest, each other. We must affirm that grace perfects nature; it does not destroy it. However, crucial to this approach is an understanding that there is no univocal account of "reason" that might be juxtaposed with "faith." Reason (or rationality) itself is always a tradition-constituted enterprise.

We also reject the irresolvable tension between faith and reason because Strauss himself rejected this tension. Stanley Rosen has noted that Strauss "never suggests that the philosopher, the archetypical citizen of Athens, is also a resident of Jerusalem." For Strauss, the "genuine philosopher can never become a genuine convert to Judaism or to any other revealed religion." In his essay "Jerusalem and Athens," Strauss notes, "According to the Bible, the beginning of wisdom is fear of the Lord; according to the Greek philosophers, the beginning of wisdom is wonder. We are thus compelled from the very beginning to make a choice, to take a stand." Rosen then observes, "No competent student of Leo Strauss was ever in doubt as to his teacher's choice. When I once asked him if he seriously doubted that Descartes was a believer, he replied with passion: 'philosophers are paid not to believe!'"[14] Rosen continues

> Strauss's own respect for and attention to the detailed statements on behalf of revealed religion were primarily intended as extensions of his own elusive propaganda for philosophy, or what he would have preferred to call his philosophical rhetoric. It was part of his attempt as a political philosopher to convince the city that philosophers were not atheists, "that they do not profane all that the city regards as sacred."[15]

The exoteric teaching that the tension between Jerusalem and Athens cannot be resolved was merely cover for his own preferred esoteric teaching that the tension could not be resolved by reason but can—and must—be resolved (in favor of Athens) by an act of will.[16]

It is this rejection of esotericism, in both form and content, which most clearly distinguishes an ecclesially based great texts curriculum from one informed and guided by Straussian assumptions and ideals. It is easy for us to reject this notion because we reject the fundamental principles on which the distinction is predicated. (1) Philosophy is capable of operating within the ambiance of faith (It is not essentially in conflict with faith.) It is not necessary that one must philosophize in the ambiance of faith (John of St. Thomas's *philosophandum in fide*),[17] but one surely may do so. In an ecclesially based university, this practice will flow naturally from the community of scholars and friends who have a common conception of the good. Since this is the case, we do not have to convince the city that philosophers are not atheists. (2) The hermeneutic of hospitality is predicated on the centrality of "telling the truth today." There is no deceit, no need for deceit.

It does not follow, of course, that one must always say (or teach) everything that one knows (or suspects), or that all intellects are capable of wrestling with the highest truths and the most difficult questions. But *phronesis* does not require esotericism. As Ernst Fortin, a most unique Straussian, noted, "Only the shallowest of persons, who has nothing of importance to say anyway, would state publicly everything he thinks exactly as he thinks it."[18] We are still quite a long way indeed from the noble lie.

Atraditional approach? This last point is also crucially important for my defense of a hermeneutic of hospitality for the reading and teaching of great texts. Two points need to be made. First, it seems clear to me that Strauss did not actually affirm an atraditional hermeneutic. Setting aside the important but general observation that there can never be a genuinely neutral or atraditional approach to the interpretation of texts, it seems that there are specific reasons to read Strauss as affirming a traditional approach to moral inquiry, especially moral inquiry informed by the interpretation of texts. Strauss, in fact, exemplifies Alasdair MacIntyre's third version of moral inquiry, namely that of tradition.[19]

In MacIntyre's taxonomy, it is quite clear that Strauss cannot be an advocate of "genealogy" as with Nietzsche (despite Strauss's many similarities and sympathies with Nietzsche). This point seems self-evident. Moreover, he cannot be located in MacIntyre's "encyclopedia" category. Strauss denies the fact-value distinction at the heart of the encyclopedia method of inquiry. If one assumes that MacIntyre has adequately delineated the three broad orientations of moral inquiry, then Strauss must be a traditionalist.

Even if MacIntyre's classification is not complete, it seems that Strauss exemplifies tradition-constituted inquiry. He is, after all, an explicit proponent of a particular perspective (i.e., the West), which finds itself in a pitched battle with conflicting views. His principal resource for addressing this conflict is the presentation and exposition of several central authorities who are given the place of privilege and are the "indispensable starting point for an adequate analysis, to be achieved by us, of present-day society."[20] This is plainly an instance of tradition-constituted inquiry as MacIntyre describes the genre. Strauss simply affirms the "tradition" of Western democratic liberalism.

Even if there were no internal contradiction in Strauss's presentation, it should be clear that a hermeneutic of hospitality in great texts education (in an ecclesially based university) must not accept this atraditional hermeneutic. The ecclesially based university rejects the hermeneutic for three reasons. First, by definition, an ecclesially based university is an instance of tradition-generated inquiry. By affirming that humanities education should include the cultivation of the *artes liberales* for the sake of human flourishing, one explicitly affirms a particular telos that guides all inquiry and practice. Second, though above I set aside the general observation that there can never be a genuinely neutral or atraditional approach to the interpretation of texts, the ecclesially based university recognizes that this observation can never be set aside. The posited goods of any inquiry will always do the heavy lifting of interpretation.

Third, and most important for my purposes, the confessional Christian identity of the ecclesially based university exists to glorify the God of grace and to form a community which, since it conceives of history (natural and social) as a meaningful intersection of all events, seeks to understand and exemplify this redemptive grace. The interpretation of texts follows explicitly from this confessional orientation, and this confession becomes the basis for the practice of hospitality.

Having said what such a humanities education is not, I now turn to example of what the hermeneutic of hospitality might look like.

Reading Wordsworth's "Ode" under a Hermeneutic of Hospitality

The hermeneutic of hospitality is guided by the same assumptions that guide and inform the practice of hospitality more generally. Hospitality is the practice of welcoming strangers in a reciprocity of mutual giving and receiving. Hospitality emerges from what Alasdair MacIntyre calls the "virtues of acknowledged dependence."[21] These virtues are the dispositions of character that enable us first to recognize and then to respond to the vulnerability and the dependence of others while recognizing and affirming their intrinsic value. Hospitality, as the receiving of guests, invites a narrative orientation to the human life as a whole (they tell us their stories; we tell them ours) and thus is well suited for the basis of a hermeneutic. And though we do not always agree, hospitality has a transforming effect on both the host and the guest.

Hospitality transcends banal notions of "tolerance" and "inclusiveness" because it is exemplified by actual hosts and guests who must engage and serve one another. As such it denies the allegedly neutral space within which tolerant political discourse longs to move. Since there is no such thing as neutral space to begin with, this means that hospitality is also more honest. Hospitality is committed to "telling the truth today." By denying the neutral space and establishing a context of reference ("Welcome to our home. Make yourself at home."), hospitality makes moral discourse coherent—or at least potentially coherent—in a way it could not be when abstracted from any intellectual community or tradition of discourse.

Confronted with a beautiful poem like William Wordsworth's "Ode" [Intimations of Immortality], Christian interpreters are naturally tempted in two directions. One may baptize the poem, emphasizing those passages where Wordsworth praises the glory of children by pointing to the Christian belief that children are in fact gifts of God, created in *imago Dei,* through whom we not only find life and blessing but also acquire insight, wisdom, and correction. This interpretation may also reflect a longing for the innocence of youth, the promise of naïveté, and the hope for life everlasting. Or, one may dissect the poem for its obvious departures from Christian orthodoxy—nascent pantheism, the divinity of the child, the immortality of the soul, life as a forgetfulness of immortal glory, and maturity as stifling custom. Here one might rightly deplore the delusion brought about through a romanticizing of childhood or even through the adult recollection of childhood. Obviously, both of these extremes fail to do justice to the poem. Recognizing that Christians are always tempted to romanticize existence, to suggest that there was a time when all was right and now we find ourselves wondering, "Whither is fled the visionary gleam/Where is it now, the glory and the dream," what can a hermeneutic of hospitality offer beyond a careful *via media* between these extremes?

Teaching and studying the poem in the context of an ecclesially based university offers a distinct advantage. One can introduce the poem to students by recognizing that the poem is inconceivable apart from, indeed its insights are parasitic upon, the Christian tradition. In an ecclesially based institution, this recognition is far more than merely an observation about the religio-cultural context from which Wordsworth wrote; it is an engagement with that which animates the curriculum and sustains the intellectual and moral community of the university. Romanticism, as a literary movement, is a response to a variety of factors, not the least of which is the hegemony of the church and the perceived inadequacies of its rationalistic doctrines to account for competing conceptions of human flourishing. The articulation of, or challenge to, Christian faith presented in this poem has an immediacy at an ecclesially based university that it often lacks at other institutions.

As with the physical practice of hospitality, the interpretation of texts under a hermeneutic of hospitality is characterized by reciprocal giving and receiving. Thus with this orientation, one seeks first to present the poem in all its fullness, both its continuities and discontinuities with Christian belief. Primarily, one seeks to learn from the poem, to see how in the "Ode" Wordsworth exemplifies an almost universal human experience, namely the loss of "splendour in the grass." Moreover, Wordsworth also articulates a deep, evocative desire to transcend the temptation to grieve over our present experience of loss.

A hermeneutic of hospitality, however, might ask what resources Wordsworth has to accomplish his objective. How do we manage "to grieve not, rather find / strength in what remains behind"? In this context, Wordsworth mentions four such resources that "remain behind:" (a) "In the primal sympathy / Which having been must ever be," (b) "In the soothing thoughts that spring / Out of human suffering," (c) "In the faith that looks through death," and (d) "In years that bring the philosophic mind." In this context I want only to examine how a hospitable hermeneutic might address the first of these resources, that which is, in some senses, the most prone to easy Christian misappropriation and the most difficult to reconcile with orthodox Christian belief.

The first and most important of these resources for Wordsworth is this "primal sympathy," his deep love for nature and his recognition of the fundamental unity of human beings with the natural world. This theme is one of the most pervasive in Wordsworth's poetry, and it is not surprising that he would express it as that "which having been must ever be." Christian interpreters at an ecclesially based university might easily resonate with this strong affirmation of the power of the created order to restore and rejuvenate one who grieves. And yet, a hermeneutic of hospitality, while able to value creation as not only plumb and sound but also representative of God's grandeur, might remain deeply skeptical of the claim that nature has the power to affect cognitive change and engender specific beliefs, or in Wordsworth's words, "to give / thoughts that do often lie too deep for tears."

The appeal to nature as the teacher of moral truth is found throughout so much of Wordsworth's poetry. In no place is this more succinctly stated than in the early poem "The Tables Turned." Here, Wordsworth notes

> One impulse from a vernal wood
> May teach you more of man;
> Of moral evil and of good,
> Than all the sages can.

Taken at its most mundane level, this claim is, of course, patently false (aptly demonstrated by the sage Wordsworth through his mere articulation of the claim). An hospitable hermeneutic seeks a more charitable interpretation, however. Wordsworth is clearly seeking to juxtapose moral truth apprehended in abstraction through books with the moral reality apprehended through nature. Earlier he had reminded us "Books! 'tis a dull and endless strife, / Come, hear the woodland linnet, / How sweet his music; on my life / there's more of wisdom in it."

And yet, there is an equivocation here in the notion of "wisdom." It is the same equivocation that occurs in the "Ode" when the poet refers to "thoughts that do often lie too deep for tears." Wordsworth does not tell us what he means by "wisdom," but it is clearly not Aristotle's intellectual virtue of *sophia*. One is tempted to interpret wisdom as some sort of "inarticulate insight," an insight gained exclusively from nature. The mistake here is to confuse tears for language, to assume that Wordsworth has in mind some inarticulate character of wisdom. But that is not what Wordsworth has in mind at all. This wisdom *is* articulated, just not by mature adults. It is articulated by the inhabitants of nature, especially those who are not tied to the earth, first the children ("trailing clouds of glory") and lastly the birds. I will take these in reverse order:

In "Tables Turned" we are exhorted to "come, hear the woodland linnet," and in the "Ode," the narrator first comes to thoughts of grief "while the Birds thus sing a joyous song." Indeed, the joyous song of the birds ("Then sing ye Birds, sing, sing a joyous song!") enables the narrator to overcome his grief and to "Feel the gladness of the May!" And yet, there is little evidence that this resource can produce the "thoughts that do often lie too deep for tears." More importantly, is there any sense—other than an emotive and evasive sense—in which this resource enables one to "grieve not, rather find strength in what remains behind"? It seems to me that the "thoughts that do often lie too deep for tears" are not really thoughts at all. Had Wordsworth referred to nature engendering "thoughts too deep for language" we might more readily recognize the thesis.

It seems to me that there is a charitable interpretation made possible by a hermeneutic of hospitality that might be helpful here. We must focus not on the birds, but on the children. By recognizing the gift and the promise of children, one is able to "find strength in what remains behind." Indeed, the child is what remains behind, and this becomes a source of hope that will enable one to "grieve not." But the strength comes from the child as she is, a child blessed and encumbered by "her earthly freight," not from any idealized *conception* of the child as divine.

There is a deep irony here. Wordsworth repeatedly and rightly points away from neat abstractions and ideal conceptions and toward those messy particulars that constitute the reality we experience. And yet, at the crucial moment of this extraordinary poem, he resorts to an abstraction, the child as the bearer of divinity and of those "shadowy recollections" that "Are yet a master light to all our seeing." Wordsworth seems to fail to see that one can only "find strength in what remains behind" in the child who is the bearer of the "inevitable yoke"; here are the real "mighty waters rolling evermore."

An ecclesially based university might offer a context for reading and thinking about this poem that recognizes its insights while offering a critique of some of its assumptions. The value of nature and of children are easily forgotten or romanticized beyond recognition. Wordsworth's poem stands as a reminder against the former while succumbing to the latter. A hermeneutic of hospitality, such as that described here, can help one recognize nature's value without idealizing it. This is, of course, being true to Wordsworth's own best insights and intentions.

▪ Conclusion

I conclude this essay with this example of how a hermeneutic of hospitality might engage and teach a text that is a grand part of our intellectual heritage and that presents both challenges and opportunities to the Christian reader. Notice, however, that one can engage this text, presenting its strengths and its weaknesses while offering contested interpretations, without resorting to exoteric and esoteric distinctions, without assuming a deep division between the deliverances of faith and of reason, and without locating its significance vis-à-vis the West.

I believe that education in the humanities at an ecclesially based university is best pursued within a great texts curriculum that explicitly rejects Straussian assumptions and ideals. Such an approach might be understood as a hermeneutic of hospitality for reading great texts.

▓ Notes

1. Josef Pieper, *In Tune with the World: A Theory of Festivity*, trans. Richard and Clara Winston (South Bend, Ind.: St. Augustine Press, 1999), pp. 8–9.

2. Linda Zagzebski and others have argued that a "motivation-based" account of the intellectual virtues need not be teleological. Space does not allow a thorough discussion of this question on the current topic. Linda Zagzebski, *Virtues of the Mind: An Inquiry into the Nature of Virtue and the Ethical Foundations of Knowledge* (Cambridge: Cambridge University Press, 1996).

3. This phrase comes from the subtitle of Joseph Dunne's *Back to the Rough Ground: Practical Judgment and the Lure of Technique* (Notre Dame, Ind.: University of Notre Dame Press, 1993).

4. Ekklesia Project (www.ekklesiaproject.org).

5. Leo Strauss, *The City and Man* (Chicago: University of Chicago Press, 1978), p. 1.

6. Ibid., p. 5.

7. Ibid., p. 3.

8. Ibid., p. 5.

9. G. B. Smith, "Who was Leo Strauss?" *American Scholar* 66:1 (Winter 1997).

10. Strauss, *The City and Man*, p. 9.

11. Leo Strauss, *The Rebirth of Classical Political Rationalism*, Thomas L. Pangle, ed., (Chicago: University of Chicago Press, 1989), p. 208.

12. Ibid., p. 217.

13. Bruce Cole, Public presentation to the American Academy for Liberal Education, Washington, D.C., March 2002.

14. Stanley Rosen, *Hermeneutics as Politics* (Oxford: Oxford University Press, 1987), p. 112.

15. Ibid.

16. For this insight, I am indebted to my colleague Robert Miner.

17. Ralph McInerny, "Cum Maria Philosophari," *Crisis* 16:11 (December 1998): 60.

18. Ernest Fortin, "Between the Lines: Was Leo Strauss a Secret Enemy of Morality?" *Classical Christianity and the Political Order: Reflections on the Theologico-Political Problem* (Lanham, Md.: Rowman and Littlefield), p. 323.

19. Alasdair MacIntyre, *Three Rival Versions of Moral Enquiry* (Notre Dame, Ind.: University of Notre Dame Press, 1988).

20. Leo Strauss, *The City and Man* (Chicago: University of Chicago Press, 1964), p. 11.

21. Alasdair MacIntyre, *Dependent Rational Animals: Why Human Beings Need the Virtues* (Chicago: Open Court, 1999), pp. 119–28.

9

Who Invited Mammon?

Professional Education in the Christian College and University

Robert W. Brimlow

Deliver me, O Lord, by your hand from those whose portion in life is this world . . .

Psalm 17:14

Introduction

As we consider the ecclesially based college and university, it becomes apparent that we also have to examine the role of professional training. I am not quite sure where this necessity comes from, other than the fact that the colleges and universities where so many of us work contain professional schools and pre-professional programs that may appear to be of eternal origin and unalterable in character. We seem to lack for other institutional models. And the necessity of examining the role of professional education seems to imply that it does, in fact, have a role within the ecclesially based college and university, and that this role needs clarification and definition.

In this chapter I will be disputing that notion, arguing that the church has no business maintaining business schools or any other professional program, both because of the nature of professional education itself and also because of the status and function of professionalism in society.

II. An Excursus to Idolatry

It is generally not a good idea to begin an essay or a book chapter with a cliché. I suppose I received that bit of advice from an editor long ago who told me that a trite lead-in bodes ill: if the author can't think of something original and insightful in the first couple of paragraphs, it is not clear that the rest of the essay will contain anything interesting either. This is unfortunate on at least two counts. The first is that clichés become clichés because they tend to be true and, therefore, should not receive short shrift. Second, I want to begin this essay with one.

The saying I have in mind is a particularly optimistic one, namely, that wisdom consists in the ability to learn from one's mistakes. This saying is especially apt, not only for those of us who are prone to err in our judgments and actions, but also for inclusion in a book like this, which offers an examination of aspects of education. American education in its broadest features is devoted to this insight about learning from mistakes, at least insofar as American educators consciously or unconsciously follow the counsel of John Dewey.

Dewey's formulation of the problem-solving curriculum, with its emphasis on process and scientific methodology, comes as close as anyone would wish or dare to enshrining the mistake as providing invaluable data to learners. In fact, Dewey says that "the opportunity for making mistakes is an incidental requirement" of schools.[1] Dewey's point is not that mistakes are desirable in themselves but simply that they are inevitable, and true learning involves the direct experience of consequences. Mistakes, in the context of trying to solve problems, often indicate that the problem has been misdefined, or show that putative solutions have unintended or deleterious consequences. We can learn from our errors—and, indeed, ought to—precisely because mistakes contain valuable information about the problems we face and how we ought to go about surmounting them.

Understanding the cliché about learning from one's mistakes from Dewey's frame of reference, it then becomes clear that heresies and heretics have gotten a bad rap. Throughout our history as a church, what has been declared heretical has been eliminated from our discourse. Even now, though heretics are rarely burned at even metaphorical stakes, some intellectuals in the church worry that their views will be similarly branded and relegated to the boneyard of condemned (or outré) doctrines. I suppose that our theologians and church leaders have their own very good reasons for wanting to eliminate all traces of the heretical from the life and thought of the church. As one theologian wrote some time ago,

> Christianity holds that this absolute truth which is salvation has communicated itself in a definitive and concrete manner, precisely as absolute truth, in Christianity: in Jesus Christ, in Scripture, in the Church. . . . This is why, we may quietly note, Christianity is most sensitive to heresy that arises among Christians. For the absolute truth that was already present, expressed in an historically unmistakable manner, is lost. It is not merely the provisional and undecided which has not yet reached its goal but what is final and definitive is again endangered or already lost.[2]

While Rahner is clearly addressing those aspects of orthodox belief that are endangered or lost through heresy, I am more concerned in this paper with the provisional and undecided—as expressed in heretical movements—which have not attained fruition. In other words, in this context I am just enough of a Deweyan pragmatist to wonder about the grains of truth that underlie the heretics' mistakes, those things we can learn from the discarded movements of our history that can be used to understand more fully our contemporary life as church. In our haste to condemn and correct we overlook the elements of truth and insight that heresies possess. In general, heresies are the responses of our sisters and brothers to problematic situations. They are attempts to come to grips with aspects of the faith that confuse, or with situations of pain, trouble, and discord. Even though some of the heretics' insights are misguided and erroneous, it is not at all the case that all of them are. Heretical movements have spoken to the needs of the people of God, are the result of serious and prayerful reflection, and are not something we should ignore by reflex or through the simple emotive response Rahner describes.

The heresies I believe should be reconsidered and reexamined are the Montanist and Donatist movements of the second through fifth centuries. In many ways they are related: each flourished in the North African church, especially in Carthage; both were responses of the community to times of state-sponsored persecution; both are characterized by a rigorous interpretation of the gospel; and both are marked by a rejection of the power, authority and culture of the Roman Empire in favor of the church and advocacy of Christian social revolution.[3]

The primary issue that divided the Montanists and Donatists from the Roman Church centered around the status of bishops and clergy who abjured the faith in order to avoid persecution and death. The Montanists and Donatists were adamant in their claim that flight from persecution was apostasy; they further maintained that Christians should be defiant in the face of persecution and accept martyrdom as the hallmark of Christianity.[4] This rigorous interpretation of the gospel and what it means to be disciples of Jesus led the movements to deny the efficacy and validity of the ministries of the lapsed clergy. They therefore argued that the bishops and priests who were apostates during the persecution of the church should not be welcomed back into the fold of the faithful until they (and all whom they had baptized after their apostasy) were rebaptized. It is not necessary to recount all the details of how this controversy was resolved except to say that the church accepted St. Augustine's doctrine of *ex opere operato*—i.e., that since such presbyters (priests) who had apostasized were instruments of the Holy Spirit, "their immoral characters did not affect the efficacy of the sacraments."[5] Augustine not only won the theological argument, he also succeeded in his advocacy of the Roman Empire's persecution of the Donatists (see, e.g., Ep 34 and Contra Epist Parm I: 10: 16), which, since the members of the movement welcomed martyrdom, must have made the state's task relatively easy.

Even though the church rejected the claims for rebaptism for apostates and the inefficacy of the ministry of apostate clergy, the church does recognize the sanctity of members of these groups who suffered martyrdom—Sts. Perpetua, Felicity, and Cyprian, to name three. It is clear, then, that not all of the insights captured by these movements are prima facie heretical. As Linwood Urban points out,[6] the controversy addressed by Augustine in the late fourth century involved both a narrow issue—the validity of the ministry of immoral clergy—and a wider one—the nature of the church's sanctity. It is this wider issue that concerns me in this essay on professional training: how the church is to be church in the world.

Tertullian stands as the bridge between Montanism and Donatism in North African Christianity.[7] Despite his being a father of the church, Tertullian's writings from his semi-Montanist and Montanist periods (approximately A.D. 206–223[8]) are too often discounted or ignored outright as heretical. His book *On Idolatry*, written circa 213, contains arguments that are not heretical but are germane to this discussion and applicable to the contemporary life of Christians. In this work Tertullian provides a definition and understanding of what constitutes idolatry and further develops an analysis of certain types of work and academic study that exhibit an idolatrous nature. In so doing Tertullian offers the contemporary church a starting point and structure to evaluate its behavior and attitude toward society and societal values.

Early in the work, Tertullian points out that idolatry should not be construed only as, or restricted only to, the worshiping of graven images. He argues that idolatry involves not only such worship, but also the maintenance of any created thing in a position that ought to belong to God alone.[9] It is clear that for Christians the notion of the primacy of God is of paramount importance; the Lordship of God over all creation is simply too obvious for much discussion. As Christians we maintain that our lives and being are sustained by God and that we derive our understanding of our identity from the fact that we are his children—heirs to the promise of Abraham by the suffering and death of Jesus. In other words, the claims of our faith are totalizing and determinative, affecting our being as well as our actions.

Tertullian goes on to maintain that the sin of idolatry extends itself to include any action that facilitates the worship of idols by others. Thus Tertullian attacks those Christians who would argue that their making of idols for others to worship is consistent with the faith, since the simple manufacture of idols for others' use does not taint the Christian worker. Tertullian responds by saying, "For how have we *renounced* the devil and his angels if we *make* them? . . . Can you deny with your tongue what you proclaim with your hands, or unmake by your words the deeds that you perform?"[10] Tertullian's position is quite clear: there can be no distinction between how we act and what we believe. It is not acceptable to divide our lives into two spheres, one in which we believe in the Lordship of Jesus and another in which we act as though Jesus were not Lord of all. To create an idol for another to worship is to sanction the worship of idols; we cannot legitimately divide ourselves into parts and deny with our minds or conscience what we affirm by our actions.

Tertullian extends his reasoning further when he maintains[11] that even those activities which, while not creating idols for others to worship, embellish the idols already created are likewise sinful. So strong is the connection, he argues, between action and belief that even the building of a temple or plastering the walls of a room where an idol is worshipped is a declaration of the legitimacy of idol worship. Any material assistance, any kind of facilitation of idolatry is just simply outside the bounds of what a Christian may do. Granting any service to idols is just the same as worship. We cannot confess that there is one God while serving the needs of other gods.

Tertullian gives a succinct formulation of this principle in chapter XI:

> For although the fault be done by others, it makes no difference if it be done *by my means*. In no case ought I be necessary to another while he is doing what to me is unlawful. Hence I ought to understand that care must be taken by me lest what I am forbidden to do be done by my means. . . . In that I am forbidden from fornication, I should furnish nothing of help or connivance to others for that purpose; in that I have separated my own flesh itself from brothels, I acknowledge that I cannot exercise the trade of pandering. . . . So, too, the forbidding of murder shows me that a trainer of gladiators also is excluded from the Church.[12]

In this passage Tertullian expands the notion of idolatry to include all trades, occupations, and behaviors that "pamper the demons." For him, idolatry is inextricably linked to all forms of sinful actions. In other words, sin is understandable and can be analyzed as forms of placing idols and the claims of idols before God and the claims of the gospel, whether in the explicit shape of other gods or especially by the deification of our own human tendencies and desires. Tertullian makes the case that there are certain trades or jobs at which Christians simply ought not work because they entail either idolatry or the facilitation of sin and separation from God. The training of gladiators is a job that Christians may not perform because by their actions such teachers condone, support, and encourage sinful behavior and activities that are inconsistent with the gospel.

This analysis is consonant with Tertullian's discussion in chapter II of Matthew 5:28: "But I say to you, everyone who looks at a woman with lust has already committed adultery with her in his heart." As he explains, this passage reduces to the claim that one's disposition to act in a certain way, i.e., looking upon a woman with lust, is the same as acting—committing adultery.[13] What Tertullian argues throughout the body of De Idolatria is that the converse is also true: acting in certain ways, though not in themselves sinful, is equivalent to having the disposition to sin under certain conditions. Thus, if one's actions make it easier for another to sin, then those actions are indicative of a disposition approving of the sin; and a disposition approving of the sin is equivalent to sinning, as the passage in Matthew indicates. Therefore the Christian who pimps commits adultery, and the Christian whose actions promote idolatrous behavior on the part of others is also guilty of idolatry.

Tertullian is more explicit for our purposes in chapter X, where he makes an interesting distinction between teaching an idolatrous discipline and learning one. He demonstrates that teachers of literature necessarily facilitate idolatry because the subject matter is such that "it is necessary for [teachers] to preach the gods of the nations" and also that the structure and operation of pedagogical techniques are linked to the celebrations of pagan feasts. The teaching of literature is so contextualized within the milieu of pagan ritual and belief that it is impossible to treat the subject in a neutral manner, let alone a Christian one. "If a believer teaches literature, while he is teaching he doubtless commends, while he delivers he affirms, while he recalls he bears testimony to the praises of idols interspersed in the texts."[14]

It is difficult to find fault with Tertullian's equation of teaching with commendation, affirmation, and testimonial. It seems obvious that teachers value the disciplines they teach, and the very fact that a subject is offered by an institution conveys the judgment that the subject is worthy of being studied. Teachers and schools implicitly affirm and commend courses and courses of study to their students. Furthermore, it is also evident that most professors at colleges and universities are affected in significant ways by their particular disciplines. Some are consumed by their subject, others are merely enamored, but almost all have internalized the values and modes of inquiry their disciplines represent to such an extent that those values and ways of looking at the world become integral to the professor's personality. It is difficult to imagine any professor devoting herself to the years of training and study necessary to teach in postsecondary education who is not thereby committed to her discipline to such an extent that her teaching bears testimony to it.

Also in this chapter Tertullian addresses an issue particularly germane to our discussion: if literature is replete with idols and idolatry to the extent that teaching it constitutes advocacy of paganism, and if the study of literature is the means of training for a complete and successful life, then how can secular studies be repudiated without adversely impacting the intellectual life of Christians and frustrating the pursuit of theological inquiry? Tertullian makes an interesting assumption here, viz., that some secular studies are not only crucial for intellectual development but also for theology. He leaves this assumption unexamined; he does not offer a list or argument for which disciplines or, more importantly, what content is necessary for those ends. Nonetheless, he does admit that in those cases it would be permissible for Christians to *learn* about idol-rich subjects, provided that the believers understand what idolatry is. In other words, if a Christian is sufficiently mature in the faith, she will be equipped to reject those aspects of the corrupt disciplines that are contrary to the gospel "as one who knowingly accepts poison but does not drink it."[15] Presumably, the mature Christian will be able to adopt those aspects of the corrupt disciplines that are necessary for her intellectual development and theological training.

▓ III. Professional Education

I think that one of the difficulties with the many discussions of Christian higher education over the past few decades has centered around the reluctance, or inability, of the disputants to examine what a Christian education should be about. Too frequently writers assume that education has a preestablished form, and the arguments focus upon whether this form or that can be Christianized. Thus, to put it very simply, some, like Theodore Hesburgh, would argue that the standard of education has been established through the evolution of secular universities in the U.S. and the church's colleges and universities ought to adhere to those standards of teaching and scholarship: "A great Catholic university must begin by being a great university that is also Catholic."[16] Others, such as George Marsden, argue for the development of a tradition of contemporary Christian scholarship. Marsden seems to believe that the distinctiveness of a Christian education can be maintained if some critical mass of scholars in an institution are confessing Christians: "[There need to be] vigorous efforts to explore the implications of Christian faith in scholars' exploration of reality."[17] What both viewpoints accept without question is that the disciplines to be taught in the ecclesially based college or university are given; they assume that there must be some way for church schools to achieve the same ends that secular schools have. This assumption leads to puzzling questions such as "What is the nature of Christian physics or chemistry?" or ludicrous labels such as "Christian law school," as though it were possible to give an ecclesial interpretation to aspects of tort law that would be acceptable to a board of bar examiners.

A positive examination of what Christian education ought to be and what it should consist of lies beyond the scope of this chapter. Tertullian's implied answer—that Christian education should be directed toward intellectual development linked to theological study—is one that deserves further consideration, though I have little doubt that it would be controversial and considered by some to be too rigorous or sectarian. Nonetheless, I think we can make some progress in framing a negative answer to this problem by discussing what it should not include.

It seems readily apparent to me that whatever the ultimate role and goal of Christian education may be, the primary thing that it must avoid is idolatry, especially in the sense that Tertullian describes. This is precisely why I wish to argue that professional education has no place within the ecclesially based college or university.

If a university or college is ecclesially based, then that description—if it means anything at all—must mean that the church recognizes the subject areas and degree programs the school offers as worthy of study. If there is a justification for the ecclesially based college or university, it must include that the work being done within the institution is important to the advancement of God's Kingdom. Professional education does not satisfy either of these basic criteria of worth and justification. In fact, I think it is fairly clear that professional education runs counter to these criteria.

If Tertullian is correct, then what the church accepts as worthy, through its colleges' and universities' curricula, it also commends, affirms, and bears testimony to. Since this affirmation, commendation, and testimonial come from the church, it also seems clear that what the church accepts it also sanctifies. "Sanctification" may appear to be a loaded word in this context and might strike some as excessive or inappropriate. After all, when we think of the church as a body that sanctifies—that "makes holy" in God's name and for God's people—most of us immediately and naturally think of the sacraments and ceremonials that mark our lives: the baptism of new members of the Body of Christ, the blessing of marriages, prayers for the dead, the consecration of bread and wine. Similarly, we see the variety of ways the church engages in sanctification as important for our life as a community. They bring us together as one family in Christ, direct our attention, and remind us of who we are, not only for the most important events in our lives but also on a daily basis. Sanctification is supposed to root us by bringing our lives together, forming our characters and dispositions, and submitting us to God.

My claim that the church in accepting and teaching the professions also sanctifies them may not appear to be a bad thing when seen in the light of the foregoing. The problem is not that the church's activity fails to root us. The problem is that it *does* root us, only it does so by inverting the relationship. Instead of submitting our lives to God in order to follow Him more closely, we instead submit God to the social order so that we may become more professional and more fully accomplished macroeconomic actors in society. This sanctification does not transform the professions into something holy, but rather transforms the church and the church school into another market niche, our faith into another commodity, and our God into another fringe benefit co-opted by the secular world and adapted to help us work better. The fundamental and inescapable point of professional education is to enable practitioners to work better. That is its aim. Underneath all the fancy talk about the moral status of professionals and the virtues of professionalization, the real issue is work, and what work ought to mean in our lives. We need to understand professionalism, and the claims it makes, in the broader context of work and the social relations that give the professions their distinctive character.

The professions have at least two aspects that make them distinctive: the affective and the formal. By affective I mean the basic way that we regard the professions, how the professions impact us whether we are professionals ourselves or interact with professionals. The affective characteristic of professionalism speaks to the way society views the professions and how professionals are different internally than other workers.

In 1985 Robert Bellah and four of his colleagues published *Habits of the Heart*, which offered a primarily sociological study of American life in a variety of aspects, one of which was the affective character of work. The authors made the point that the affective character of work encompasses three distinct classifications:

1. One may regard one's work as a job, i.e., as a way to earn money and support oneself and one's dependents. Not surprisingly, one would define success on the job by material accomplishment—does the job in fact provide enough of a wage and benefits for self-support?
2. The second classification of work was labeled as career. When work is classified in this way, the focus is not solely on the money one earns and the material things that money can buy, but rather on one's accomplishment in an occupation. Success in careers, according to the authors, encompasses not only one's social standing and a certain amount of social prestige that depends on others in society valuing the career, but also on one's own recognition that the career itself is a source of self-esteem.
3. In the final category the authors speak of work as a calling. As a calling, "work constitutes a practical ideal of activity and character that makes a person's work morally inseparable from his or her life. It subsumes the self into a community of disciplined practice and social judgment whose activity has value and meaning in itself, not just in the output or profit that results from it. . . . A calling links a person to the larger community, a whole in which the calling of each is a contribution to the good of all."[18]

There are several things about this last category that need comment. First of all, I believe that the aim of professional education is to form students to see their work as a calling. Certainly the public perception of the professions is as callings, since professionalism connotes a serious long-term commitment and dedication to a particular function within the moral order of the civic community. The problem with the accounting practices of Arthur Andersen in particular, and other recent auditing scandals, is that those professionals betrayed their calling by abjuring the trust of the public in favor of the material gain of themselves and their clients. Professionals in general are not expected to pursue their work only as a means to their economic enrichment, but also—and primarily—for the public good, even when doing so harms their own personal economic well-being.

Secondly, the authors of *Habits* have given us an interesting example of the way spiritual imagery and language have been appropriated and used for the civil religion. It demonstrates that the appropriation has been so effective and complete that we hardly notice the images' or words' spiritual provenance. In their discussion of work as a calling, the authors of *Habits* do not directly state that one is called by God to a particular task. Nor, for that matter, do we notice that the term "profession" originally derived from its use in the monastic orders of the Middle Ages when monks and nuns publicly proclaimed their religious vows and commitments, which went beyond the religious commitments of the other members of the Christian community who did not make professions.

Although the authors of *Habits* lament the decline of religion and churchgoing in the U.S., their concern is much more about the preservation and maintenance of social cohesion and the civic community than it is a concern for the state of our souls. The church functions as a provider of many of America's ideological roots and also as an instrument whereby the body politic may achieve greater civility, stability, and connectedness. Clearly their point is not that the kingdom of God needs to be advanced. The authors make no claim that some divinity is doing the calling or that one's acquiescence to the call is a sign of discipleship and fundamental commitment to the community on God's behalf.

That is not quite correct. There is a divinity that calls, to whom professionals render allegiance and discipleship: the secular social order. The claims of society's good, as society understands it and expresses it, is the kingdom that is advanced. In using the images and language of calling and profession, society evokes memories of Moses as well as the prophets—Samuel, called while he slept; Elijah, reluctant to respond because of his youth—and the apostles. The apostles responded to their call by following Jesus to death, even to the point of undermining the civility, stability, and connectedness of the communities in which they lived and preached. The gospel does not provide a blueprint for community-building or the development of better civic political unions. The call of persons to membership in the Body of Christ and the profession of faith is not for the purpose of social cohesion or what the state means by "common good."

The second aspect that makes the professions distinctive is formal. It is through the structure of the professions and the particular training they require that candidates are transformed into professionals and their identities defined and maintained. It is through this structural characteristic that every profession maintains its autonomy, which is expressed by the profession's freedom to govern its own affairs, define its own range of service, and determine its own conditions of practice and excellence. Through the professionals' possession and use of special skills or a body of technical knowledge, they stand in roles of authority over their clients. Because this authority is born of a particular expertise, most professions claim that only their own professionals ought to monitor, judge, and certify the activities of practitioners.

This structural characteristic is mirrored in professional educational programs.[19] It is clear that the professional activity rests primarily upon a body of knowledge capable of being formulated in principle and taught primarily in a classroom (unlike other technical occupations such as plumbing), even if some period of apprenticeship is required before final admission into the profession, e.g., certified public accounting. Second, the professions claim that, because the occupation rests upon such a specialized body of knowledge, only expert practitioners are able to teach the professional activity to candidates. This also leads to the third aspect of professional education, that only expert practitioners can examine and evaluate the candidates' proficiency and judge whether the candidate has attained a level of mastery sufficient to be admitted into the profession.

We must bear in mind that the purpose and goal of professional programs is to ensure that students who complete the course of study are admitted into practice; this is the defining measure of a program's success. The programs focus in on developing qualifications and teaching the norms of the profession that the candidates are expected to internalize. The programs are designed to facilitate the understanding, acceptance, and conformity to the social roles of practitioners as defined by the socially derived standards.

Throughout this essay I have intentionally blurred the distinction between colleges and universities, primarily because it is not the case that professional programs are limited to the graduate schools of universities; some, like education or accounting, are applicable to undergraduates. The other reason I have included colleges in this discussion is that undergraduate education in general is affected by the proliferation of graduate professional programs and the importance that is placed on them. If we consider that the primary purpose of education is helping students gain the knowledge requisite to earning a living, then the role of undergraduate education should be focused, in the main, upon facilitating the professional development of students. The function of the undergraduate college, then, will be determined by how well it serves the needs of professional education. As Robert Paul Wolff has pointed out, from the perspective of the professions, undergraduate colleges should perform three functions:

1. They need to begin the initial sorting of prospective candidates into the group that is acceptable for admission into professional programs and those who are not.
2. They need to rank acceptable candidates "along a scale of excellence in aptitude and achievement in order to facilitate a fair and efficient distribution of scarce places in more desirable professional programs."
3. They need to adapt undergraduate curricula so that candidates may be prepared for graduate professional work. This means that an undergraduate curriculum must include courses required as prerequisites by the graduate professional schools, and the value of undergradu-

ate majors and programs are determined by their ability to prepare students for graduate professional work.[20]

If this analysis is true, and it certainly appears to be, then undergraduate education has been subordinated to the aims and goals of professionalism. The professions' autonomous structure leads to a division of loyalty even in the secular academy. The tuition gleaned from robust enrollments in professional programs fund other programs in the college or university to such an extent that faculty and administrators are loath to challenge the curricular decisions of professional programs or the mandates of professional certifying agencies. The effectiveness and value of undergraduate education is increasingly defined by the proportion of graduates entering professional graduate programs. Even in the liberal arts, where one might expect to find some level of resistance to this process and the posing of an alternative view, faculty are redefining their disciplines. For example, English literature and philosophy are now described in terms of skill sets such as "effective expression" and "critical thinking" in order to make the case that the liberal arts are, in fact, relevant to those students who are focused on securing a career.

It is not clear to me why, given the autonomous structure of professional programs and the external public agencies that certify programs and graduates, these programs exist even within secular colleges and universities. It seems they would be able to perform their function just as well if they would set up shop as independent professional schools. But even if we accept that their proper place does lie within the traditional academy, I think it is clear that they do not belong in the ecclesially based university or college.

On the most practical level, there doesn't appear to be a need for the church to train students to be accountants, lawyers, physicians, or managers. There are fine secular institutions like Stanford, Michigan, Princeton, Notre Dame, and Georgetown that are quite proficient at producing corporate and civic leaders.

On a more theoretical level, we have to return to the question of what an ecclesially based college or university ought to be and do. Whatever else is included specifically in the answer to that question, these colleges and universities ought to require a commitment of their members to God, the gospel, and the church; the focus of their activities should be the advancement of the kingdom. As I have argued elsewhere,[21] the goals of the church are not the same as that of liberal society or especially of the professions. And even if there are some areas where the requirements of the gospel do not conflict with what professionals do, Christian educators should be focused on helping their students become better Christians rather than better professionals.

Conclusion

Earlier in this paper I argued that we ought to attend carefully to the mistakes Christians and the church have made in the past because there is a grain of truth even in heretical movements from which we can learn. It should be obvious at this point—especially after the rhetorical shot I took at my brothers and sisters at Notre Dame and Georgetown Universities—that I think the church has erred in including professional education in its schools. It remains, then, for me to examine what the grain of truth is in that erroneous endeavor.

There are a variety of reasons why church-based schools began including professional programs in their curricula. For example, for a long time during the nineteenth and twentieth centuries in the U.S., Roman Catholics were excluded from Protestant dominated or secular institutions of higher education. In order to facilitate upward mobility socially and economically for its members, the Roman Catholic Church developed medical, law, and business schools. What this evidences in general for all denominations of Christians is that the church is concerned for the well-being of its members. This is good and valuable and should not be lost: a measure of concern for the material welfare of Christians and non-Christians is required of us by the gospel.

But if we reflect on the discussion about work I cited from *Habits of the Heart,* we need to be careful, in helping one another earn livings and support families, that we do not support the affective implications of careers and callings. The church needs to emphasize work as *job.* The church errs if it maintains the notion that a career is a significant source of self-esteem; the church behaves sinfully if it supports the notion that a person's work is morally inseparable from his or her life, or that it constitutes a practical ideal of activity and character. This is nothing other than idolatry, and it is where professionalism leads.

If we are to take the grain of truth and learn from our mistakes, perhaps we should include within the mission of the ecclesially based college and university a different kind of professional education. Rather than take Christian men and women and turn them into professionals, we ought to take professionals and turn them into Christians: teaching lawyers how sometimes the gospel requires us to go to jail; teaching accountants the Christian value of poverty; teaching physicians the blessings that come from suffering and death. We can then understand the concern of the church for the well-being of its members in the countercultural way of Jesus and the early church.

■ Notes

1. John Dewey, *Democracy and Education* (New York: Free Press, 1944), p. 197.

2. Karl Rahner, *On Heresy* (Freiburg: Herder, 1964), pp. 19–20.

3. W. H. C. Frend, *Saints and Sinners in the Early Church* (Wilmington, Del.: Michael Glazier: 1985), esp. pp. 71–72 and 106–107.

4. Frend, *Saints and Sinners*, p. 96

5. Linwood Urban, *A Short History of Christian Thought* (New York: Oxford University Press, 1995), p. 327.

6. Ibid., 324.

7. Frend, *Saints and Sinners*, p. 97.

8. William A. Jurgens, *The Faith of the Early Fathers,* vol. I (Collegeville, Minn.: Liturgical Press, 1970), p. 111.

9. Tertullian, *On Idolatry*, trans. S. Thelwall (with revisions by the author). http://www.ccel.org/fathers2/ANF-03/anf03-07.htm accessed Feb. 2004, (chapter IV).

10. Ibid., chapter VI.

11. Ibid., chapter VIII.

12. Ibid., chapter XI.

13. Ibid., chapter II.

14. Ibid., chapter X.

15. Ibid.

16. Theodore Hesburgh, C.S.C., "The Challenge and Promise of a Catholic University," in Theodore Hesburgh, C.S.C., ed., *The Challenge and Promise of a Catholic University* (Notre Dame, Ind.: University of Notre Dame Press, 1994), p.5.

17. George M. Marsden, "What Can Catholic Universities Learn from Protestant Examples?" in Hesburgh, *Challenge and Promise,* p. 197.

18. Robert N. Bellah et al., *Habits of the Heart* (Berkeley: University of California Press, 1996), p. 66.

19. Robert Paul Wolff, *The Ideal of the University* (Boston: Beacon, 1969), p. 10.

20. Ibid., p. 14.

21. Michael L. Budde and Robert W. Brimlow, *Christianity, Inc.* (Grand Rapids: Brazos, 2002).

10

The Role of Scripture in an Ecclesially Based University

Stephen Fowl

I have been asked to discuss the role of Scripture in an ecclesially based university. Within the life of such a university as we might imagine it, Scripture will play numerous and diverse roles, influencing a vast range of policies and practices well beyond the curriculum. I will touch on some of those issues, but not at first. I will begin by focusing on what I take to be the curricular heart of any ecclesially based university, the core curriculum. I realize that there are church-related universities that do not currently have a core curriculum. I expect, however, that these are in the minority. In defense of beginning here, I will simply note that I take the rationale for an ecclesially based university to derive from something like either Paul's admonition to take every thought captive to Christ (2 Cor. 10: 5), or Aquinas's claim that one should aim to think about all things in their relationship to God [see 1a.1.7. ad 2], or Ignatius of Loyola's compelling hope that by traveling in the company of Jesus, one would learn to find God in all things.

The considerations and proposals I offer here reflect my hopes for what might happen were we to begin an ecclesially based university from scratch. On the one hand, these are hopes, dreams, and aspirations. On the other hand, my hoping is shaped by several considerations, the first of which is my own experience of fifteen years of teaching in a Jesuit university. Without a doubt, that reality shapes both my best hopes and worst fears. In addition, while some of my suggestions clearly will have an eschatological tinge to them, I think others might be capable of embodiment in current ecclesially based universities. Nevertheless, the confessional and institutional variety of ecclesially based universities may make some of these proposals inconceivable in their present form. I hope, however, that they will be capable of being extended and modified analogically to be of use to other sorts of ecclesially based universities.

While Paul's demand to take every thought captive to Christ is incumbent on all Christians, the ecclesially based university provides a distinct context within which Christians can be introduced to the habits, practices, and dispositions that will enable them to think Christianly across the entire spectrum of knowledge. There is no aspect of human knowing that Christians can rule out of bounds. Christians should not, thereby, assume that they should embrace all aspects of human knowing. Christians can, however, engage all aspects of human knowing, if only to offer a prophetic critique. At its best, a core curriculum provides an essential foundation for this larger mission to which the ecclesially based university contributes.

To the extent that ecclesially based universities do not share in some form of this larger aim, they will find that both the rationale and the execution of their core curriculum will become more and more fragmented and incoherent. In such cases, there is little point in talking about the curriculum until it has a clearer relationship to the university's mission. Most of us live and work in institutions where there is not a clear rupture between mission and curriculum. Even when missions are vaguely articulated and weakly embodied, there is some attempt to have the mission influence the curriculum. My reflections here presume a sort of ideal case for the purposes of sparking our imaginations and discussion.

Teaching Scripture Theologically within the Core Curriculum

Within the core, I have come to see that it is crucial that we teach students to read the Bible theologically. That is, it is crucial to teach Scripture as shaping and being shaped by the church's ongoing struggle to live and worship faithfully before the Triune God. There are several interrelated components to this task. Initially, students must be introduced to "the biblical story." Those who are professional biblical scholars will immediately want to raise questions about this notion of "the biblical story"—and rightly so. Let me say a bit more about what I do and do not mean here. First, I do not mean to imply that there is a single narrative substructure to the entire Bible that is perfectly evident to all reasonable people of good will. Further, I see no point in arguing that discrete biblical authors understood themselves to be contributing to this grand story. Moreover, in presenting "the biblical story" we must be careful to avoid training students to read from such a great height that they end up unable to see the details of any particular text. Christians have a theological obligation to read closely. This is true with regard to all texts, but especially Scripture. Hence, I do not take the notion of presenting students with "the biblical story" as a way of denying the obvious diversity of Scripture or its textual richness. Rather, I take it to be a shorthand way to refer to the interpretive results of ordering the diversity of Scripture in the light of the economy of salvation as articulated in such ordering principles as the Rule of Faith or the creeds.[1]

The question is not whether there is diversity in Scripture. This fact is really too obvious for comment. The question is, how can and should one order that diversity? This is not a new question. Irenaeus saw the question of how a diverse Scripture is to be ordered as the essential issue in his disputes with such characters as the Valentinians. In Irenaeus's day many felt that some sort of philosophical scheme such as the one offered by Valentinus provided the proper way of ordering Scripture's diversity. Today, most so-called biblical theologians argue that some sort of historical or social scientific scheme is the proper way to order it.[2]

We cannot answer this question about how to order or regulate our reading of Scripture without first answering the prior question of the purposes for which we are teaching the Scriptures in the first place. If one's larger purposes are historical, then some sort of historical or social scientific scheme will be the best way to organize Scripture's diversity. As the history of biblical theology shows, however, one who retains a strictly historical approach will thereby say little of theological interest. If one fudges the historical scheme, one can say something theologically significant while simultaneously calling down the wrath of critics and reviewers.

If, however, in the light of the larger mission of the ecclesially based university, one's aims are theological, then one must primarily teach students how to order Scripture's diversity in the light of theological considerations. Teachers must at some early point in a student's learning begin to present to them both the basic content and structure of "the biblical story" and the theological considerations and concerns leading Christians to order their reading of Scripture that way rather than other ways. This need not and should not result in the view that there is only one meaning or possible interpretation for a specific passage. Reading in the light of the Rule of Faith can generate a plurality of interpretations, so long as they conform to the Rule. Done well, this sort of theological interpretation of Scripture produces a harmoniously ordered diversity of readings. This contrasts with the agonistic struggle of interpretations characteristic of the work of someone like Derrida.[3]

This suggestion about how Scripture should be taught within the core leads to several potentially dramatic consequences for the curriculum. First, the two testaments of Christian Scripture must be taught together. Pragmatically, there are a variety of ways to do this. In any case, the OT must be taught in the light of the NT; the NT must be understood in the light of the OT. There is no point in teaching Isaiah without reading it christologically. The christological need not be the only way of presenting the text, but one cannot simply defer that question onto a different course. Presenting the Bible as two autonomous testaments, each taught in isolation from the other, can only frustrate the larger ends of a core course. Second, the teaching of Scripture cannot be separated from the teaching of theology. Specifically, the teaching of Scripture cannot be separated from teaching about the doctrines, practices, and ends of the Christian life. Again, one cannot simply defer questions about the Trinity in a discussion of John 1 or Philippians 2.

Of course, while these two curricular consequences do not really pose problems for most students, they pose quite large problems for most faculty. This is because graduate training in Bible and theology—even in ecclesially based universities—has adopted the modern professional model of training scholars in discrete disciplines. These disciplines largely retain their own integrity by keeping other disciplines—especially theological disciplines—at arm's length. Hence, if Scripture is to play its proper role in the core curriculum of ecclesially based universities, then faculty are going to need to learn how to teach against the grain of their professional training.

I recognize that there are numerous possible ways to accomplish this. At Loyola I think we have developed one promising way: All of our students must take two theology courses and one ethics course—students can take this latter course in either theology or philosophy. All students must take Introduction to Theology as the first of those two theology core courses.

We have (or aim to have) eleven or twelve full-time faculty. Each of them has academic training in a specific theological discipline. All of us, without exception, must teach Introduction to Theology. While we allow each other to teach to our strengths, all of us must teach Scripture, some parts of the tradition, and some contemporary texts. In addition, we take one text each year and make that the focus for our Intro course. For this common text we alternate between a biblical text, a text from the tradition, and a contemporary text. For example, this past Fall the common text was the Epistle of James; the year before that it was Catherine of Siena; the year before that it was the papal encyclical on the Sabbath, "Dies Domini." Because the demands of our curriculum run counter to our graduate training, we are forced to talk regularly with each other about the texts we are teaching. While there are formal occasions when we do this, the vast majority of these conversations are informal and ad hoc. It is not unusual for me to walk next door to my colleague in medieval theology to argue over a text in the *Summa*, an argument that may draw in others. Later that afternoon one of our contemporary theologians might ask me about a text in the Gospel of John to be taught the next day. Thus, the health of our contribution to the core depends on the quality of our collegiality and our common commitment to teaching these courses in a particular way. My point here is not to be self-congratulatory. Rather, I simply want to remind us that, especially in ecclesially based universities, we cannot think and reflect on the curriculum apart from its maintenance and execution by a concrete community of scholars. What and how we teach shapes and is shaped by the sorts of people we are, the friendships we form, and the departments and institutions we inhabit.[4]

We at Loyola are by no means the only or even the best model. I regularly confront the numerous ways in which our courses, and student learning within them, are inadequate. I can, however, say that students who go through our core classes are presented with some of the theological and interpretive habits that can enable them to read Scripture theologically as a whole. Moreover, I am happy to recognize various ways of teaching students to read Scripture as shaping and being shaped by a larger theological task. Nevertheless, any way of teaching the Scriptures in core courses that leaves the disciplinary distinctions of our graduate training intact will largely fail to teach the Scriptures in ways that enhance the mission of an ecclesially based university. Obviously, there are issues of teaching more specialized courses in Scripture for majors and other sorts of students. I will try to say a few things about those issues later.

Teaching Scripture theologically in core courses is to teach Scripture in the light of the larger aims and purposes of the ecclesia. Teaching Scripture theologically will lead one to talk about Scripture's role in the formation, maintenance, and re-formation of concrete Christian communities. Moreover, in the course of such teaching, an attentive student picks up two key points. The first is that Scripture makes rather extraordinary demands and claims on the lives of Christians. The second is that, as Christians struggle to attend to and embody these demands, they will become less and less suited to life in contemporary America. Moreover, the attentive student will also note that there may well be numerous aspects of the life of an ecclesially based university that run counter to the claims and demands that Scripture exerts on the lives of Christians. If this fact is taken seriously, it raises issues for the university as institution, for faculty, and for student life outside the classroom. I would like to spend some time looking at these issues.

Issues for the Institutional Life of the University

To help understand the role of Scripture in the institutional life of an ecclesially based university, I want to borrow from Alasdair MacIntyre's discussion of practices, goods, and institutions in *After Virtue*.[5] Following MacIntyre, let us think of a practice as a coherent and complex cooperative human activity directed towards the achievement and advancement of the goods internal to the practice itself. Institutions are those structures necessary to sustain practices. Institutions typically sustain practices through the ordering and distribution both of resources that enable and advance the practice, and of rewards, status, and power that are external to, but attendant upon, the practice. While institutions largely deal with goods external to a practice, they are, at the same time, necessary for sustaining practices and the goods internal to the practice:

> No practices can survive for any length of time unsustained by institutions. Indeed so intimate is the relationship of practices to institutions—and consequently of the goods external to the goods internal to the practices in question—that institutions and practices characteristically form a single causal order in which the ideals and the creativity of the practice are always vulnerable to the acquisitiveness of the institution, in which the cooperative care for the common good of the practice is always vulnerable to the competitiveness of the institution.[6]

For the purposes of my discussion, the practice of educating and forming people in ecclesially based universities achieves its good as, and to the extent that, members of the university are formed to bring every thought captive to Christ, or to think all things in relation to God, or to find God in all things. The ecclesially based university as an institution is charged with acquiring and redistributing the goods and resources needed to sustain this practice. We can all recognize how easy it is for an institution like a university to substitute the pursuit of the goods and resources external to the practice of education for the achievement of the goods internal to education. If the curricular role of Scripture, however, is in good working order, then one can expect that students, faculty, and administrators will be formed in ways that will enable them to resist the corrupting tendencies within the institutional life of the university. Moreover, in those cases when ecclesially based universities act in ways that will frustrate rather than enhance the practice of this sort of education, students, faculty, and administrators formed by Scripture taught within a larger theological framework can speak prophetically about the institutional life of the university. Such prophetic speech will both articulate sinful practices and habits and call for repentance. These issues can range from a university's investments to the wages and conditions it provides to it custodial staff to the ways in which the university relates to its neighbors.

▓ Issues for Faculty

If Scripture is taught theologically, its formative role will also implicate faculty beyond their normal teaching duties. As I indicated above, and as I know from experience, a number of students (perhaps quite a small number) will undertake to embody what they are learning in the classroom. If faculty members are not to leave students in the lurch, they will need to be intentional, confessional, and pastoral.

Faculty will have to be intentional in that they, too, will have to come to grips with the claims of Scripture. I suppose it is theoretically possible that either a nonbeliever or a Jew might teach Scripture theologically without seeking to embody their scriptural interpretations. In their teaching they would simply lay out the theological logic that Christians bring to Scripture and the ways in which Scripture might shape and be shaped by Christian theological considerations. They would, presumably, present various ways in which Christians in particular contexts might embody their interpretations of Scripture. All of this teaching, however, would be done under some disclaimer like, "This is the way I would be compelled to think and act if I were a Christian, but I am not." There are such characters out there. I think of people such as Scott Davis, or Jews like Peter Ochs. These people are, however, quite rare.

For the rest of us, our identities as Christians join us to that ongoing debate, struggle, and discussion within the church about how to order our lives in the light of our interpretations of Scripture. When such Christians are faculty teaching Scripture in ecclesially based universities, they are not exempt from the struggle that is theirs by virtue of their baptism. Hence, the call to be intentional about embodying one's scriptural interpretations is incumbent on all Christians. For those teaching Scripture within an ecclesially based university, this call to be intentional will lead them to also be confessional in their classrooms. Let me be clear about what I take this to mean. I am taking "confessional" here primarily in the sense of bearing witness. To the extent that teachers are confronting students with the formative claims of Scripture on the lives of believers, such teachers must also be prepared to speak concretely about their own practices, their successes, and their failures. The point need not be to present oneself as an exemplar to be imitated—though, of course, that has scriptural precedent. Rather, the point is to provide concrete examples that might encourage, enliven, and sharpen the imaginations of students so that they may fruitfully embody Scripture in their own lives. In this light, the confessional role of the faculty member need not simply or primarily be focused on the faculty member's life. Such confession can involve bearing witness to the faithful, saintly lives of others who might otherwise pass without notice. I cannot stress how important this matter is. In time my students will come to accept that attending to Scripture in the ways Christians must will put them at odds with the cultures in which they live and move. They also contend, however, that it is inconceivable that real people today might try to embody Scripture in any of the ways we have spoken of in class. Speaking of things my family and I do, especially our failures, contradictions, and tensions, is often helpful. It is even more helpful to present them with people living close by to them who are embodying Scripture in ways they find inconceivable.

Obviously, faculty must be prudent about when and how they do this. Nevertheless, unless one is willing to do it, one runs several risks. At the very least, students will be left with the sense that Scripture exerts all sorts of claims on their lives but that such claims are incapable of embodiment in "the real world." In the worst-case scenario, without some kind of confessional witness, students confronted by the formative call of Scripture may end up pursuing a variety of sinful practices in the mistaken assumption that they were faithfully responding to what they had confronted in the classroom.

Confessing or bearing witness, of course, invites response. Faculty should not be surprised if students either inside or outside of class will respond with their own questions and struggles about how they might both interpret and embody Scripture in their own lives. In this respect, faculty must be prepared to play a pastoral role in the lives of their students. Because issues about how one ought to live often arise out of classroom encounters with Scripture, faculty have a responsibility to address these questions rather than passing them on to campus ministers and chaplains. Indeed, I am deeply intrigued by Stephen Webb's account of the rise of the chaplain's post at Wabash College in *Taking Religion to School.*[7] As Webb tells it, the chaplain became necessary as the confessional and pastoral components of teaching religion at Wabash got pushed out of the classroom. Wabash is not an ecclesially based university, and I am not arguing against having chaplains in principle. Nevertheless, if the teaching of Scripture is not to be fragmented into an intellectual component on the one hand, and a moral and spiritual component on the other hand, then faculty must be willing to engage both Scripture and their students at all of these levels.

Issues for Student Life

If Scripture is taught theologically within an ecclesially based university, the call to embody scriptural interpretation will raise at least two central issues for student life. One of these issues represents an opportunity for ecclesially based universities; the other poses a challenge to them. First, ecclesially based universities can nicely supplement the curricular role of Scripture through their support of certain types of service learning.

There are many pitfalls to service learning. When it is done badly, the service remains disconnected from the curriculum. If service is not accompanied by rigorous, disciplined reflection, it works to reinforce a split between intellect and affect in students. If it is not driven by a theological vision, it can do as much to confirm student prejudices as to challenge them. Nevertheless, ecclesially based universities have a unique opportunity to bring together disciplined theological attention to Scripture in ways that can generate and be closely integrated with specific types of community service. I would not argue that this is essential in all cases. Alternatively, the ecclesially based university that will devote time and resources to enabling faculty to provide this curricular option can greatly enhance the role of Scripture in the life of the university.

If ecclesially based universities have the distinct benefit of being able to integrate service into curriculum in particular ways, they also face a distinct challenge stemming directly from attempts to enhance students' prospects for embodying scriptural interpretation. This challenge lies in the temptation to begin to confuse participation in the life of an ecclesially based university with participation in the ecclesia. In particular I am thinking of participation in concrete local manifestations of the body of Christ. As I have already indicated, teaching Scripture theologically will raise issues of ecclesiology. At the very least, it will become clear that the church, under the Spirit's guidance, generated and formed Scripture. At the same time, attention to Scripture, again, under the Spirit's guidance, forms and sustains the body of Christ. Scripture both shapes and is shaped by the life of the body of Christ. If Scripture is taught this way, then it seems natural that students will find through their engagement with Scripture a concomitant call to be part of an ecclesial community. Indeed, participating in the body of Christ is not something one simply decides to do and thereby accomplishes. The manner in which one is part of the body of Christ is something that is learned and formed in the course of participating in distinct local manifestations of Christ's body over the course of one's life. If the ends of the Christian life are directed to ever-deeper communion with the Triune God and with others, then participation in the local forms of the church of God is a requisite element of growing in communion.

Alternatively, an ecclesially based university is not a local congregation and it should avoid the temptation to try to become one. Students should be encouraged to join local congregations. It is there that they will encounter Christians different from themselves. If nothing else, they will encounter both small children and older adults in ways that they will not in their lives on campus. More important, they will encounter families and single people with whom they can form friendships that are capable of drawing them into deeper communion with God, as well as providing them with exemplars of faithful living outside of the rather rarefied and limited contexts that the university provides.

Issues for Majors and Advanced Students

Thus far I have been reflecting on the role of Scripture in ecclesially based universities in terms of their core curriculum and in terms of the broader life of the university. I should also speak about the role of Scripture in more advanced courses. In core courses I have argued that Scripture should be taught theologically as part of a larger theological program. Obviously, students majoring in theology should continue to learn to interpret Scripture theologically. At the same time we must recognize that this is not the way most upper-level and graduate courses in Bible are taught. Historical, social scientific, and secular literary concerns currently dominate professional biblical studies. Ecclesially based universities must introduce upper-level undergraduates to these concerns along with larger philosophical and methodological issues surrounding textual interpretation in general.

It is crucial that we teach these issues honestly and charitably. Even if some of the particular methods of professional biblical studies are inadequate to their own stated ends, the concerns of professional scholars are, for the most part, serious intellectual matters. Ecclesially based universities will simply replicate the worst sort of bible college education if they engage professional biblical scholarship simply in order to debunk it. Christians bring every thought captive to Christ with the aim of treating it with Christ's charity and subjecting it to Christ's lordship, not with the aim of annihilating difficult or unpalatable ideas.

Nevertheless, there is a great deal of mystification surrounding the practices of professional biblical scholarship. Historical and social scientific concerns are often presented as necessary activities. Their results are often presented as unquestionably true and absolutely objective. Moreover, a very narrow notion of historical analysis often drives these concerns. In addition, question begging and incoherent accounts of textual meaning abound within the profession. Teaching advanced courses in Scripture at any university will involve training in demystification. Learning about the various concerns of professional biblical scholarship is an important intellectual activity. Yet such learning should also help students identify overheated or confused scholarly claims. In this way students who pursue theological ends in their approach to Scripture can appropriate the work of professional biblical scholars on an ad hoc basis.

Conclusion

In offering these concerns and reflections about the role of Scripture in ecclesially based universities, I have tried to indicate that there may well be a variety of ways in which such concerns and reflections might be taken on in the concrete life of any particular ecclesially based university. Confessional histories and differences will play a significant role here. Moreover, as I indicated, my suggestions are offered as if we were constructing an ecclesially based university *de novo*. Instead, we all work in ecclesially based universities with complex histories. They have constructed, altered, and reconstructed their missions. Faculties, policies, and practices are already in place and may not be easy to move, even slightly. Nevertheless, I offer these consideration and reflections in the hope of sparking ideas and raising issues that might find their way in some form into the lives of the real ecclesially based institutions that we represent.

Notes

1. For a fuller account of ways this might be done, see S. Fowl, "The Conceptual Structure of New Testament Theology," in S. Hafemann, ed., *Biblical Theology: Retrospect and Prospect* (Downers Grove, Ill.: InterVarsity Press, 2002), pp. 225–36.

2. You can find examples of Irenaeus making this sort of argument in *Against Heresies*, 1.8.1 and 1.9.4.

3. John Milbank makes a version of this case in *Theology and Social Theory*, part IV (Oxford: Blackwell, 1990).

4. I take it that this is what Michael Baxter was getting at in his review of George Marsden's *The Outrageous Idea of Christian Scholarship*. See *First Things* (May 2001): 14–16.

5. Alasdair MacIntyre, *After Virtue: A Study in Moral Theory*, 2d ed. (Notre Dame, Ind.: University of Notre Dame Press, 1984).

6. Ibid., p. 194.

7. Stephen Webb, *Taking Religion to School* (Grand Rapids: Brazos, 2000), ch. 6.

IV

Formation and the Ecclesially Based University within a Liberal Democratic Society

11

Moving Beyond Muddled Missions and Misleading Metaphors

Formation and Vocation of Students within an Ecclesially Based University[1]

Michael G. Cartwright

Thanks in part to the pervasive influence of the liberal democratic society in which we live, faculty and administrators of ecclesially based universities have come to think about the missions of church and university in disjunctive ways—as if the benefits we have to contribute to the formation of a student's vocational self-understanding are entirely separate. In the process, we have often lost sight of the opportunities that are already at hand to make a difference in the lives of those we would like to think that we are serving. One of the sad ironies of the transformation of higher education in the 1960s and 1970s is that in many instances the racial integration of colleges and universities took place at the price of *segregating* the church's mission from that of the university. During that era it became common for university faculty to say that the church's task is to "do evangelism" and the university's purpose to "do education."[2]

While I am sympathetic to some of the reasons university faculty and administrators of that era sometimes felt it was necessary to make such a division of labor, I have come to believe that such distinctions are confused at best. I also believe that such an answer to the question of how we distinguish the missions of church and university is wrongheaded and misleading for all concerned—students, faculty, and administrators.[3] One of the consequences of this kind of unimaginative and/or reductionist thinking is that it often leads to little or nothing being done about the Christian formation of students, an ironic result when juxtaposed with the original purposes of most church-related colleges and universities.

In fact, I have come to believe that we have allowed ourselves to be captive to a host of very unfortunate metaphors about *who we and our students are* as participants in the formation process and *what our universities are about* in the context of the wider arena of American higher education. In this paper, I want to challenge six sets of metaphors that I believe have contributed to our distorted thinking about the formation of students. In my conclusion, I will point toward more imaginative ways of thinking about the formation of students that may be helpful as we create new models for vocational reflection in ecclesially based higher education.

Before I proceed, however, I need to clarify the particular environment of church-related higher education that I have in view. Such clarification is necessary, I believe, because we find ourselves participating in several different debates that are going on at the same time but are not necessarily constituted by the same sets of issues or focused in the same ways. For example, the recent debate about what constitutes Christian scholarship is not the same as the debate about what it means for church-related colleges and universities to seek excellence.[4] Although I believe that these debates certainly overlap in ways that are important for one another, I also think we must be able to distinguish these concerns at certain points in order to avoid creating more confusion than may already exist about what it might mean for us to envision and work toward the realization of ecclesially based universities in the best senses. That having been said, both sets of concerns must be kept in view as we move forward.

As Michael Baxter, CSC, has observed in a perceptive review of George Marsden's book *The Outrageous Idea of Christian Scholarship* (1997), it is by no means clear "what the outcome . . . will be" of the recent discussion of the place of Christian scholarship in American higher education.[5] Baxter is forthright in stating his disappointment with Marsden's advocacy of a university ordered by "pragmatic liberalism." Using an image originally articulated by William James, Marsden describes the typical American university as being more nearly like an innumerable set of chambers, each housing a particular scholar practicing a particular mode of inquiry. "But,"

James writes in the passage quoted by Marsden, "they all own the corridor, and all must pass through it if they want a practicable way of getting into or out of their respective rooms." Baxter rightly calls attention to the price to be paid for such an arrangement; namely, there can be no overarching substantive beliefs held in common by all faculty but only an agreed upon set of procedures, which might be imaged as the corridor outside the office doors of autonomous scholars whose only necessary reason for interaction would be to make their way to "the restroom, the copy machine, the classroom, or the next conference." [6]

In addition to disputing Marsden's assumption that there is common agreement about what constitutes the procedural rules for the operation of the university as a community of inquiry, Baxter advocates a more robust vision of Christian scholarship, "a comprehensive Christian intellectual vision, wherein all branches of knowledge—the humanities, the social sciences and the natural sciences—would be brought into a complex but unitary account of the truth of God's creation as understood by the best scholarship up to this point. Its primary mission would be to foster Christian scholarship, and its institutional structures—its curriculum, departmental arrangements and divisions, and so on—would be ordered to this end." [7] Whatever else might be said of Baxter's sketch of the mission of a "comprehensive Christian" university, its mission is not the product of muddled thinking. Further, it is clear that the faculty who would meet one another in the corridors of Fr. Baxter's university *would be able to have arguments* that are oriented by a set of metaphors ("from the heart of the church," [8] etc.) that stand in contrast to those that emerge from Marsden's pragmatic vision.

I am confident that Baxter's "more outrageous" [than Marsden's] account of Christian scholarship would also pose positive challenges for the wider spectrum of church-related higher education. In his book *Quality With Soul: How Six Premier Colleges and Universities Keep Faith With Their Religious Traditions* (2001), Robert Benne offers a typology of church-related colleges [9] that locates the major divide between those institutions that use "the Christian vision as the organizing paradigm" and those universities that use "secular sources as the organizing paradigm." With regard to the former category, in *Orthodox* institutions, the Christian vision is "pervasive from a shared point of view," whereas *Critical-mass* universities give the Christian vision a "privileged voice" in the ongoing conversation that constitutes such a community of learning.

By contrast, those church-related institutions that are oriented within the secular paradigm can best be described as *Intentionally Pluralist* where the secular paradigm provides the Christian vision "an assured voice" in the ongoing conversation. By contrast, in *Accidentally Pluralist* universities the Christian vision will either be voiced in random ways or it may be al-together absent from the ongoing conversation. In certain respects, Benne's argument can be read as an attempt to provide the kind of conceptual resources keep institutions that are "intentionally pluralist" from sliding over into the *Accidentally Pluralist* category.[10] At the same time, Benne thinks it is important to be clear about the important ways the *Orthodox* and *Critical-mass* types are to be differentiated from *Intentionally Pluralist* type of church-related colleges.

To the extent that Baxter's vision can be correlated with Robert Benne's typology of church-related colleges and universities, it would seem that Baxter has in view either a *Critical-mass* university or an *Orthodox* uni-versity, namely an institution of higher education in which Christianity is clearly the organizing paradigm. By contrast, the argument of this paper has in view the kind of *Intentionally Pluralist* institutions of higher educa-tion where the organizing paradigm remains secular but where it is also possible to frame the mission of the institution in ways that not only are consonant with the Christian vision but also make available Christian articulations of that vision in a variety of forms accessible to students and faculty alike.

I write from the context of my experience of having founded a "center for Christian vocations" at the University of Indianapolis (with the aid of outside funding from Lilly Endowment, Inc.), where I now serve as the executive director of *The Crossings Project,* another Lilly Endowment-funded effort to foster theological exploration of vocations in conjunction with this particular ecclesially based university's historic mission of "education for service." It remains to be seen how successful this venture will be. Like Robert Benne, however, I argue that we should not assume that *Intention-ally Pluralist* colleges and universities cannot also be "ecclesially based" in substantive senses. I hasten to add a caveat. Making the case that something is conceptually possible cannot suffice for an actual case in view. In the future, institutions such as the University of Indianapolis may or may not actualize this possibility.

Those ecclesially based institutions that would aspire to the kind of comprehensive vision espoused by Baxter et al. might want to think about vocation and formation of students in richer, more imaginative ways than I will suggest. I believe, however, that much of my argument in this paper could be said to apply to these institutions as well, given that "conjunctive thinking" is also necessary in these precincts, even if, as I would readily concede, the patterns of conjunction quite likely would take shape in dif-ferent ways at an "orthodox" college than at an "intentionally pluralist" university.

I. Collegiate "Relay Races" and Segregated "Missions"— Metaphors of Means and Ends in Church-Related Higher Education

As alluded to in the introduction, segregated missions rhetoric in college catalogs is one of the byproducts of the social transformation of colleges and universities during the civil rights era. In the course of a decade, some church-related institutions of higher education went from having policies of refusing to accept federal aid to becoming heavily dependent on such aid. This was the era when the designation "nonsectarian" began to be applied in broader fashion,[11] and institutions began to include clauses in their admissions propaganda making it clear that students were not discriminated against on the basis of sex, race, or religion in order to remain eligible to administer federally granted financial aid. Indeed, some church-related institutions became so practiced in saying what they were not that they sometimes failed to register the significance of their own missions as ecclesially based universities. In the process of these changes, the vision of *the ends* of church-related higher education also became a bit more confused.

The results of these changes have been ironic—where noticed. For example, one of the most notable features of *Intentionally Pluralist* church-related colleges and universities is the rhetoric of segregation about mission that can be found in the academic catalogs of such institutions right alongside rhetoric of holistic education that pay homage to the goal of educating "whole persons." In many cases, the matrix within which these holistic visions have been articulated is explicitly Christian. For example, my alma mater's motto is a phrase taken from Ephesians 4:13—*eis andra teleion* ("to the whole man," or, after 1975, translated more inclusively as "to the whole person"). Even more ironic, I might add, is the fact that very few people who know the motto of my alma mater recognize the Ephesian vision of the *eis metron elikias pleromatos tou Christou*—translated in the NEB as "measured by nothing less than the fullness of the stature of Christ"—which properly speaking, was the grammatical referent to which the "wholeness" of personhood was to be directed.

Why such selective amnesia about the mission of church-related higher education? In the kind of social environment that I have been describing, it is simply easier for institutions to "make ends meet" (financially speaking) if they use a secular rhetoric of self-description, which in turn has the ironic effect of *reinforcing* segregationist metaphors of mission and identity (where the "ends" of church-related higher education don't always seem to meet!). We now find ourselves in a circumstance in which we will need to be clear about the ends of church-related higher education if we are going to be able to provide the kinds of opportunities for vocational exploration and Christian formation that are so needed. Or to put the point more directly, we need to learn how to articulate *the formative and vocational significance* of "the fullness of Christ," the proper referent of church-related liberal arts college mottoes like "to the whole person."

This confusion can also be found in the ways in which we think about *the linkage* of what a church-related college or university is doing with respect to the particular concern of educating Christian leaders (lay or clergy) for service in the church. In a perceptive essay on the "ends of theological education," L. Gregory Jones calls attention to the "'relay race' understanding of education for Christian leadership." As the metaphor suggests, each of the "players" has a specific role to play in the formation of the student, which for the purpose of this metaphor is imagined to be a "baton." Churches are responsible for initiating future leaders into Christian beliefs and practices. Colleges and universities are to prepare students for seminary education by giving them solid training in the liberal arts, teaching students to write and think critically about a wide range of topics (including their faith). Seminaries, which take the baton during the critical third stage, are supposed to teach them the "critical thinking and leadership skills that will equip them for their professional roles." Once trained, it is up to the church's own judicatories, "boards of ministry," and congregations to complete (and/or correct for mistakes made during earlier legs of the race) the process of formation for ministry and service.[12]

According to Jones, the "relay race" motif has dominated the way churches, universities, and seminaries have thought about the preparation of ministers for much of the twentieth century. Although Jones's primary purpose is not to discuss the role of colleges and universities in the formation of students who may one day be (lay and clergy) leaders of congregations, the image he has laid out does invite further reflection about this matter. What are the "ends" of church-related higher education as it exists in colleges and universities? Granted that it is no small thing to teach students to think critically and write coherently about a wide range of topics, including their faith, are there more adequate ways to describe the role of church-related liberal arts colleges in the formation of Christian leaders? I believe there are better metaphors available to us, but I doubt that we will make progress until we clarify in what sense—if at all—we aspire to seek the "fullness of Christ" for ourselves and our students.

Here we simply have to be candid with ourselves and the churches to which we are related. Too much has been assumed in the past about what other members of the "relay team" were doing in the Christian formation of the students who have attended our institutions. If we can manage to wean ourselves from our dependency on the other "players'" making up time for our slow efforts, perhaps we can become clearer about what our role actually should be and begin to work with churches and seminaries, where practical to do so, to create new kinds of collaborations. In the process, maybe we can locate *better metaphors* to describe as the missions of colleges and universities related to churches that also support seminaries and theological schools training persons to become pastors.

One of the first things we have to do is to reorient the way we think about the relationship of time to Christian formation of students. One of the unfortunate features of the relay race metaphor of church-related higher education is that it tends to reinforce a set of assumptions about the temporal duration of the university's role. If the goal is simply to "hand off" the student-as-future-Christian-leader to the next player on the "relay team," then the quicker we do so, the better. But if we think of Christian formation as a timeful process, in which both church and university play more complex roles, then "handing off the baton" will not be an adequate way to image the process to which we contribute. In some instances, students may need to linger with us longer than we are accustomed to having them, and we will take seriously that what it takes to help students discern their vocation is not identical with the development of critical thinking skills and effective composition habits.

By contrast, Michael Budde has proposed that we think about Christian formation in the context of a "lifelong catechumenate."[13] We can no longer act as if Christian disciples can be "mass-produced," and we might as well renounce the visions of Christendom that led us to think that it was possible in the first place. As Budde puts it, "the way from here" is likely to look like a "workshop of witnesses" in which Christians are formed "one person at a time, with different groups of people requiring differing modes of training and teaching—with the further wrinkle that the craftspersons themselves are unfinished, are themselves 'on the way' of Christian discipleship and practices."[14]

While the full implications of Budde's proposal for ecclesially based universities have not been worked out to date, one very clear implication of this initiative would be that we can no longer act as if the church and the college can operate in isolation from one another. My own way of unpacking Budde's challenge for church-related higher education has been to say that *Christian formation of students is more about apprenticeship than it is about knowledge acquisition, more about craft than technique, and more about cultivating wisdom than about career-training.* If the faculty of ecclesially based universities were to think of our students who are Christians as apprentices to the craft of Christians discipleship, and ourselves as called to cultivate wisdom in the lives of our students in the course of practicing that same craft, we would expect more of ourselves and our institutions than tends to be the case at present.

What is also clear is that we have to reenvision the telos of church-related higher education with respect to the eschatological imagery of the fullness of Christ. To do so may not be as daunting as we might initially think. In fact, as I have already pointed out, at least some church-related colleges and universities have mottoes that gesture toward the desire for holistic education of mind, body, and spirit. Just as my own alma mater once upon a time had to engage the apparent sexism of its motto, it now finds itself faced with the opportunity to reengage the theological dimensions of what it means to educate "to the whole person" within the eschatological horizon of the "fullness of Christ."[15]

Such language *invites* vocational reflection by students and faculty alike. Indeed, as a metaphor for the destiny of the church, this term has a rich and complex history that is closely related to how Christians have thought about Christian vocation. This image of the "fullness of Christ" has inspired and befuddled—as well as resisted attempts at domestication by—Christians through the centuries. As such, it can be seen as both a site for ecclesiological confusion and a source of vocational debate—debate that emerges in the context of different ecclesial visions of how God goes about enacting divine purpose in the world through the people of God.[16] Nevertheless, I believe the Ephesian metaphor of the *pleroma* or "fullness" of Christ not only can be meaningfully registered in the context of my alma mater's mission as a church-related liberal arts college, but also can provide conceptual resources for thinking more imaginatively about the vocation and formation of students at ecclesially based universities.

I would go so far as to argue that those institutions that cannot make sense of why they should make it possible for their students to have opportunities for theological reflection about Christian formation and vocation exploration have an impoverished sense of their mission as a church-related college or university. However, with a few notable exceptions, until recently not much had been happening in education for Christian vocations. With the infusion of more than $150 million in grants from the religion division of Lilly Endowment, Inc., for theological exploration of vocations programs since 1998, church-related colleges and universities have begun to take this role more seriously. Many observers believe these kinds of initiatives will serve as the catalysts for fostering conversation about what it means to be an ecclesially based university, but it remains to be seen whether these changes will be sustained once funding from the Lilly Endowment is no longer available.

▓ II. The "Unencumbered Self" and the "Business" of the University: Liberal Metaphors

I submit that *Intentionally Pluralist* church-related colleges and universities will not bother to undertake these kinds of challenging engagements if we (continue to) treat our (Christian and non-Christian) students as "unencumbered selves" devoid of religious convictions, beliefs, desires, and practices. According to the political philosopher Michael Sandel, this conception of the self, which has evolved out of the stew of liberal political theory, is cast as "the author of the only obligations that constrain." "Freed from sanctions of custom and tradition and inherited status, unbound by moral ties antecedent to choice," this vision presents human dignity as consisting solely "in being persons of . . . our own creating, making, choosing."[17] The political metaphor of the *unencumbered* self appears to offer liberation, and no doubt it is well suited for living in a consumer society that constructs virtually everything—including higher education—as operating within the sphere of sovereign choosing.

Unfortunately for those colleges and universities with faculty and administrators who think this way, the liberal metaphor of the unencumbered self does not provide a sufficient basis for participation in an ecclesially based university, nor can it account for the moral bonds that characterize Christian congregations. In this respect it is also important to notice what is denied by this vision of the self. "What is denied to the unencumbered self is the possibility of membership in any community bound by moral ties antecedent to choice; he cannot belong to any community where the self could be at stake. Such a community would engage the identity as well as the interests of the participants, and so implicate its members in a citizenship more thoroughgoing than the unencumbered self can know. More than a cooperative arrangement, community in this second, stronger sense describes a mode of self-understanding that partly defines the identity of the participants."[18] This latter conception of community is *constitutive*.

What might it mean for us to treat our students as if they were persons of conviction or persons who (yearn to) embody beliefs, desires, and practices? To aspire to treat and educate our students as having convictional selves is to take very seriously their Christian and non-Christian commitments and aspirations. I think it also would mean to think about our students and our community of learning in ways appropriate to what theologian David Ford has described as the "soteriology of abundance." As Ford points out, in the Letter to the Ephesians, where the word *pleroma* or "fullness" is used to describe the mystery of salvation that has been wrought in the life, ministry, death, and resurrection of Jesus Christ,[19] the best description of the self that is being transformed is a "worshiping self" or "singing self" whose life makes sense within the "economy of superabundance" made possible through God in Christ. Although it is not possible to spell out all the ways that this theological focus would define ecclesially based universities, I do want to gesture toward two particular features of the approach I am advocating.

First, I believe it would be plausible to think of what we are doing as practicing a particular kind of hospitality, one marked by evocative metaphors and symbols of Christian servanthood. Here we still have much to learn from Benedictine communities, where men or women have received strangers as if they were receiving Jesus Christ himself. Indeed, as Carney Strange and Harry Hagan, OSB, have persuasively argued, the values of Benedictine communities are applicable to how we think about the way universities shape student affairs' activities.[20] Here, I think it is especially significant to recall that Benedict charged those who followed the Rule with the task of washing feet, a practice that simultaneously reminded the monks of their proper focus of concern while also orienting them to the One who sustains them in this "school for the Lord's service."[21]

At the University of Indianapolis, when we put together the liturgy for the first Commissioning Service for graduates of the Lantz Center for Christian Vocations program, we deliberately had the seven students who were being commissioned offer their commitment statements in the context of both the Great Thanksgiving of the church and the washing of feet (John 13). In these simple but profound liturgical gestures, students and faculty alike were reminded of the kind of hospitality that we must be able to give to and receive from one another if we are to make it possible for one another to discern how God is calling us to live out our lives as Christian disciples. Faculty and students alike in an ecclesially based university will need to make themselves vulnerable to the One who washes our feet[22] if we are going to be able to foster the kind of community that is hospitable to all.

Second, if we were to think of our students as being persons of conviction, we would have to think of what we do (as a university) as something other than "product delivery" in the sense of a business selling widgets. Over the past two decades it has become more and more common for faculty and administrators alike to think about the university as "a business." But as more than one insightful analyst pointed out, there are senses in which the university is more than a business.[23] If we do not know how to name these distinctions in ways that register with the substance of the mission of church-related higher education, then we leave ourselves—and our students—vulnerable to the corrosive effects of the commodification of education. Granted that virtually all church-related colleges and universities now find themselves in a struggle to "survive" in a highly competitive "marketplace" of higher education, we dare not transmit to our students the cynicism and hopelessness displayed in the statement: "you do what you have to do to survive." If we do so, then we are inculcating truncated imaginations.

The kind of moral and spiritual formation advocated by the programs offered through the Lantz Center for Christian Vocations presumes that students who elect to participate do so as—at least partially—constituted selves by virtue of their membership in church and university; as Christian disciples they are ready to engage the prospect of being formed by their participation in the constitutive practices of this university and the church. But in order for this kind of initiative to succeed, it requires that we offer a particular kind of hospitality—to treat our students with appropriate care for the host of convictions that constitute who they are. In the process, we also have to resist the consumption-oriented environment that encourages prospective students to value an institution of higher education solely for what they as consumers want to get out of it. We cannot afford to let church-related colleges and universities become institutional versions of the "unencumbered self." This concern, I would argue, probes to the very heart of what it means to be an ecclesially based university in the first decade of the twenty-first century.

III. "Consumers" and "Puppets"—Metaphors of Student Identity and Relationships

Too often our habit of using tired metaphors of segregation to describe the missions of church-related colleges and universities has left us blind to the corrosive effects of consumerism in both church and university and vulnerable to letting our missions be defined by interests that distract us from those concerns that we have in common.[24] Over the past decade it has become increasingly common for church-related colleges to image students as "consumers" and themselves as "product providers" seeking to provide "customer satisfaction" in education. In the midst of the competition for students, church-related colleges and universities have been known to downplay their relationship to the church (in some instances to "erase" the relationship) in order to compete in the marketplace. Similarly, churches are more and more encouraged to use the metaphors of "personal spirituality" instead of "organized religion," as if vital piety is not embodied socially in ways that are not easily "marketable."[25] But of course, those who counsel the congregations to "market" their churches to those persons who are most apt to be responsive to such marketing campaigns rarely have a sense of what it would mean to "sell out" the church by employing means that thwart the mission of making disciples of Jesus Christ.[26]

Students already struggle with impoverished imaginations about what it is possible to be and to do in a world driven by hypertrophic patterns of consumerism. The question is whether we will give them the resources to begin to image themselves in other ways. In working with the students who are enrolled in the Christian vocations program, we deliberately invite students to consider what metaphors have shaped the way they see themselves in relation to God and their sense of vocation. Oftentimes, we discover that students are locked into patterns of thinking that represent themselves as "puppets on a string" who think of God's will rather woodenly as a matter of "either/or," which in turn reinforces their own feelings of helpless passivity. We encourage them to seek more heuristic metaphors to shed light on their experience. In particular, we challenge them to begin to think of themselves as persons who are capable of responding to God's gracious initiatives.

One of the readings we assign students for discussion in the Christian Vocations curriculum offered through the Lantz Center is a moving reflection by Frederick Buechner, excerpted from his memoir *Telling Secrets*.[27] As he reflected on several painful episodes in his family history, Buechner came to realize that he had been locked into a view of himself as a passive instrument of God. "As I [now] see it, in other words, God acts in history and in your and my brief histories not as the puppeteer who sets the scene and works the strings but rather as the great director who no matter what role fate casts us in conveys to us somehow from the wings, if we have eyes, ears, hearts open and sometimes if we don't, how we can play those roles in a way to enrich and ennoble and hallow the whole vast drama of things including our own small but crucial parts in it."[28]

If we can help our students learn to see themselves as capable of responding to God's initiatives, then we can help them to move beyond binary ways of thinking, which tend to be paralyzing. The value of such a metaphorical shift is that students begin to see themselves as agents *in relationship,* which is crucial in helping them to begin to see the importance of grace as the first move that God makes in calling us. As David Ford has shown, the question of self-image is closely related to the issue of whether we are able to grasp the importance of our identity as "worshiping selves" whose lives exist in relationship to the God who saves us by grace. Therefore, students at church-related colleges and universities must have opportunities to learn to see themselves as "singing selves" in the context of public worship opportunities.

Here the ecclesially based university will take responsibility for fostering an environment within which Christian worship is possible. That does not necessarily mean, however, that the chaplain of the university will be given that responsibility. Nor need it always be led by clergy, except where the need for a pastor or priest is required (e.g., for the celebration of Eucharist). Indeed, where university faculty tend to see the existence of the chaplaincy as constituting the primary locus of the "assured voice" for Christianity in the life of the university, it would be very important that other members of the faculty and staff be involved in leading worship on campus. Here the availability of space (for prayer and worship) and time (in the daily schedule) may be more important than personnel, although there is no question that fostering religious life on campus will require people who are set aside to make this happen on behalf of the university. Whether or not there is a chaplain on campus (see Wes Avram's chapter), students should be encouraged to be involved with Christian congregations outside the precincts of the university community rather than gathering solely with folks from the university. At the same time, students should be given opportunities to participate in "prayer and study" communities within the residence life program, or they can be invited to participate in the "daily office" along with other members of the university community.

These ways of gathering for worship, in turn, can open up new perspectives for the imaginations of students and faculty alike to resist the commodification of church-related higher education. Given the liberal democratic society in which we live, however, we are likely to continue to find ourselves facing the commodification of "liberal learning." In some precincts, it may be that a direct result of helping students imagine themselves in relation to God as "worshiping selves," not consumers, will be to foster subversion of liberal values. Regardless, church-related colleges and universities should not accede to the use of liberal and/or capitalist metaphors in the descriptions we offer about the identity and relationships of our students (to us and to God).

■ IV. "Parents" and "Professionals"—Metaphors of Faculty Roles

At our best and our worst, university faculty know that our students do not come to us devoid of metaphors that have implications for how they understand their relationship to us. Much of the time, we display ambivalence about the roles we may play in students' lives. For example, most faculty are quite adept at communicating to students that we are not their parents, and that they need to learn to live autonomous lives. Whether we realize it or not, what students may actually learn from us is how to compartmentalize their lives. Whether we believe it or not, to some degree these students are shaped by our words and actions, regardless of what metaphors we may choose to use. Lurking alongside the myth of autonomy is the image of faculty as "professionals" who exhibit such independence.

More likely than not, our students already are living lives populated with images of themselves (and God) that are limited, even distorted. It requires a feat of imagination to be able to see an alternate future for oneself. Not surprisingly, some students are surprised to discover that the Christian faith can be seen as an adventure. And in fact, this way of envisioning one's Christian formation and vocation is likely to remain a remote abstraction if students do not have opportunities to see it embodied in those around them. That is precisely where the role of faculty as a "mentoring community"[29] in fostering theological reflection about vocation is so important to take into account. In effect, the faculty of the ecclesially based university constitutes "a community of imagination, affirmation, and invitation" for students who are uncertain where they are in the landscape of their pilgrimage. Yet the prospect of participating in mentoring communities[30] evokes the fears of many faculty members.

In a sense, I want to say that faculty at a church-related university have the privilege of serving as "vocation exploration guides" in our own version of "Interpreter's House"—a place where pilgrims stop on "the Way" to Zion, the City of God, in John Bunyan's *The Pilgrim's Progress*.[31] Our role is not to tell students what their vocation is. Our role is more modest but no less valuable—to guide by asking questions to open up possibilities, by evoking metaphors to enrich imaginations, and by engendering courage in the students who dare to consider "options" not previously known and to reconceive of themselves as persons who are graced with the image of God. In doing so, we practice the kind of hospitality that invites students to embrace the adventure of living lives of Christian service to church and community. And when our students leave, we do what a mentoring community should do, we join with the congregations from which they come in affirming their call to service and send them forth in the confidence that we have fulfilled our mission to educate for service.

Of course, not all faculty are prepared to participate in this kind of Christian vocations mentoring community, and no doubt some colleagues would question the wisdom of playing such a role. After all, they may object, faculty no longer serve *in loco parentis,* nor should we try to do so. At the same time, we cannot act as if (all) our students are already formed as adults and leaders, much less as disciples of Jesus Christ. In fact, some educators would argue that part of what it means to teach after the demise of *in loco parentis* is that professors must help orient the students we teach to the moral world around them. In that sense, David Hoekema argues that all faculty have become "moral educators" whether they accept that role or not.

Hoekema contends that in the contemporary environment of American higher education, the university "community" plays an indispensable role in shaping the moral universe of its students.[32] "Those of us who are faculty members and administrators . . . need to explore how best to *demonstrate* to students what it is like to commit oneself to learning and teaching in community. When we have found effective ways to do that, we will have brought to the campus an atmosphere of moral accountability and mutual respect that can rightly demand their engagement and allegiance."[33] Unfortunately, Hoekema laments, "The structure of most colleges and universities . . . nurtures the fiction that the members of the campus community live their lives in independence and isolation from each other."[34] It is precisely because of the discrepancy between what our students need and the fact that most universities are little more than "a community of strangers" symbolized by vast parking lots, that faculty must take on the challenge of being mentors for students who are trying to get their bearings in a bewildering landscape of cynicism and commodification.

Building on Hoekema's argument, William Willimon and Thomas Naylor have called upon faculty to think of themselves as engaging their students *in loco amicis*—that is, we should aspire to be "wise friends" of the students we have the privilege of teaching. Just as Aristotle believed that friendship was the kind of intellectual virtue that could hold states together, Willimon and Naylor argue that liberal arts colleges and universities need to become places "where people are allowed the time and space for friendship to develop, where the virtues required of friends are cultivated, and where we all become adept in the art of relating to one another not as strangers, adversaries, clients, customers or care givers, but as friends."[35] Whatever else may be said about the proposals found in their book *The Abandoned Generation: Rethinking Higher Education* (1995), Willimon and Naylor are surely correct when they call faculty to the task of being wise friends. And there are many alumni of church-related colleges and universities that could testify to the wisdom of particular faculty persons who have served this role for them in past years. Given the pressures students face at the dawn of the twenty-first century, however, it is imperative that faculty of such institutions take purposeful steps to make this the rule and not the exception.

To some extent, I believe this will require that faculty *turn away* from the image of faculty as dislocated professionals who are committed only to excelling in the practice of their discipline or field of expertise. As Wendell Berry has argued, one of the unexamined aspects of the contemporary struggle in American higher education is the crisis of the vocational identity of those of us who live out our lives in the academy. "As long as the idea of vocation was still viable among us, I don't believe it was ever understood that a person was 'called' to be rich or powerful or even successful. People were taught the disciplines . . . to enable them to live and work but as self-sustaining individuals and as useful members of their communities and to see that the disciplines themselves survived the passing of the generations."[36]

Berry thinks he has identified one of the most important factors that has led to demise of this way of thinking. "Now we seem to have replaced the ideas of responsible community membership, of cultural survival, and even of usefulness, with the idea of professionalism . . . the context of professionalism is not a place or a community but a career . . . The religion of professionalism is progress and this means that . . . professionalism forsakes the past and present in favor of the future, which is never present or practical or real."[37] I would argue that "professionalism" need not be understood in such a way as to exclude the possibility of faculty serving *in loco amicis* for their students. Unfortunately, however, some of the same forces that lead our students to feel bewildered and alone in their pilgrimages also have shaped faculty in ways that leave them blind to the fact that they have, in effect if not intent, abandoned their students—and often their colleagues—in the interest of advancing their careers.

Accordingly, any church-related college or university that attempts to foster theological exploration of vocations for its students not only will need to have sufficient faculty and curricular resources to make such an initiative plausible but will also need to provide opportunities for faculty to engage in vocation exploration and formation. What is required is *not* that a certain number of university faculty be ordained, but rather that there be faculty whose lives provide demonstrative examples of the "adventure" of Christian discipleship at a variety of levels. The faculty person who participates in the ecclesially based university's monthly Eucharist is a role model in ways that are just as important as the faculty person who teaches theology and ethics. The faculty person who leads work team trips and fosters opportunities for service-learning is playing just as important a role as the nursing instructor or the history professor who leads a class where theological exploration of vocation takes place.

These diverse contributions must be acknowledged and supported, because none of these efforts can succeed simply by benevolent nods. The power of modest acts cannot be underestimated if they display authenticity, moral imagination, and Christian character. The university president who prays a humble prayer of gratitude for the gift of collegiality of faculty and staff at the annual Christmas gathering of the university community adds value to a ritual that might otherwise have grown tired and stale if left only for the chaplain and other ordained faculty to offer. The faculty person who offers a prayer at the beginning of the monthly faculty meeting gives renewed significance to the practice of prayer when she thanks God for the students she has the privilege to teach and reminds her colleagues that we are to approach our daily pedagogical duties in the awareness that we encounter God in the lives of our students. The college chaplain who reminds the faculty at the end of their monthly meeting that some of the students are struggling with serious issues and bids them to remember these ongoing struggles in their interactions with such students—and even pray for them[38]—is exercising his office as pastor to the learning community in reminding these would-be "wise friends" of the needs of their students.

Faculty who are tempted to regard the proposal that they understand themselves as acting *in loco amicis* as a reversion to the days when faculty were expected to inhabit the role of parents must be corrected and redirected. When such colleagues protest against what they perceive to be a revival of the *in loco parentis* conception of the faculty role, they should be reminded of the more powerful role being played by the liberal metaphors of the marketplace in the lives of our students as well as in our classrooms. At the end of the day, if we no longer believe that faculty at church-related colleges and universities should aspire to cultivate "wise friendships" with their students, then perhaps church-related higher education in American culture doesn't deserve to survive after all.

V. Monks, Managers, and "Manifest Destiny"—Vocational Metaphors

But even if we should find ways for faculty to reorient themselves to be "wise friends," conversation about the formation of students nevertheless is likely to run into the problem of inarticulacy about whether or *how* to use the language of "vocation" on campus. With few exceptions, faculty and student affairs professionals at church-related colleges and universities are not well-equipped for giving direction to students who may come to us with vocations to be contemplative servants of God. In many church-related universities, a student with a (monastic) vocation to prayer is more likely to be directed to a career services office (if not to counseling services!) than he is to be encouraged or taken seriously by faculty. By contrast, in a liberal democratic society, no one seems to be puzzled about how to deal with the student who tells his or her faculty advisor that he wants to be a manager. Here also, disjunctive thinking contributes to confused thinking about mission and vocational identity *as if it makes sense* to talk about the "vocation" of a manager apart from an identity anchored in convictional commitments.

Given the current environment of consumerism, leaders of church-related colleges and universities are likely to continue to struggle with the use the word "vocation"—considering its conflicted history within Christianity as well as within liberal democratic societies. For this reason alone, some faculty and church leaders are tempted to discard the concept as no longer useful and quite possibly an unnecessary obstacle for a church already struggling to attract candidates for ordained ministry. Ironically, this can be said to be an ecumenical problem in Christianity inasmuch as Protestants, Catholics, and Orthodox Christians have generated their own patterns of distortion of Christian vocations. The publication of the Os Guinness's book *The Call: Finding and Fulfilling the Central Purpose of Your Life* (1998) almost a half century after Elton Trueblood published his classic work *Your Other Vocation* (1952) marks a discernible shift in Protestant reflection about Christian vocation that I believe has important implications for ecclesially based universities.

When the Quaker educator Elton Trueblood wrote his collection of essays at mid-century, he saw himself pointing the way for a movement, which he believed was part of a "new reformation" of the church. Writing in the midst of a post-World War II economic boom, Trueblood was combating "the chief occupational disease" of that time—boredom. Using the Protestant Reformation as his principal analogy, Trueblood called upon his readers to "change gears again" and "open the ministry to the ordinary Christian in much the same way that our ancestors opened Bible reading to the ordinary Christian."[39]

Trueblood, whose life of scholarship and teaching was spent at Earlham College, cared deeply about the role of church-related colleges in fostering Christian vocations. He was sharply critical of the secularization then occurring at most church-related colleges, which he said had neglected their mission. "The chapel may still stand in the middle of the quadrangle, but it is only in a geographical sense that it is central; in every other sense it is peripheral. What is really central is the basketball court or the ballroom floor or the technological laboratory. . . . At the same time a sentimental reference to the Christian *background* of the institution is still printed in the catalog."[40] Trueblood, who was by nature an optimist, also pointed to the fact that there were church-related institutions that were seeking to "reverse" this trend.

The disestablishment of Protestantism in American culture was simply not as discernible at the time that Trueblood wrote as it now is. This is perhaps most evident in the signature phrase of the book—*your other vocation*. "Whatever a person's ordinary vocation in the world, whether salesmanship or homemaking or farming, the ministry can be his other vocation, and perhaps his truest vocation. Most vocations are incompatible, but the ministry is compatible with all others, providing they are productive of human welfare."[41]

Trueblood understood that there was widespread confusion about vocation in his time, but he also believed that the sense of Christian vocation remained intact despite a diminished sense of calling in the sense of occupation. He also assumed the stability of career paths while fostering what he believed was a growing awareness of the meaning of Christian vocation. As a result, he focused attention upon what it would mean for Christian laypersons to recover "the ministry of work" and "family life" while pursuing education as *non*professionals in ministry.[42]

Trueblood the educator envisioned that various "training centers for lay ministry" would be founded. He understood, even then, that such ventures would need to take into account the time constraints of the men and women who would participate in these courses of study. While Trueblood understood the need to equip lay leaders with practical opportunities for learning, he forthrightly declared that "the chief subject of study must be theology." He even dared to offer a "five year plan" of theological education for laity, and he called upon pastors to exercise their responsibility to teach.[43]

Although that lay ministry movement Trueblood attempted to direct did produce some successes, including the "Yokefellows" initiative and several lesser known experiments, it must be said that the "revolutionary" ferment that Trueblood and company thought was coming to pass appears to have dissipated, if it ever fully existed. Reformation of the church remains a possibility not yet fully enacted, just as the apostolic image of "the fullness of Christ"—the phrase from the Letter to the Ephesians (4:13) that points to the *universality* of Christian ministry—has not yet been exhausted.

Indeed, to read Guinness's book, *The Call,* against the backdrop of what Trueblood wrote about with such exuberant confidence in the early 1950s, is to remind ourselves that we remain at some distance from grasping the radical promise of the ministry of the laity. Whereas Trueblood's book sought to remedy the distorted sense of vocation by reinvoking the Protestant conception of the "priesthood of all believers," Guinness goes further to explain ways in which Protestants have become confused about vocation. Indeed, he identifies two historical patterns of distortion, each of which reflects the basic divisions of Western Christianity.

By the *Catholic distortion,* Guinness means that in the course of Christian history, the holistic character of calling has often been distorted in an élitist way that elevates the spiritual at the expense of the secular, resulting in a host of dualisms—higher vs. lower, sacred vs. secular, perfect vs. permitted, contemplation vs. action. As Guinness rightly observes, "Sadly, this 'two-tier' or 'double-life' view of calling flagrantly perverted biblical teaching by narrowing the sphere of calling and excluding most Christians from its scope."[44] The result has been a tendency to think of monks as having "religious vocations" in ways that seem to imply that laypersons either do not have a vocation at all, or exist deficiently with only partially realized vocations.

Guinness wisely does not permit his readers to make the mistake of thinking that this spiritualizing distortion only occurs in those congregations that are in communion with the bishop of Rome. Indeed, his point is to remind them that all too often Protestants have themselves succumbed to this mistaken separation. Indeed, as he pointedly notes, in their zeal to commend "full-time Christian service" many evangelical Protestants do not see the irony that this very pattern of thought reproduces *a Protestant version* of the "Catholic distortion."[45]

In fact, Guinness argues that the "Protestant distortion" is even worse because this secularizing dualism diminishes our understanding of the primacy of Christian vocation. "Under the pressure of the modern world," Protestants have separated "the secular from the spiritual altogether, thereby reducing vocation to an alternative word for work."[46] What was only a "latent imbalance" in Puritanism grows into a full-blown distortion. "Slowly such words as work, trade, employment and occupation came to be used interchangeably with calling and vocation. As this happened, the guidelines for callings shifted; instead of being directed by the commands of God, they were seen as directed by duties and roles in society. Eventually the day came when faith and calling were separated completely." The early Christian awareness of the call of Jesus to discipleship "was boiled down to the demand that each citizen should have a job."[47] When Christian vocation comes to mean little more than that Christians make good "managers" who find their work to be meaningful, then vocation has been secularized in ways that render Christian discipleship innocuous.

In my judgment, *The Call* provides an accurate diagnosis of our diseased condition in church-related higher education. For example, Guinness calls attention to the ways in which the nineteenth-century notion of "Manifest Destiny"[48] has debased the sense of calling both for the individual citizen and the nation-state of the U.S. Ecclesially based universities should be the kinds of learning communities where such debased senses of "vocation" can be identified and named as such. Here again, one of the ways to unmask the deleterious effects of nationalistic visions of Manifest Destiny would be to enable students to participate in the kind of Christian formation that aspires to a different conception of human flourishing—such as the Ephesian vision of the "fullness of Christ"—where their giftedness is oriented not by visions of individual success (e.g., the "self-made" man or woman) and nationalist dominance but by the vision of the ecclesial community's vocation to *point beyond itself* to the reign of God.

Guinness's book also reflects on the question of how to orient career interests without allowing such aspirations to dominate his reflections. "As followers of Christ we are called to be before we are called to do and our calling both to be and do is fulfilled only in being called to him. So calling should not only precede career but outlast it too. Vocations never end even when occupations do."[49] At the end of the twentieth century, churches and universities alike find themselves struggling to engage challenges ranging from changing gender roles in church and society to the "downsizing" in the workplace (which has been enabled by the extensive use of information technology). The combined effect of these changes is forcing us to reimagine work itself, with many people changing careers several times over the course of their lifetimes. As a result, some are saying that it is no longer viable to think of Christian vocation as "your other vocation."

All the more reason why we should heed the wisdom of Os Guinness's words: "Calling is the truth that God calls us . . . so decisively that everything we are, everything we do, and everything we have is invested with a special devotion, dynamism, and direction lived out as a response to [God's] summons and service.[50] These stirring words pose challenges to church-related colleges and universities insofar as we have tended to oversimplify the task of Christian formation and vocational exploration while overextending the capacities of "career services" and "student affairs."[51] What it will mean to provide our students with the kind of imaginative opportunities for them to reflect about their vocations will require that we rethink what it means to "graduate" students in the context of the larger challenge of a *lifelong* Christian formation.

VI. "Graduations" and "Confirmation Classes"—Terminal Metaphors of Formation

The notion that alumni have completed a course of study that constitutes an adequate education is dear to those of us who inhabit church-related colleges and universities. Students have been judged to have "measured up" to the established standards—or not. The fact that some have "graduated"—and others have not—assures us that we have fulfilled our responsibilities individually and collectively. Maintaining the curricular standards for graduation, in turn, assures us of the integrity of our pedagogy and provides crucial evidence for maintaining our professional standing among peers as professionals who have also measured up to the established standards. Indeed, it is not too much to say that we are dependent on "terminal metaphors" for how we understand undergraduate education.

And yet, most of our institutions also want to pay tribute to the virtues of lifelong learning—if for no other reason than that they give us a foothold in laying claim to the allegiances (not to mention wealth!) of our alumni. This is one of the ways that we take a bow toward our "liberal arts" heritage—if we have one. Lifelong learning is supposed to be embodied in the lives of faculty who continue to acquire degrees, rank, and honorifics. Evidence of lifelong learning is also part of what we assess when we judge candidates for honorary degrees, which of course are conferred upon these recipients at the commencement exercises at which students are graduated. However much we may value "life-long learning" though, faculty and administrators at church-related colleges and universities tend to think of this kind of journey as beginning with them. In sum, we assume that we are the proper context for measurement and accreditation of all—earned and unearned—"degrees."

With such terminal metaphors of educational formation in view, many faculty at church-related colleges and universities take a rather condescending attitude toward the kind of Christian formation that they associate with the practices of "Sunday school" and confirmation classes. Thinking that students must be challenged to think "critically," university faculty sometimes dismiss whatever formation a student may bring with him or her. (Churches and their leaders are not immune to this truncated way of thinking. Indeed, many congregations and more than a few pastors act as if the completion of a confirmation class brings an end to discipleship training.) Faculty who would seek to be "interpreters" for students who have already embarked on a lifelong journey of Christian formation will have dispositions appropriate to those who understand that the role of the university in this process, although necessary and important, is by no means sufficient. At the same time, such faculty will understand that the portion of the student's journey in Christian formation that is spent as a member of the ecclesially based university may very well be a time when the student's vocational self-understanding is integrated in ways that will prove to be generative for all concerned.

Responsibility for Christian nurture and discipleship training—whether understood as the challenging adventure of a "lifelong catechumenate,"[52]as proposed by Michael Budde, or more minimally regarded as the task of teaching a one-time "membership training" class—must continue to reside with the church at both congregational and conference (or diocesan) levels. The church-related university can make a contribution to this process, however, precisely at the point that its faculty takes purposeful steps to enable students to engage in "reflective conversation with their past(s)" with a view toward enabling them to discern their future as persons of conviction. The most appropriate way to begin this process is by educating both Christian and non-Christian students about the significance of religious practices.

Here it is important to be clear about how students who are not professing Christians are to be engaged in this process. An "intentionally pluralist" college or university will invite students whose identities have been shaped by other religions (or no religion at all) to engage in reflective conversations that honor their identity as persons of conviction. However, such students should also be given the opportunity to understand the significance of the practices that make it possible for this particular community of learning to be hospitable to that student's presence. In other words, even non-Christian students should be given opportunities to understand the significance of the kind of Christian formation and vocation exploration opportunities that the university makes possible. Where these opportunities are constituted with reference to the university's mission, non-Christian students can be invited to consider the significance of Christian vocation for understanding the university's purposes as well as to consider what it is that they should be able to expect their Christian friends and neighbors to do and be as persons formed "in Christ." Not to provide this kind of educational engagement for non-Christian students will contribute to shaping these students to believe that a particular ecclesially based university's education is a commodity to be purchased without regard for the stated missional purposes of the university or its religious heritage.

A church-related university that provides students with opportunities for vocational reflection and discernment in the context of conversation with their past must take seriously the fact that in some cases those students who are professing Christians probably will not have been exposed to the practices being discussed in the curriculum it provides for students. In some cases, students may never have had any exposure to the practice of foot washing; in other cases, the congregations from which they have come may have practiced sacraments such as the Eucharist in less than optimal ways. Where this is the case, students can be given opportunities to practice such disciplines along with as contemplative prayer, fasting, and spiritual direction in retreat settings held in conjunction with Christian vocations courses.[53] But such learning opportunities should not be limited to the transmission of information.

As noted above, *Christian formation is more about apprenticeship than knowledge acquisition.* Accordingly, ecclesially based universities will enable students to participate in formally arranged apprenticeships including—but not limited to—service-learning opportunities and internships. But we cannot afford the self-deception of thinking that apprenticeship can be contained within the provisions of the university's curriculum. Where faculty, staff, and administrators understand themselves as constituting a mentoring community (for one another as well as for the students who enter and leave this learning community), they will understand their relationships with students as oriented by the mission of the university. This means that whatever gnosis students may have acquired in the course of their academic journey must be regarded as penultimate. As judged in the light of the *pleroma* of Christ, the kinds of knowledge acquisition that students experience in college have value inasmuch as they are conducive to the wisdom of the cross.

Christian formation is more about craft than about technique. At some levels this is easier to practice in church-related higher education than others. Ultimately, it has to do with how we think about the "means" and "ends" of ecclesially based education. Too often, the focus of Christian formation tends to be located in terms of technique, but instrumental values are not the only ways to register the importance of formative endeavors. Just as some practices are done for their own sake and not as means to other ends, so also the vocation of Christian discipleship is to be understood as the proper context for locating the importance of those practices of discipleship. The proper way to locate the value of the craft of forgiveness or the craft of peacemaking is to frame it in terms of the vocation of Christian discipleship, where all gifts are intended for the "building up of the body of Christ" (Eph. 4:12).

Christian formation is more about the cultivation of wisdom than about career training. When we cultivate wisdom in students who are enrolled at ecclesially based universities, then we will render plausible the imaginative vision of human destiny found in the Letter to the Ephesians—"until all of us come to the unity of the faith and the knowledge of the Son of God, to maturity, to the measure of the full stature of Christ" (4:13)—even where this may not correlate with the existing common sense about careers. As would-be wise friends, faculty will guide students in ways that make apprenticeship in the gospel possible even where that means that they will need to help students see *beyond* the guidelines for professional certification and postgraduate standards. This may take a variety of forms, but in every case it will mean valuing Christian vocation above the established "career paths" of a liberal democratic society.

▧ VII. Conclusion

As my arguments in this chapter suggest, I believe it is time for us to move beyond the misleading metaphors that have populated too much of the thinking about what it means to form students in the context of vocational discernment. As my arguments have shown, unimaginative thinking—often informed by misleading metaphors—has too often contributed to what might be called the "muddled missions" of contemporary church-related colleges and universities. I offer the following six directions for future endeavors of church-related colleges and universities in the hope that those of us who live out our days in the precincts of "intentionally pluralist" communities of learning will be able to embody our vocations as Christian disciples so as to persuade those communities to continue to understand their missions in ways that provide "an assured voice in an ongoing conversation."

1. *Instead of assuming segregated missions, church-related colleges and universities must begin thinking conjunctively about their missions in relation to the church's mission.* The missions of the two clearly are not identical. They are distinct in their scope, but they do not have to be segregated from one another, and if they are—in actuality, or in effect—entirely separate, then it will be difficult for intentionally pluralist institutions to avoid the slide into the "accidentally pluralist" type of church-related colleges and universities. In the midst of such distinct but overlapping missions, church-related colleges should take steps to image this relationship in ways appropriate to their history and relationship. I take it for granted that the most appropriate metaphors and imagery for such collaboration will need to arise out of particular traditions and practices of ecclesial-based universities. But I am confident that metaphors exist that could be used that we simply have not noticed.[54] Further, I am convinced that in many cases, mission statements and mottoes can be recontextualized in ways that recover at least some of the significance of the Christian vision that informed the institutions when they were founded.

2. *Instead of acting as if students are "unencumbered selves" ecclesial-based universities must learn to think of faculty and students alike as persons formed by conviction.* However much the metaphor of unencumbered selves may populate the thinking of public colleges and universities, ecclesially based colleges and universities must resist the pressure to think in such a reductionist fashion. Where we take seriously that persons are constituted by their convictions, we will be in a better position to understand ecclesially based universities as "communities of conviction" with missions that are also oriented by their relationship to the church.

3. *Instead of enabling students to continue to think of themselves as consumers or puppets, the ecclesially based university must help them be reoriented as explorers on a quest for self-understanding or as actors in a drama with multiple "acts."* Buechner's metaphor of God as stage director of a drama is certainly not an adequate metaphor for how students should understand their relationship to God, but it might serve as a means to the end of reorienting

students toward the vision of human flourishing to which Christians bear witness.

4. *Instead of seeing themselves as "professionals"—rather than parent-substitutes —the faculty of ecclesially based universities need to reimagine their relationship to students as "wise friends."* Faculty occupy the role *in loco amicis*—not the role of the "dislocated professional" who has no commitments to place or persons. The faculty of a church-related college should think of themselves as residents of "Interpreter's House" and members of mentoring communities that include administrators, support staff, and even the students themselves. This mentoring community will foster the imaginations of students to seek the fullness of Christ.

5. *Instead of using metaphors that spiritualize or secularize "vocations," ecclesially based universities must invite students into an open-ended exploration that involves "everything we are, everything we do, and everything we have."* In other words, we will aspire to do more than gesture at the "impossibility" of monastic vocation or the secular feasibility of the managerial "calling." We will dare to engage students, faculty, and staff in an ongoing conversation that takes seriously the mystery of the Spirit's "blowing" people's lives where it will. This will necessarily mean that we be open to the transformations that occur whenever we dare to embrace the call to Christian discipleship. The effects of such discernment cannot be predicted nor controlled. Some students may elect not to go to Wall Street because they feel drawn to work in the streets of Gary, Indiana, or East St. Louis. Still other students may find ways to work within the corporate structure while practicing "monasticism beyond the walls." Some faculty and administrators may discover in the midst of their middle-aged meanderings that they are called to a life of prayer as an oblate of a monastic order or more informally as a contemplative. Faculty and students alike will find themselves drawn together as practitioners of a common craft—the craft of discipleship.

6. *Instead of using "terminal metaphors" to describe their role in the formation of students, ecclesially based universities need to think of what they are doing as contributing to a "life-long catechumenate,"* etc. This will mean that they acknowledge that there is a standard greater than they would seek for their own narrow self-interest. By framing their mission in relation to the "economy of abundance" imaged in the Ephesian metaphor of the *pleroma*, leaders of ecclesially based universities will be able to see their institution's contribution to the lifelong learning of students not so much as the beginning of a new journey, but rather as one of several kinds of formative endeavors that contribute to a student's Christian formation.

This way of thinking about the role of ecclesially based universities may not be "more outrageous" (in Michael Baxter's sense), but I would hope that it might be more imaginative than some of the ways faculty and administrators still tend to talk about the identities of students, the roles of faculty, and the importance of vocation exploration in the context of the missions of their institutions. In an economic environment in which many college administrators are prone to use "survivalist" rhetoric with respect to institutional future, to think in these ways may initially feel as though church-related universities are being asked to "choose their fate" rather than seeking to "control their destiny." I would argue, however, that we do not have to accede to fatalistic thinking, and after all, it is a theological mistake to think that our destiny ultimately depends on us. The fact that ecclesially based institutions do not control our destinies does not mean that we have no destiny; it simply means that our destiny (and that of our students) is most meaningfully located in the context of a mystery—the mystery of the *fullness* of Christ. Any ecclesially based university that is serious about carrying out a mission explicitly including the Christian formation and vocation exploration of students will be *at least* this imaginative.

▨ Notes

1. This chapter is a thoroughly reworked version of arguments originally presented to a gathering of church and university leaders at the University of Indianapolis on October 26, 2000, and March 28, 2001. Subsequently a revised version of my comments was distributed to participants in the United Methodists IN-Conversation at the University of Indianapolis in the form of a booklet entitled "What Happened on 'the Way' from Interpreter's House? Protestant Reflections on Christian Vocation" (Indianapolis: University of Indianapolis, 2001) as first publication in the *Vocare* series of "Occasional Papers for Theological Exploration of Christian Vocations," published by the Lantz Center for Christian Vocations at the University of Indianapolis.

2. See my unpublished paper "Who Will Lead Our People Out of the Wilderness?" about the relationship of Hendrix College and the North Arkansas Conference of the Methodist Church during the Civil Rights struggle in Arkansas from 1954 to 1964. Originally presented at the Quinquennial Conference of the Historical Society of the United Methodist Church, Madison, New Jersey, in August 1993, this study explores the changing roles of the church and the college in the struggle to integrate this particular college and Methodist churches of the North Arkansas Conference. A copy of the paper is available from the Hendrix College Archives in Conway, Arkansas.

3. This kind of distinction invites us to adopt reductionist views of what the church and the university are both about and further contributes to uncertainty about how to collaborate with one another in those areas where our purposes do converge. Indirectly, such dichotomies contribute to the loss of the distinctiveness of church-related higher education and leave congregations, students, and university faculty alike with the impression that the only options are to be secular public universities or to be members of the Christian College Coalition. Our missions can be distinguished without creating an ultimate separation.

4. Here I have in mind the kinds of initiatives that have been taken by the Lilly Fellows Program in Humanities and the Arts. A modest literature has emerged from the

series of annual meetings, with selected papers from keynote speakers published in the summer issue of the *Cresset*. One of the concerns that marks the Lilly Fellows program is how to foster the development of Christian scholars as pedagogues who will be teaching in church-related colleges and universities upon the completion of their postdoctoral fellowships at Valparaiso University. By contrast, in many instances the debates about "Christian scholarship" appears to be focused on questions of research methodology and ideological bent. Clearly, pedagogy and research do not have to be seen as separate concerns, but it is interesting to observe how the metaphors used often suggest that such divisions are operative in the thinking of advocates for "Christian scholarship" and "excellence in Church-related higher education."

5. Michael Baxter, CSC, "Not Outrageous Enough" in *First Things* (May 2001): 16.

6. Ibid., p. 14.

7. Ibid., p. 16.

8. Ibid., p. 16. In the conclusion of Baxter's review essay, he uses the expression "*ex corde Ecclesiae*"—presumably an allusion to the recent papal encyclical by the same title that has laid out the conditions under which bishops may give permission for faculty to teach students at Catholic colleges and universities.

9. Robert Benne, *Quality With Soul: How Six Premier Colleges and Universities Keep Faith With Their Religious Traditions* (Grand Rapids: Eerdmans, 2001). While Benne lays out his typology of church-related colleges in the third chapter (pp. 48–65), the information is neatly summarized in four columns on p. 49.

10. Benne makes this fairly explicit at the beginning of the third chapter of his book, where he states: "It is my contention that these partially secularized schools are not fated to complete the process of secularization. Not only should we appreciate the schools that have not succumbed completely to secularization, we should find ways to strengthen the partial connections they have to their sponsoring traditions and to find new connections that have never existed before." (p. 48). While there is no question that Benne's project has value at the level of tactics, I would argue that it also has strategic significance insofar as it enables the kind of conversation about the mission of the university within which the issues of vocation and formation of students can be registered forthrightly. How well these matters can be clarified in the midst of political concerns will of course vary with the setting and (faculty and administrative) personalities of each college or university.

11. For an example of a church-related college where this took place, see Michael G. Cartwright, "A Holy Experiment in American Higher Education," in John Westerhoff and Stanley Hauerwas, eds., *Schooling Christians: Holy Experiments* (Grand Rapids: Eerdmans, 1992).

12. L. Gregory Jones, "Beliefs, Desires, Practices, and the Ends of Theological Education," in Miroslav Volf and Dorothy Bass, eds., *Practicing Theology: Beliefs and Practices in Christian Life* (Grand Rapids: Eerdmans, 2002), pp. 185–186. For the purposes of this chapter, I have adapted Jones's metaphor of the relay race slightly to emphasize the role of the church-related college in this process. In doing so, I do not mean to suggest that ecclesially based universities will play the primary role in the process of Christian formation in the future, but I do want to stress that we have assumed *too much* about how much we can rely on other "players" to do Christian formation. Our role should never be primary, but neither should we assume that we need play no role in this process because it is being taken care of by others.

13. Michael Budde, *The Magic Kingdom: Christianity and the Global Culture Industries* (Boulder, Co.: Westview, 1997).

14. Ibid., 130.

15. In November 2001, Hendrix College was awarded a $2 million grant by the Religion Division of the Lilly Endowment to create a theological exploration of vocations initiative on campus during the next five years. The college's motto was the focus of the program proposal.

16. Within the Catholic tradition, such imagery has often been registered liturgically, particularly with respect to the sacraments. In such contexts, the Ephesian imagery of mature Christian existence has a rich resonance for what it means to be *the Corpus Christi*—the provisional embodiment and "signpost" of God's reign in the world. At the same time, the social shape of ministry has tended to be not only focused narrowly with respect to the priesthood but also categorized Platonically, which has sometimes resulted in a curious kind of split between the monastic communities and the ordinary lay people, instead of these being two foci of an integrated whole within which roles are differentiated functionally. In the process, the myth of "Christendom" also focused attention away from congregational life, thereby dislocating the social dimension of the Christian faith and diminishing the significance of "the people of God" as the bearer of the good news. (For a thorough discussion of the social character of the ministry of the church as "the people of God" See Gerhard Lohfink's book *Does God Need the Church?* [Collegeville, Minn.: Liturgical Press, 2000]).

From a Protestant perspective, at the time of the Reformation an attempt was made to restore the significance of the ministries that laity embody insofar as Luther and Calvin came to believe that secular callings were in fact Christian vocations. This calls for a different kind of spiritual formation. Not coincidentally, congregational singing experienced a kind of rebirth in the life of the church as Protestants embraced their vocations as participants in the "royal priesthood" of the church. The practice of congregational singing is itself a form of witness to the gospel as we embody our eschatological vocation to worship the Lamb as described in chapters 5 and 7 of the Revelation of St. John.

To some extent, the Reformation notion of the "priesthood of all believers" can be said to have been an attempt to discern the "fullness of Christ." Those churches of the "radical Reformation" (Mennonite, Brethren, Quakers, etc.) took this a step further in seeking to see all Christians as being gifted for ministry. Today churches of the Believer's Church traditions continue to bear witness to the vision of "universal ministry." Some theologians (John Howard Yoder) have gone so far in their criticism of Christian traditions to say that the Pauline vision of universal ministry has yet to be "consciously and consistently lived out" (see Yoder's *Body Politics* [Nashville, Tenn.: Upper Room, 1991], p. 57). This criticism is not without its point; however, in my view, it prematurely consigns the gatherings of Catholic, Protestant, and Orthodox congregations to a faithlessness without taking into account the rich senses in which they too have embraced this multidimensional metaphor of Christian ministry.

While the "free church vision" of the gathered company of disciples-in-ministry has an expansive view of the participation of all members of the Body of Christ, I argue that it too quickly discards the offices of bishop, presbyter, and deacon as incompatible with the "fullness of Christ" (Yoder, *Body Politics*, p. 47) just as it jettisons the sacraments as acts of God in the church. Because Believer's Church theologians tend to have sharply limited conceptions of the "means of grace" and/or the sacraments in the formation of Christians, it is not uncommon for such theologians to regard all priestly roles as attempts to control "access to the divine." This view is misleading given that it prematurely excludes the possibility of the existence of thriving Christian congregations that have both priestly roles and mutual accountability at the same time.

I grant that it may be easier to act as if the "both-and" conception of the fullness of Christ (understood as manifest sacramentally as well as embodied in diverse ministries) is nonexistent. I would argue, however, that to maintain the hope that God can work through the church's ordinary means of grace as well as in the gathering of faithful disciples is to embrace the multidimensional work of God that is always more than we can ask or imagine.

17. Michael Sandel, *Democracy's Discontent: America in Search of a Public Philosophy* (Cambridge, Mass.: Harvard University Press, 1996), p. 12.

18. Ibid.

19. David Ford, *Self and Salvation: Being Transformed* (New York: Cambridge University Press, 1990). Later in this study, Ford develops the intriguing idea of what it would mean to think of singing as a "transformative practice" in the context of communities and institutions. What this would mean for ecclesially based universities is by no means obvious, but we should not discount the possibility that this could be developed.

20. "Benedictine Values and Building Campus Community," by Carney Strange with Harry Hagan, OSB. It appeared in the *Cresset* (1998), Special Issue, Lilly Fellows Program in Humanities and the Arts.

21. The phrase "school for the Lord's service" is used in the "Prologue" of *The Rule of St. Benedict.* See *RB 1980* edited by Timothy Fry, OSB (Collegeville, Minn.: Liturgical Press, 1982), p. 18.

22. Jean Vanier's book *The Scandal of Service: Jesus Washes Our Feet* (New York: Continuum, 1998) provides a very provocative account of the most "ecumenical and interfaith" sacrament that we might imagine. The fact that Vanier's reflections arise from his own ministry with mentally handicapped adults in the L'Arche community where they wash one another's feet is also noteworthy.

23. Robert McCauley, "The Business of the University," in *Liberal Education* 68, no. 1 (1982): 248–255. This article originated in an address at Indiana Central University where McCauley taught from 1978–1982.

24. To mention but a few of these, why is it that in the church we have clung to the metaphors of "mainline" Protestantism as if our ministries have only been on Main Street? Why do we think we need to see ourselves at the center of the American project? Why have we not been able to see the distorting effects of American mythology of Manifest Destiny on both personal and ecclesial senses of Christian vocation?

25. After all, it was John Wesley who taught us that there is no holiness but social holiness!

26. For a witty and incisive analysis of the dangers of church-marketing, see Philip Kenneson and James L. Street, *Selling Out the Church: The Dangers of Church Marketing* (Nashville, Tenn.: Abingdon, 1997).

27. The chapter "The Dwarves in the Stable" is included in the collection of writings *Listening for God: Contemporary Literature and the Life of Faith,* ed. Paula J. Carlson and Peter S. Hawkins (Minneapolis: Augsburg Fortress, 1994), pp. 40–55. This piece was originally published in Frederick Buechner's memoir *Telling Secrets* (New York: Harper Collins, 1991).

28. Buechner, *Telling Secrets,* pp. 53–54.

29. In discussing the roles of the mentoring community, I am drawing on the essay of James R. Zullo, FSC. Zullo describes the mentoring community in terms of fostering

imagination in the context of faith formation, inviting giftedness to be expressed in service, and affirming promise in the midst of vulnerability. According to Zullo, a mentoring community that succeeds in doing these things will engender faith, hope, and love in the lives of young adults, which are in turn the conditions for the possibility of their flourishing as twenty-first-century Christian leaders. See "God and Gen-X: Faith and the New Generation" by James R. Zullo, FSC, in *Listening: Journal of Religion and Culture* (Fall 1999). This resource is available from Lewis University, a Christian Brothers University in Romeo, Illinois.

30. For an example of the growing literature that focuses on the creation and sustenance of mentoring communities in higher education as well as elsewhere for young adults, see Sharon Daloz Parks, *Big Questions, Worthy Dreams: Mentoring Young Adults in Their Search for Meaning, Purpose, and Faith* (San Francisco: Jossey-Bass, 2000). On pp. 158–172 Parks focuses on the challenge of institutions of higher education creating mentoring communities for young adult students.

31. See my related booklet "What Happened on 'the Way' from Interpreter's House" (Indianapolis: University of Indianapolis Press, 2000).

32. David Hoekema, *Campus Rules and Moral Community: In Place of In Loco Parentis* (Lanham, Md.: Rowman and Littlefield, 1989), p. 159. Hoekema observes: "Morality on campus today is . . . formed and shaped *in dialogue*. We cannot restore the ethical dimension that has largely vanished from the campus demands by reimposing the paternalistic rules of an earlier generation . . ." (p. 164) However, he observes that "Respect for the autonomy of students does not entail surrender to a wholly individualistic conception of morality. . . . The ideal of the independent individual accountable to no laws save those he imposes on himself—an ideal drawn from philosophical liberalism that underlies much of modern politics and psychology—distorts our moral experience and misrepresents our ethical selves. . . . We are moral beings because we are beings who live in community and who shape our ideals in dialogue" (p. 164).

33. Ibid., 166.

34. Ibid., 164–165.

35. Willimon and Naylor, *The Abandoned Generation*, pp. 93–94.

36. Wendell Berry, *Life Is A Miracle: An Essay Against Modern Superstition* (Washington, D.C.: Counterpoint Books, 2000), p. 130.

37. Ibid.

38. I am grateful to University of Indianapolis President Jerry Israel for this example. This incident took place during his tenure as President of Morningside College in Sioux City, Iowa.

39. Eldon Trueblood, *Your Other Vocation* (New York: Harper & Row, 1952), p. 32.

40. Ibid., p. 17.

41. Ibid., p. 38.

42. Ibid., see pp. 57–105. These concerns were the focus of the third and fourth chapters of Trueblood's book. Looking back at Trueblood's essays from the vantage point of those who have now seen the end of the twentieth century, one is struck both by the wisdom of his words about the importance of family life and by his lack of awareness of the need to reconstruct gender roles. But then, there is much about the last fifty years that few could have anticipated in 1950. The fact that almost half of seminarians today are women is but one of the salient facts that must be confronted in our time.

43. Ibid., see pp. 106–125.

44. Os Guinness, *The Call: Finding and Fulfilling the Central Purpose of Your Life* (Nashville, Tenn.: Word, 1998), pp. 32–33.

45. Ibid., p. 32.

46. Ibid., pp. 39–40.

47. Ibid., p. 40.

48. For a very helpful discussion of the American myth of Manifest Destiny and its power to shape the vocational sensibilities of self and nation, see Roger Betsworth, *Social Ethics: An Examination of American Moral Traditions* (Louisville: Westminster/John Knox, 1990).

49. Ibid., pp. 243–244.

50. Ibid., p. 29.

51. At the same time, there are offices of career services and work-study programs in church-related universities that have been able to reconfigure the way they go about engaging students by reframing what they do in terms of vocation. For a good example of the way one church-related university has reconfigured its career-services office, see Paul Gabonay at the University of Indianapolis. Val Pederson-Knopp's "Life-Study" program at St. John's University, Collegeville, Minnesota, provides an imaginative example of how a collegiate work-study program can be reoriented with the category of vocation in view.

52. For a helpful discussion of the significance of the lifelong catechumenate as a form of resistance to consumerism, see Michael Budde, *The Magic Kingdom,* pp. 131–151.

53. At the same time, students who learn about such spiritual disciplines, and who begin to practice them, may return to their home congregations with questions that disconcert the laity and clergy of the church. Such interaction, in turn, can evoke an awareness that the congregations themselves may need to consider focusing more on a "spirituality of practice."

54. For example, at the University of Indianapolis, on the gable above the portico of the oldest building on campus, there is an image of two lamps burning. The lamps face one another. Elsewhere I have suggested that this imagery might be used to prompt thought about the contributions of the church and the university to the vocation and formation of students whose lives we share.

12

With Friends Like These

Pathetic Chaplaincy and the Ethos of the Ecclesial College

Wes Avram

My operative question is this: If institutionally appointed chaplaincy is to be advocated for an ecclesially based university or preserved elsewhere, how might it be imagined to avoid the revenge effects against the church that too easily accompany it now? By "revenge effects" I mean those ways in which a practice or institution produces some of the ills it is meant to redress. The terms "iatrogenesis" and "paradoxical counterproductivity" have also been used to describe this phenomenon.[1] In this essay I use a narrative frame to describe some of those revenge effects and offer several suggestions for rethinking the work. These suggestions amount to an image of chaplaincy taking an ironic position and confessional tone. In discussing these iatrogenic effects, my focus is on institutionally appointed and funded full-time chaplaincies at liberalizing colleges or universities.[2] By "liberalizing" institutions I mean those schools that are either largely or increasingly rationalized under the presumptions of classically liberal notions of education—sublimating faith commitment, religious community, and related notions of learning in service to the church, and through the church to the world, to the values of democratic pluralism, technological culture, individual agency. Where it acknowledges that religion might be other than an anachronistic holdover, liberal culture tends to accept religion as little more than optional sets of symbols and varied organizational techniques useful for meaning-making, need-meeting, and, to a lesser degree, individual moral formation. It interprets the work of chaplaincy in these lights. First, a narrative description of chaplaincy's paradoxical counterproductivity.

A Tale of Disestablishment: A New England Case in Point

Between 1990 and 1996 I was the college chaplain of a once American Baptist, now unaffiliated liberal arts college in the Northeast. The school sits in one of the least "churched" parts of the country, with the crumbling material trappings of the once dominant Protestant and Catholic establishment all around. On the campus, in the midst of red brick Collegiate Georgian buildings and converted Victorian houses spanning out from a stately nineteenth-century quadrangle, there sits a beige stone English Collegiate Gothic chapel, styled after King's College, Cambridge (a 1912 gift to the college of Mrs. D. Willis James). Not what you'd expect in Maine. The chapel holds a large sanctuary, two storage rooms, a machine that runs belfry chimes, and a fine pipe organ of recent vintage. No offices for the staff, no classrooms, no program or service space for religious organizations. No Xerox machine. Not even a public telephone.

In the sanctuary of this chapel, Charles Connick stained glass windows show Madame Curie, Shakespeare, Roger Bacon, Aristotle, Copernicus, daVinci, Euclid, and other "saints" of Enlightenment. In the rafters above the nave one finds seals of schools to which the Free Will Baptist leaders of Bates College aspired at the beginning of the century: Bowdoin and Williams, among others. The twelve disciples of Jesus can be found in the chancel. At the back of the chapel, in the narthex, hangs a permanent dedication:

> To the Glory of God
> And the Worship of His Son
> This Building is Forever Dedicated.

The plaque presents a simple purpose held in a limiting frame, exhibited in the building by a rather odd, even contradictory, set of symbols.

The incongruent architecture of this chapel can be easily read to represent unsurprising cultural aspirations for rural New England Baptists, though it is still interesting to note how those aspirations gave religion the weight of late medieval memory while the rest of the college looked back to Colonial times. But quite aside from the architectural feint, one can also surmise a theo-educational rationale for the now quite inconvenient layout of the building—having, as it does, no space but worship space.

That fate of that theo-educational rationale can be seen in the history of the college in relation to its chaplaincy.[3] This is a history that is remarkable only for the way in which it demonstrates a process that has either developed or is now developing, with only modest variations, in church-related colleges and universities all over the country. For, at the time the chapel was built, there was no college chaplain at either this college or nearly any college. The first chaplains had been appointed at two institutions in the middle of the nineteenth century, but very few others were hired until a light wave of appointments after the turn of the century, two or three equally small waves between the world wars, and then a tidal wave immediately following World War II.[4] As was true of many colleges of its kind, the first presidents of Bates were clergymen of the denomination to which the college was bound. This was the case for about ninety years. It was not until right after World War II that the first layman, still a Baptist, was inaugurated. An Episcopalian layman took the helm in the 1960s. A Presbyterian cum Unitarian assumed the presidency in 1990, and he hired me. I was only the third fully installed chaplain at the college, as Bates had established the office only after it had hired that first non-Baptist president and had fully broken any remaining associations with its denomination.

With this story, the symbolic significance of the chapel may be coming clear. For, again, not unlike other church-related colleges in its time, for most of Bates's life it had been assumed that the location for the integrating Christian zeal, church identity, moral formation, pastoral concern, and the work of higher education lie nowhere in particular at the college. It was assumed to lie everywhere. The building on the Quad was not a chapel as much as it was the *sanctuary* for the chapel, the chapel being the whole campus. The president regularly preached in that sanctuary, where he also gave the annual baccalaureate sermon. Nearly all faculty lived within walking distance of the college and were assumed to bear teaching, counseling, advising, and formation responsibilities toward students. They were the elders of the chapel-campus. The local American Baptist congregation, with its building a couple of miles away, demonstrated its personal and pastoral connection to the college by placing its parsonage on campus. The relationship was rather seamless.

The ethos of the place was shaped by loving struggles among education in Enlightenment rationality, training for civil leadership, and formation in Victorian piety. As the pressures of liberal culture slowly transformed the college, this ethos slid over to pathos, which, when come to the present day, may be all that is left of this earlier integration. It is now left to individualized feeling, vague reminiscence, ceremonial recollection, and redefined sentiment—pathos. No longer even partially the basis of character, credibility, or responsibility—ethos.

This may reflect developments regarding religious life throughout New England, but it is how these developments change this college that takes my interest here. For onetime specifically theological warrants for Bates's practices—always admitting women as well as men, admitting black students as well as white, privileging rural poor over urban well-heeled and first-generation over third-generation college-educated applicants, forbidding fraternities and sororities, preferring local residents over those from away (and, on the perhaps less noble side of things, restricting Jews and Catholics)—were either lost or redescribed in terms of vague "tradition," unclarified "heritage," or expressed "values." They were rewritten into a discourse of "excellence" and the promotion of secularized versions of social "progress." The language of a self-congratulatory egalitarianism replaced that of a Christian mandate, and the role of the founding clerics was referred to in college publicity by their status not as pastors, but as abolitionists (an accurate, but rather reductionist claim). As on many campuses, the secularizing impulse of the Protestant spirit had its way at Bates.

In time it became necessary to clarify (and so quantify) the significance of the religious warrant for the college and complete the shift from viewing the traditions that gave birth to the college as ethos-forming practices, however ambiguous they might have been, to viewing those traditions as purely optional resources for those pathos-forming values alluded to above. The faculty diversified, sought a national profile, and largely moved out of town. Chapel services were deregulated and moved to Sundays, the administration was expanded and rationalized, and religious life was professionalized along with other offices.[5] Student health and counseling services were soon to follow. In making this move, Bates did not follow the full rejectionist tactic of either mothballing its chapel or removing explicitly religious symbols and transforming it into an activities center with vague preference to religious activities or a museum and concert space. Bates may be credited for that. But the fact that it followed those colleges that took a more seemingly benign course should not hide the fact that it was nonetheless sealing rejection and disestablishment. It simply took the course of condemning religion through a feint of welcome. The key is that the direction of welcome is now reversed, no longer from the church toward the academy, but now from the academy toward a highly qualified and limited expression of church. As this pattern develops, faith is marginalized by being sentimentalized and ritualized. Chaplaincies unwittingly collude. Bates is typical in this regard and less aggressive than many colleges.

This process can be watched as one traces how denominational identity is or is not preserved. One of the last vestiges of such identity is often a stated preference toward hiring chaplains from the founding denomination (and possibly the gesture of putting that denomination's hymnal in the chapel pews). With the severing of denominational affiliation at Bates being nearly coincidental with hiring the first chaplain, there the pattern worked in an opposite, though still structurally related way. Perhaps, at Bates, beginning with a Baptist chaplain would have felt too much like a sign of remaining association; and so among the four installed chaplains and three acting chaplains Bates has had over thirty years, only one of the *acting* chaplains (working as a part-time interim after I left) has been Baptist. The others have been Congregationalist, Presbyterian, United Methodist, and Episcopalian. The Baptist came only at a time when any hint of Baptist association was long gone. With all of this, the statement implied by the chapel that the whole campus is ecclesial is also long lost. And however aesthetically pleasing the chapel may be in a quaint sort of way, it is now both functionally obsolete and rather inconvenient—a long walk on a cold day in Maine and far too large for the worship that actually takes place there.[6]

To summarize the case, I'm suggesting that despite some differences from institution to institution, the history of chaplaincy in most colleges and universities tends to find that at some point, either from its founding or from a point at which a reconfiguration or personnel change prompts a transformation of purpose, chaplaincy begins to serve three interconnected liberalizing developments at the college. These developments complete the basic disestablishment of ecclesial identity, first, by *professionalizing religious life* so the college can more comfortably get on with its business; second, by *moving theological claims* and pastoral responsibility from the space of ethos to the mediation of pathos on campus; and, third, by a development that has not been reviewed here yet, which is *underwriting the centrality of service provision* as the primary practice by which relationships among students, faculty, and administrators are mediated. The role of chaplaincy in shaping ethos thus returns, though now emptied of its theological texture and remade in the shape of consumer values. It is only on this basis of those values that chaplaincy is accepted.

The services the chaplain provides hover about events or problems that other professionals on campus are uncomfortable addressing, such as providing rituals surrounding death or disaster, being the resident counselor for students presenting "religious" or "spiritual" questions (according to culturally acceptable definitions of "religious" and "spiritual"), providing ballast in times of war, forging connections between the college administration and religious organizations in the community, providing symbolic comfort for alumni or others who might cling to anachronistic religious claims on the college, or releasing pent up political anxieties through organizing relatively harmless political demonstration. Thus chaplaincies tend to be interpreted by analogy to other offices on campus—whether in academic affairs, student activities, counseling and student health, or community and alumni relations. The offices from which a chaplaincy borrows its identity might depend on the disposition of a particular chaplain or the inclinations of the person(s) to whom a chaplain answers (a president, a student or academic dean, a development or alumni officer). On the whole, the chaplain's authority, or "voice," on campus is no longer derived from his or her ecclesial status, but is, rather, earned through standards of professional competence and personal charisma derived elsewhere than from the church. So the deal is sealed, and a hidden curriculum is shaped by which an implicit and operative ecclesiology is taught without being subject to the least critical reflection. It is simply a part of the liberalizing givens that increasingly shape the place.

If I see this often-repeated pattern, within variation, as ominous for the interconnection of ecclesial practices and ecclesial identity at church-related colleges, *which I do,* must I not also admit more benign motives in the establishment of these professional chaplaincies? Must I not acknowledge the good, even essential, work that nearly all of these chaplains do? Of course I should, and so I do. Even chaplains limited to counselor-activist-cheerleader-affirmer-ceremonialist roles touch lives and do good. (Bates's chaplains have had larger roles than that, and the current chaplain works with integrity, effort, and imagination.) Nevertheless, I would argue that despite any intentions to the contrary, and despite the good they do, professional chaplaincies still tend to mediate, if not even facilitate, the withdrawal, or at least sidelining, of ecclesial imagination from the life of the college. They thus serve a paradoxical counterproductivity—in fact limiting religious expression as much as encouraging it. Like so many trappings of liberal practice, they risk undermining the very reality they are thought to embody. So conceived, they are a useful as a case in point for the very dynamics of establishment, secularization, and possibilities for new grounding of religion in ecclesially related institutions around which this volume of essays is gathered.

■ Examples of Chaplaincy's Revenge Effects

Among the revenge effects of professionalizing religious life into an activity organized through an office, sliding of arguments for and by chaplains from ethos to pathos, and reinforcing consumer models of intergroup interaction, consider the unstated but universally understood responsibility of the chaplain to serve the values and comfort of the college by authorizing some forms of religious expression and discouraging others. Following the liberalizing impulse of most historically Protestant colleges, it becomes clear that chaplaincies like mine are informally, but every bit as urgently, charged with the task of helping naïve students and misbehaving faculty adjust to new givens. We are to take over-passionate or embarrassingly pious members of the "college community" (as though students and faculty had no primary communities outside the college) and gently liberalize them into their new cultural privileges and interpretive responsibilities. We are, in effect, to usher them out of any thick kind of ecclesial identity that would make prior, countercultural, claims on them. And we are to assist them into a religious identity much thinner and more congruent with the new ethos. Again, along my definition of pathos, this means bringing them into a more supplementally value-centered than fundamentally conviction-centered view of believing. With this, they are to be socialized into a more proximate, civility-centered morality than an ultimate, responsibility-centered ethic.

Stating that chaplains socialize students, and sometimes faculty, into the dominant ethos may seem to contradict my earlier emphasis on the chaplain serving pathos rather than ethos, but on a closer look one sees that this way of serving the institutional ethos depends, in fact, on foregrounding the pathos-centered nature of the chaplain's work. For the religious discourse that a chaplain represents no longer shapes the ethos she or he mediates. The chaplain thus represents the pathetic place of religion in the dominant ethos, and so models acceptance of that relegation. Thus the marked shift from the confessional professing of denominational orthodoxy to the subtle managing of antiliberal sentiment goes without challenge. This chaplain manages, or at least monitors, potentially subversive religious claims by advocating the good of liberal education over against the good of ecclesial formation. Policing evangelism on campus is one very public example of this role. Quieter aspects include steering beliefs through conversation, through supporting some events on campus and withholding support from others, taking publicized advocacy positions in national ecclesial and/or political debates, teaching and preaching in a certain way, developing programs and sponsoring lectureships, intervening officially in religious conflict, and performing an effectively Unitarian or Universalist theology in public prayer and ceremonial leadership. The enemy most often claimed here to be worth excising from the campus is religious "fundamentalism," which is usually taken as a loose descriptor of any expression of faith that does not share liberal premises. Never mind that fundamentalism is a historically identifiable religious movement, representatives of which are rarely found on liberalizing campuses in the first place. The point is to render any religious expression that does not accept the limitations put upon it by classical liberalism extremist and indecorous.

During one of the years I was at Bates I received a call from one of our sister colleges. This college also had Baptist founding, even earlier than Bates's. It has also broken its ties. The college has never had a full-time, institutionally situated chaplain. Instead, it outsources religious services for selected constituency groups. Local pastors, rabbis, and other religious leaders who might be available are provided a small stipend by the college (unless paid by their own denomination) to be minimally available for counseling. Out of their legitimate sense of mission to students, local religious leaders are, as far as I know, quick to oblige. A couple of groups have weekly worship. Some administrative support is also provided.

The chapel is of later design than Bates's. It is bold in its profile and well appointed with program and office space. It is an integrated chapel complex in New England Congregational style, in marked contrast to the beautiful anomaly at Bates. It has a large white steeple bearing a prominent cross.

The person calling me was seeking advice, knowing that I was a fully appointed chaplain and had likely encountered the problem he was working on. Seems that a group of non-Christian students (and faculty?) had lodged a complaint with the administration over the overbearing cross in the center of campus. They wanted it removed, warranted by the value of pluralism and argued for in the discourse of multiculturalism. Perhaps the right cause, even if for the wrong reasons. An ad hoc committee was hastily formed by the college and alternatives were investigated. The live option at that moment involved placing other religious symbols along the front of the chapel and the building and converting the building into a multi-faith center (never minding that the placement of other symbols on the steeple might suggest a Christian triumphalism that the cross alone did not). The interdenominational mainline Protestant group was in strong support, the Roman Catholic group did not object, Jewish students (largely liberal-reformed) approved, as did Hindu students and others, as I recall. All seemed well, until Muslim students were consulted. There stiff opposition arose. "If you want to affirm us," the college was informed, "don't put a symbol of Islam on the front of a Christian chapel and lay a few prayer rugs on the floor. It's a church. Let it be a church. For us, build a mosque." The plans began to unravel.

I was being called not, first, for an opinion about the plan, but for advice on how to deal with the uncomfortable particularity coming from Muslim students. Too bad they didn't have a college chaplain who was vested enough in the institution to be able to handle such awkwardness. For while the dominant narrative would tell us it is desirable to have Christian, Jewish,

Muslim, and other students of faith on campus, it is most desirable if they hold their beliefs with a bit of a wink. The wink says, without saying, that while they honor their culture and tradition and believe a certain secularized and pluralized version of their faith's claims, they would never take those claims too literally. Religious differences are rendered more aesthetic than substantive. But a witnessing Christian, or an orthodox Jew (or an anti-Zionist one?), or a Muslim who doesn't wink when saying that Allah is God—while tolerable, are not authorized. And so while accommodated in certain ways, such belief is to be gently reminded that it is, in fact, only tolerated. A chaplaincy might have helped the Muslims become less inclined to interrupt the party. I resisted that topic, however, and gave no advice but to compliment the Muslims for understanding their particularity and suggest that perhaps the college should, in fact, build that mosque. I might have supported the building of a dedicated space for Muslim prayer at Bates as well.

I don't believe multifaith universalism to be, in and of itself, a negative presence on campus. It is one particularity among others and deserves to be respected as such. I believe it becomes pernicious, however, when it does not take its purported universalism with the same wink it demands of others. It becomes its own fundamentalism, and tends to recruit chaplaincy into its service.

Consider interfaith chapel worship as another example. My fear is that by subtly normalizing Disney-World-like values, such worship can also contradict aspects of the very discourses it is meant to unify.[7] In my view, there may be no greater harm to living, thick traditions of belief and practice than theme-park dabbling—however noble the motives are for providing a variety of "spiritual experiences" to aesthetically interested and spiritually starving seekers. The leaders may have sophisticated theological foundations and approaches, but the participants rarely do. Participation may be more emotive and aesthetic and may not lead to theological substance. It may teach something quite different from responsive engagement and risk quietly authorizing the student who insists when questioned during his senior year that, well, he's now "into Buddhism," but whose strongest statement after visiting a monastery is, "too much orange." Now persons in thick, tradition-based worship may also participate out of emotive or aesthetic impulse, of course, but they also have places to take their impulses outside of the college as they continue to mature. This does not seem to be the case when interfaith or even homegrown ecumenical worship is the norm in a campus chapel.

By ecumenical worship I mean worship that strives to be generically Christian (or Jewish, or Buddhist, or the like) without identifying any particular traditional expression of the faith as its source and frame. In a

Christian expression, ecumenical worship begs a host of questions, as it is largely only liberal Protestant worship that can bear the weight of such posed inclusiveness without betraying one or another essential aspect of itself, such as the Mass, the altar call, a certain style of preaching, expressed gifts of the spirit, particularities of ordained leadership, lack of ordained leadership, an iconostasis, etc. If only liberal Protestant forms of worship can bear an ecumenical intent, then the worship is not, in fact, as ecumenical as it promises. It is ecumenical in reference to a prescribed set of liberal Protestant denominations. And so when advertising itself as ecumenical, it renders most of the church helpless. Worship that is intentionally interfaith, which seeks a similar inclusiveness across religious traditions of the world by borrowing and recontextualizing disparate liturgical actions, cannot even promise a minimal level of ecumenical inclusion. It does not in the end affirm the living and internally diverse traditions it seeks to include but instead builds a certain kind of firewall against them in the name of re-presenting them for interested investigators.

Even practices as seemingly benign as renting a chapel for weddings of couples not affiliated with the college has paradoxical effects as it symbolically undermines bonds of particularities. The limousines parked in front of the building and the photographers snapping photos speak loudly of the college privileging social civility over ecclesiality. One can marry in a religious space with no religious affiliation, and so imitate the thin view of religious ties characteristic of what the college authorizes for those it would school. At my college, for instance, where there were on average more weddings in the chapel in a given year than there were worship services, students tended to see more activity outside the chapel for weddings than they did for specifically religious activities. That may be fine according to the ecclesial rationale described earlier, in which the building was the sanctuary for the chapel that was the college. Yet free of that ethos, such continual activity around the chapel teaches, without stating explicitly, that the chapel, and hence the church, is not here, first, to serve Christ, whose name rests in the center of a world-framing narrative, but is here, first, to provide a public service (for a fee). Local clergy who made themselves available for such ceremonies (also for a fee) simply sealed the deal. And so some quarters of the church might ask whether with friends like chaplaincies they really need enemies.

Now one cannot discount the pragmatic concerns, or even pastoral exigencies, that shape chaplaincies in particular places—the renting of chapels for weddings of persons not affiliated with colleges being a small example. There may be overriding reasons to affirm certain apparently anti-ecclesial practices for the sake of preserving other pro-ecclesial possibilities. This may be especially so where neither the local religious culture nor the college or university administration will likely adopt a rhetoric of radical ecclesiology any time soon. Without accompanying practices, testimonies, and apologetics to make sense of church-affirming gestures, the meanings of such gestures can go as easily awry as the liberalizing symbols they're seeking to counteract.

Closing the doors of the chapel to the public may, in this case, not be so quickly interpretable as an affirmation of locality or communal faithfulness. It might not look like a recognition that Christian (churched) marriage out of context is oxymoronic. It may be sooner read as simple aloofness and indifference, even mean-spirited exclusion. In this case, as in so many others, so much more would need to be done to allow a more coherent set of practices to avoid, themselves, doing mischief. Nevertheless, I mean to illustrate the fact that as chaplaincies shape their programs out of pathos-directed pastoral inclination and value-centered institutional priorities, they are always teaching. They cannot but teach. And central to what they teach is ecclesiology—whether of a vague Christian sponsorship of compulsory universalism or of a freedom to embrace the aesthetics of church without the identity-shaping work that makes church church. We then graduate students who have absorbed a markedly minimalist ethic of religious identity without ever having to be directly taught it. A secularized university might want to do just that, but an ecclesially based one will not.

Contingency and Possibilities for Rethinking

During years of attending professional gatherings of college chaplains, I never heard a conversation about the hidden curriculum of our chaplaincies. Despite differences among how our offices and programs were configured, or our relative freedom of action, or our lingering church affiliation, or how much support we received from our employers, we shared a general consensus about the basic and unquestionable value of our work. We would discuss strategies for defending chaplaincies where they were under assault—by presenting ourselves as skilled mediators of "spirituality," or upholders of the "values" (not convictions or truth-claims) upon which our colleges are loosely based. We encouraged each other to organize student enthusiasm, provide individualized services like counseling or spiritual direction, direct ecumenical or interfaith worship when allowed, mediate relationships with religious organizations outside the college, manage the claims of outside groups to proselytize, advocate for minority religious groups against perceived Christian hegemony, and convene interreligious dialogue. We had practical discussions about how to increase our market share through innovative publicity, novel programming, or improved networking. We also complained about the generally retrograde states of our denominations. We reminded ourselves how important it was to correct the various theological or political deficiencies students brought with them from home. I joined in.

These conversations worked to the good in some ways, but, as noted above, they consistently missed many of what I am arguing are the essential matters put at stake by the very presence of a chaplain as an officer of the college or university. We failed to appreciate what we were teaching whether we intended to teach or not. And we equally failed to talk about what extraordinary opportunities most of us really had to demonstrate ecclesial commitment in intellectual pursuit, and to embody that demonstration in works of love and respect for others, and to underwrite those works to the point where they might shape ethos rather than simply chase pathos. And never, in my memory, did we discuss ways of responding to that student who understood herself totally free of faith, but who walked into any one of our offices on any afternoon saying, "Something happened to me last night. Pretty frightening. I think it was Jesus." We were simply, for whatever reason, too comfortable with our roles to question them at a deep level.

Now, again, in the face of the real contingencies most chaplaincies face, one might be more generous than skeptical regarding the good they do. For the fact remains that few colleges are prepared to unequivocally define their religious identity and move in either the administrative or academic directions that make such identity the psychological, political, and philosophical space in which they dwell (their ethos). Even fewer are likely to allow a chaplain to lead such a redefinition, given that chaplains are not normally hired for having such skills (though it might be good if they were). And given the intractability of liberal polity and its dominance in the culture of higher education (quite despite competing "right wing" or "left wing" pieties), there is little chance our colleges and universities will retrace the steps that positioned chaplaincies as they are. Moreover, the handful of colleges that retain a doctrinal understanding of their Christian identity and enforce that identity through such things as student discipline and faculty codes may not present the most desirable alternative. Their relative success, however, has largely been purchased by the practice, and in some cases the articulated doctrine, of ecclesiastical and academic separation—resisting association with persons or groups who would challenge or engage their dogma in even sympathetic debate. To the chagrin of many, there may be things an ideal ecclesially based institution may yet learn from places like Grove City College or even from universities like Oral Roberts or Bob Jones, but I would not advocate their model either in general or as a context in which to reimagine chaplaincy. The lack of practical models, therefore, makes prospects for rethinking all of this rather strained. Nevertheless, I want to imagine an ecclesially based university marking its dwelling place not according to the borders of enforced or presumptive belief, but according to an institutional ethos shaped through a set of rhetorical practices. This essay is rounded out by some ideas on how these rhetorical practices might relate to institutional chaplaincy.

▓ Rethinking Chaplaincy without Harm to the Church

My realistic qualification has not been fully addressed. For despite the demonstrably iatrogenic effects of official chaplaincy in some aspects, aren't we still better off having a designated clergyperson assigned the task of meeting certain needs presented on our campuses, especially if the likely alternative is leaving those needs unattended or wrongly attended? And aren't we better off doing what good we can in facilitating *some* form of ecumenical worship on campus and embodying at least the *idea* that the college still acknowledges a place for religion in the life of the mind, even if only pathetically? And shouldn't we take advantage of whatever welcome we can still find to demonstrate that persons of faith may yet organize for study and action?

Perhaps so, but an understandable "yes" to those questions need not rule out attempts to imagine steps toward reducing the iatrogenic costs. I want to imagine chaplaincy that continues to meet such needs and interests, but does so differently. This means taking an ironic stance and positioning chaplaincy in more than one place at once so as to help keep the dominant conversation about spirituality on campus going long enough and well enough to conspire against its presumptions. This means working both within the pathetic givens and toward new commonplaces—toward available nicks of difference or irregularly placed spots of possibilities that open up, and calm down, and widen the horizons in which our colleges move.[8] Here chaplaincies meet their pathos-driven demands while suing, or wooing, the institution to become more genuinely and nonviolently hospitable for shared testimonies to absolute realities. And it means doing this in service to Christ and the church on the wager that it is in such an environment that the Holy Spirit will most readily do her work.

The task may begin with the self-presentation of the chaplain, resisting with a studied honesty the easy, even lazy, interpretations of chaplaincy we inherit.

"Oh, you're the chaplain?"

"Yes, I guess I am."

"I know what you do. You take care of spirituality: the 'Zen of tennis' and all that."

"Well. No. That's not really what I do. I actually know very little about spirituality. I really don't even know what 'spirituality' is. But I am interested in religion, even the old-fashioned kind, with all its jewels and all its warts. And I'm especially fascinated with the kinds of things people believe absolutely, no questions asked, even you, even here. So what do you believe that way?"

Or to the chief administrator who asserts during your brief presentation on campus religious life: "You know, I don't mind religion on campus. I just don't like proselytizing. I've always assumed it was the chaplain's job to keep people from proselytizing, yes?"

"Well, perhaps, but to tell you the truth, I just don't see that as my job. I actually like proselytizing very much, even in the classroom. I tend to think that every syllabus is in some form or another a statement of faith, and even a kind of evangelizing. It's at least a platform. I am much more interested in *how* proselytizing happens than *if* it happens. You see, I actually *want* it to happen. You may disagree with me, of course, but I do think that proselytizing is part and parcel of lively discourse and open exchange. Are we fair to each other? Are we discreet enough to respect the settings in which we speak? Are we open to conversion even as we seek the conversion of others? Are we nonviolent in our speech and of integrity in our actions? That's what matters to chaplaincy. That is part of the kind of ethos I want to promote. Let the games begin! Does that help?"

With these staged conversations I am trying to imagine chaplaincy speaking into the college through an attention to ethos not as denominational affiliation or doctrinal frame but as a set of communication practices. How might chaplaincy effect a certain texture of discourse on a campus so that the full dynamism of Christian faith, free of the presumptions of compulsory liberalism, might be an ever-present, available, and winsome possibility for Christians and non-Christians alike—on both the campus and in the wider world? One way is to foster an environment in which alternative discourses are attended to in their thick particularities. This implies that where they are incommensurable, these discourses need not be subsumed within an imposed ideological pluralism. Their incommensurability may stand, with all the pain those differences may bring. Resolution may prove less significant to the Christian ethos of the college than clarified rules of engagement.

In other words, chaplains need be neither ideological managers nor rhetorical reconcilers. They need to be, in some measure, referees. But as referees they are also argument makers, sometimes helping groups make better arguments about convictions that the chaplain does not herself or himself share. Being this sort of referee requires three things: 1) institutional authority without power, 2) the skills to embody, and so model, theologically formed passion in ways that invite passion in others, and 3) a knack for silence.

First, authority without power. Organizationally, the kind of chaplaincy I am imagining will be both hidden, in the sense of being difficult to locate on an organizational chart, and ubiquitous, in the sense of finding "place" or welcome in any area of college life that affects the institution's mission. This means that the organizational independence of the chaplaincy remains important. Placing a chaplain under the supervision of a dean or vice president of student affairs, for example, invites the assumption that the chaplaincy is framed as a student-services office. Moreover, not having the chaplain a full part of the faculty, however small the assigned teaching load, invites another set of assumptions about the role of chaplaincy in relation to the core academic work of the college. And in association with this last point, there seems no need to assume that a chaplain will, by necessity, hold an academic appointment in either a religious studies department or a divinity school (if there is one). Such isolation, again, serves the hazards of professionalization. A chaplain should hold an academic appointment in whatever area of the university his or her academic training suggests—be that philosophy, political science, the natural sciences, communication studies, nursing, theology, religious studies, or elsewhere. This symbolizes the claim of faithful affirmation in all areas of intellectual life. Consequently, the old model of the chaplain as a fully invested member of the faculty and answerable directly to both president and ecclesial authority probably remains the best model for an ecclesially based university. So situated, the chaplain should poke her head in all over the place—with due discretion, of course!

The accountability an ordained chaplain holds to ecclesial authority outside the college is an important reminder to the ecclesially based college or university that its own authority is derived. Rather than finding it a necessary inconvenience to get a clergyperson as chaplain, the prudent move thus being to hire a chaplain from a denomination that makes few claims on its clergy, an ecclesially based college will embrace a chaplain's dual accountability and support it. The denomination might be fully consulted in the regular review of the chaplain's work. Service to the church outside the college might be accepted as qualifying academic work for the chaplain. As already happens on some campuses, a worshiping congregation in a chapel might affiliate in some appropriate way with a denomination or, perhaps even better, form partnerships with local congregations and then do the hard work of interpreting those partnerships. Related to this, I believe that regular ecclesial patterns of approval for sacraments, baptisms, weddings, and such should be honored in the work of the chapel, not to add burdens but to teach that the church counts and the college is not free of structures of obligation outside itself. I have experienced the pastoral difficulties of such affirmation, however, and have erred by being either too much the defender of principle or too little. These difficulties need to be engaged as essential to the ambiguities of the work, and mistakes must be confessed.

I also want to argue that chaplaincy in an ecclesially based institution should carefully resist staking its claim to attention by virtue of its role as a counselor, interpreter, or activist. Not that a good chaplain won't counsel, interpret, and organize, but I think chaplaincy loses it anarchic potential when it seeks to derive its authority from any of those three. This is terribly difficult for most of us chaplains. We are pastors, after all. And universities pretend to understand themselves as communities of interpretation, after all. And, after all, the critical spirit, available energy, and relative immunity from outside critique that is the college makes it such an easy place to organize for action. It is also the case that the vast majority of chaplains have an extraordinary amount of freedom in their work, possibly more than anyone on campus. The price we often pay for this freedom, of course, is marginalization. We then try to heal that marginalization through these activities. It would be a mistake, however, to think that such effort really heals this marginalization at all.

By extension, a chaplaincy that does not derive its status by analogy will also resist deriving it from the "crisis experiences" or "limit questions" of college life in which it will be regularly engaged. As noted earlier, these are the experiences about which other offices at least provisionally acknowledge their lack of competence—death, war, uncertainty, certain kinds of conflict or violence, meaninglessness. By taking one's stake as the answer-person in such limit situations, one unwittingly underscores the force of progress in liberalizing colleges whereby any office, at any time, can claim pride of place over one or another of a chaplaincy's functions as soon as that office can assert that it is more appropriate, more fit, or more resourceful than chaplaincy. It is finally self-defeating to let a chaplaincy be defined by what others cannot do. It forces a chaplain to chase ambulances, ferret out issues not yet claimed by others, or plead a place at one table or another after the table's been populated. It defines the chaplaincy according to needs rather than strengths or purposes.

Again, it must be stressed that my argument is not against compassionate counseling, astute interpretation, or the expression of both of these in conscientious activism. Nor is it against chaplaincies that are actively present to engage limit questions and limit experiences on campus and in the world. I would see all chaplains engaging their minds most fully and acting from their consciences with full heart and passion. My argument is with hanging one's chaplaincy in any measure on these, for fear that by doing so one is interpreting the significance of one's work on something other than the unique and potentially anarchic discourse of the church. We do this work freely, as an expression of our primary ecclesial identity and an act of responsibility and witness to the anarchic power of the gospel. We don't do it as a way of making or earning a place. We gently remind the institution of that fact whenever possible.

Second, toward a confessing chaplaincy. As an alternative view of authority, or "voice," in chaplaincy, I would follow my description of ethos as rhetorical dwelling place and argue for a "confessing chaplaincy." By this I mean a chaplaincy whose work and presence on a campus is textured by a rhythm of affirmation and assertion, attention and response, self-definition and welcome, so as to elicit affirmation and assertion, attention and response, self-definition and welcome from others, and by so doing to affect the quality of discourse that characterizes the college. This assumes that there is no all-inclusive perspective or rhetoric by which every religious need, every community, or every interest can somehow be represented in, or by, a chaplaincy. There are ways of negotiating differences so as to preserve the integrity of the differences negotiated and also preserve the freedom, and burden, of judgment. That way is not the way of always arguing. Nor is it the way of never arguing. I believe it to be a way of *tending* to arguments, including one's own.

Outside of the continuum of dogmatism (whether liberal or conservative) or relativism (whether playful or cynical), confessing chaplaincy in an ecclesially based university will seek a university life textured by moral engagement, exchange of passions, and mutual openness to conversion. It will encourage discourse textured by assertion, counterassertion, charitable listening, experimentation, affirmation and confession, disputation and discretion, questioning and truth-telling, provisional and sometimes lasting judgment. It will assume all of these within an ethos of faith in Christ and trust in the church, in all the complexities of both, as the confession toward which the various discourses of the college are in responsive relationship. For only by offering testimony, on behalf of the church *and* the college, can the chaplaincy model how the college would welcome confession and testimony as part and parcel of its discursive life. This modeling is significant for persons and communities of faith as well as those of little or no faith.

This image adds up to chaplaincy that is convinced of the prospect that all words, and all ideas, and all claims to truth are rhetorical, by which I mean contingent, rendered for and from positions of intent, imagination, urgency, hope, and experience. It also recognizes that such rendering can be systematically distorted, which is why it remains open to making judgment and continually describes rules of nonviolence. Confessing chaplaincy confesses these convictions as an essential part of its ministry.

In order to accomplish this, confessing chaplaincy will take the metaphorical courtroom to be the characteristic situation of Christian witness, with the one interpreting the faith sooner a witness giving testimony than a judge upholding community values, or, for that matter, a jury meting out verdicts, or an attorney advocating a case, or a defendant seeking release, or a plaintiff seeking redress. As the one giving testimony, the confessing chaplain is a witness to faith—as tradition, as practice, as a set of generative conflicts, as a chorus of testimonies. And as a witness, the chaplain respects the frame of the courtroom she or he did not create. She offers words only when welcome, and speaks of what she hears or sees as though the trial of knowledge, culture, church, and the educational enterprise might be swung one way or another. This witness lacks the power of advocacy dreamed by counselors or prosecutors, or of interpretive judgment dreamed by the jury, or of control dreamed by the activist judge. The authority the witness holds is the authority of response and responsibility enacted through the giving of an account. That is the authority of the confessing chaplain.

Third, a knack for silence. The confessing chaplaincy imagines the college as such a courtroom. This is how it shapes ethos. It sues for a court where conflicting absolutes can peaceably engage each other and so also include skepticism, questioning, and even studied indifference when patience and compassion require. It therefore takes less pleasure in first being correct than it does in first doing no harm. Even so, it desires to know and tell the truth. Consequently, it enjoys good arguments, but not for their own sake. It loves good arguments as space in which the Spirit of Christ might be revealed. It also honors silence, but not from fear. It honors silence for the virtue of discretion it promotes.

The discretion a confessing chaplaincy models is worth noting, for it is basic to the kind of careful hopefulness it can embody on the campus. This discretion shapes hospitality by not confusing ethos-shaping compassion with pathos-chasing empathy. It is the respect for differences that allows the chaplain to speak without needing, necessarily, to speak for everyone. It includes a striving for awareness of the positions from which people take part in the discourse and a willingness to gently remind people that they, too, might benefit by also becoming aware. It includes a sense of the limits of the university and a publicly articulated respect for discourses of moral formation and intellectual inquiry outside the university. This allows the possibility that things thought, and taught, outside the college can be as potentially worthy as things thought, and taught, within it.

As a related practical example, discretion might even suggest challenging the current nearly universally accepted notion that getting as many students out into the community doing "volunteer work" in "service" to the needy is an unequivocally good and pedagogically sound thing. It might not be, for such an effort might prove indiscreet. It risks reinforcing patterns of power and disabling, even humiliating, some of the very people it is meant to serve (including the student volunteers). Actively demonstrating the catholicity of the church, on the other hand, and facilitating ongoing opportunities for students to witness significant works of Christian discipleship, and contribute to those works only when they are both mature enough and able, may prove more discreet, and so possess greater ecclesial integrity than privileging extravagant reports of numbers doing community service. Against nearly every cultural code that would suggest that the chaplain should at least cheer if not actually coordinate service learning, perhaps it is the chaplain who should raise questions when service is celebrated uncritically and out of context. Perhaps it is the chaplain who should find ways of helping the college say to students, "No, you may not be ready. Listen for a while. Watch. Reflect. Even pray. Don't *do* quite yet."

Yet another expression of a confessing chaplain's knack for silences would be a studied sense of humor. This holds the potential of undermining much of the competitive ethos upon which universities and colleges are built. For humor that does not fall into sarcasm or cynicism requires a sense of open-ended possibilities coupled with impeccable timing. Such timing is developed only via a certain patience, an awe of silence, and a cultivated attention to curious irreconcilables. It is a way of seeing. And it is a way of knowing what *not* to say as much as what *to* say. This allows the other enough time to get the joke. Such a sense of humor serves nearly all the purposes laid out here by opening the college, whenever possible, to a reality and a story older than its own founding and larger than its own mission. A sense of humor can open a loophole or two.

Shaped confessionally and handled ably, a strong chaplaincy may prove essential to the ethos of an ecclesially based university. Shaped otherwise, it might be measured by standards inimical to ecclesial affirmation. If so measured, I believe it will be counterproductive. Yet with imagination, prayer, humor, and a willingness to risk, it surely *can* be shaped confessionally. With this good possibility in mind, the prospects for chaplaincy within an ecclesially based university are hopeful indeed.

Notes

1. This notion is heavily influenced by Ivan Illich and John McKnight. On "iatrogenesis" and "paradoxical counterproductivity," see Illich, *Medical Nemesis: The Expropriation of Health* (New York: Random House, 1976). Also see Illich, et al., *Disabling Professions* (New York: Marion Boyars, 1977), and John McKnight, *The Careless Society: Community and its Counterfeits* (New York: Basic Books, 1995). On "revenge effects," see Edward Tenner,

Why Things Bite Back: Technology and the Revenge of Unintended Consequences (New York: Knopf, 1996).

2. It should be noted that by using the term "liberalizing" rather than the simpler "liberal," I mean to acknowledge that no institution maintains a single discourse within it. The colleges and universities that retain chaplaincies are often currently or formerly church-related, and so retain echoes of previous discourses and hints of remaining possibilities. Conversely, even institutions with continuing denominational ties are often effectively secular in outlook and ethos, thus suggesting that they may be as much in a process of "liberalizing" as those that have formally severed their ties. I also use the term "liberalizing" rather than "secularizing" because secularization, meaning the creation of a public square free of specifically religious claims, is but one aspect of the liberal tradition.

3. For a helpful and pointed account of the history of the college, with emphasis on its ecclesial ties, see the dissertation by Bates's second chaplain, Richard Crocker, "Belief and Unbelief: a Pragmatic Pastoral Perspective," (Ph.D. diss., Vanderbilt University, 1988).

4. For this information and more on the founding of chaplaincies, see Seymour A. Smith, *The American College Chaplaincy* (New York: Association Press, 1954), pp. 10–45.

5. It was not uncommon for church-related colleges to hold weekday chapel convocations but studiously avoid Sunday services in order to encourage students to attend local congregations, thus recognizing that the college affirms, and is in fact bound to, communities of religious and moral formation outside its borders. Some colleges still do this today. Establishment of Sunday worship is another irony, appearing to be ecclesially affirming, but in action a paradoxically counterproductive effect of liberalization.

6. I take this pattern to follow in surprising accuracy the template of disestablishment laid out by George Marsden. See *The Soul of the American University: From Protestant Establishment to Established Nonbelief* (New York: Oxford University Press, 1994).

7. See David Lyon, *Jesus in Disneyland: Religion in Postmodern Times* (Cambridge: Polity Press, 2000), pp. 1–14.

8. The language of "nicks of difference, or irregularly placed spots" is loosely drawn from Edward Said, *After the Last Sky* (New York: Pantheon, 1986), p. 63.

V

The Witness of a Church-Related University within a Liberal Democratic Society

13

The Last of the Last: Theology in the Church

This paper is dedicated to the Archbishop of Canterbury, Rowan Williams

John Milbank

Should theology owe its prime allegiance to the academic community or to the church? Should it function primarily as a "public discourse" answerable to the critical norms and liberal values of free society in the West or should it articulate the faith of the church seeking understanding according to a logic indissociable from this faith?

Faced with such stark alternatives, many people are likely to propose a compromise. Recent philosophy, analytic and continental, has tended to conclude that the notion of a contextless reason, without presuppositions and affective practical commitments, is a fiction. Therefore, it is with and not contrary to reason to suggest that a well-established community and tradition may undertake to articulate its own implicit reasonings. If this reflection is not to be merely self-regarding, however, then it must also be subject to critical reflections coming from external sources, for example, the diagnosis of "ideologies." Yet this compromise piles up a double problem and compounds it with contradiction. One is still left with the question of an uncritical solipsism and of the fictional perspective from nowhere.

If the two are combined, then one is trying to believe at once that reason founds itself and that this is impossible.

At this point some theologians have had recourse to semi-Hegelian solutions, often inspired by Jurgen Habermas. Critique is imminent. One must begin with a tradition and assumptions, but gradually drive toward a universal logos through a negative process of unraveling contradictions in the first deposit. Yet this solution leaves us in no better plight. The idea that a tradition will edge toward the universal through the outworking of contradiction, or conversely that a foundation will finally emerge at the conclusion, is itself contradictory. Traditions unfold by acts of hermeneutic discrimination as well as by the overcoming of contradictions. Something subjective and feeling-imbued is just as involved in development as in inheritance, in continuation as in origin. And however long the process of formally objective logical negation, this cannot alter the positive status of the beginnings. One remains entirely inside a tradition. Conversely, if a logical process is still the only criterion for socially acceptable truth, then one is persisting with placeless, formal, and self-founded criteria for reason. One again has a compromise between two perhaps unsatisfactory positions that sustain the unsatisfactoriness of both and adds to this the unacceptability of downright incoherence.

Is it possible to do better than this? To overcome this impasse, we need to understand that Scripture, tradition, and reason were simply *not* seen as separate sources prior to 1300. Yet, first of all, should we want simply to *return* to this earlier perspective, or must we return with difference, given a certain validity to some of the newer post-1300 considerations? Second, how do we handle a situation in which there is a real secular sphere, as there was not in the Middle Ages? Can a certain earlier pre-1300 fluidity between faith and reason still help us out in our modern predicament?

Three headings—the supernatural, the *corpus mysticum*, and allegory—may help us understand the transformation of theology from the pre-1300 situation to the modern one. Through all these headings runs a fourth, which will not be explicitly considered on its own: this is participation. What is at issue under the first heading is theology between faith and reason; under the second, theology under ecclesial authority; under the third, theology between Scripture and tradition.

The Supernatural

It is a correct Catholic view, proclaimed since the time of the church under persecution, that truth should be freely pursued, since all knowledge points toward God. Coercion into understanding defeats its own object, since the divine truth freely shines out everywhere. There is no question, then, but that the church is on the side of free scientific enquiry.

Since at least the Counter-Reformation, however, the Catholic Church has tended to construe its support of science in terms of a duality of the realms of reason and faith. In the thought of Cardinal Cajetan, the Thomistic paradox of a natural desire for the supernatural, a desire that must be already the lure of grace, is lost.[1] Instead, Cajetan underwrites the late medieval and unthomistic espousal of a purely "natural beatitude" accessible by philosophy, according to which the latter is supposed to be able to attain by natural powers of intellect and will to some sort of positive knowledge and contemplation of the divine. By comparison, Aquinas had spoken of a philosophic reach to a negatively defined first cause. In other statements, though, he indicated that even this reach is inseparable from a divine drawing forth by grace that defines humanity as such.[2] Cajetan instead espoused in effect a "closed humanism" with its own transcendental reach that was essentially unrelated to the arrival of revelation. Since there was no longer any natural anticipation of grace, faith was now construed in very extrinsicist terms as assent to a series of revealed propositions. Gradually, revelation also lost its integration of inner experience with interpretation of outward sign and was bifurcated between one or the other.[3] The realm of grace now concerned external positive data superadded to the conclusions of reason, or else an ineffable realm of inner "mystical" experience, equally positive and equally subject to experimental testing for reality of "presence."[4]

Olivier Boulnois correctly radicalizes de Lubac's reading of Aquinas to show that the paradox of natural orientation to the supernatural in Aquinas is in fact in continuity with an entire cosmology and ontology that takes up themes from the Greco-Arabic legacy, even though it transforms them in terms of a much stronger grasp of the idea of divine creation.[5] Thus it is not simply that, as natural, we desire the supernatural. It is also that *intellect* as such, on the model of the angelic intellect that moves the celestial spheres, drawn in ceaseless perfect motion by the immovable, only exists in the space of this paradox. Indeed, while all finite motions are proper to specific natures, nature as a whole is only in motion because it is drawn beyond itself by higher powers towards a stilling of motion. The motion of human intellect is like a more intense and reflexive influx and concentration of natural motion as such, while the celestial spheres combine the inwardness of the intellect of the separate substances that move them with the totality of circulating finite motion. In this way, the natural human destiny toward the vision of God is only the outworking in a conscious, knowing, and willing created nature of the paradox of creation as such. Of itself it is nothing, and only exists by participation. Therefore everything, not just humanity, is already as itself more than itself, and this more is in some sense a portion of divinity. It is not that something more is added to the natural human soul—it is rather that the psychic is the conscious concentration of the paradoxical nature of every *ens* as such. Here, even though Aquinas rejects the Arabic doctrines of a single superhuman active intellect, he still nevertheless takes over their concern to attend to the phenomenology of thinking, which notes that we are never in charge of thought: thoughts occur to us, and so thinking is certainly something thinking in us, as well as something that we think.

The collapse of the paradox of the natural orientation to the supernatural was an aspect of the collapse of this entire cosmology and ontology. Aquinas had sought a cause for finite being, *esse commune,* as such. But in the later Middle Ages this was deemed a question that made little sense, since *esse* was no longer thought of as something superadded to essence. Thereby an arriving accident paradoxically was rendered more fundamental than the essential itself in the constitution of the creature.[6] Instead, one could now only ask for the final cause of finite being in its given finite circumstances. But something finite as existing—the dog in its existing dogness, rather than the why of there being a dog, for example—was now regarded as making full sense in its own finite terms. To know that a truth was from God was no longer held, as it was for Aquinas, to change the very character of the truth that was known. This new space of univocal existence, of sheer "thereness," quickly became as much thereness for mere entertained thought as for ontic reality. Ideas and fictions now started to acquire ontological equality with real being as all equally "things" constituted through their self-understanding.[7]

The new univocalist/representational space was the space that could be explored as the realm of pure nature. It extended beyond the finite. Indeed, as Boulnois points out, Duns Scotus found it contradictory that Aquinas had combined the view that the primary object of the human intellect is sensory with the view that every act of understanding is orientated toward the supernatural. Instead of Thomas's aporias and conundra, he substituted the view that the human intellect in its pure prelapsarian essence is naturally capable of the grasp of nonmaterial essences. This reach of our intellect is then the natural base for the reception of positive supernatural information.

The combination of a univocalist and representational conception of understanding—our intellect represents "things" which are simply there in their differential exemplifying of a bare "presence" outside participation—with the idea of a natural beatitude permitted theology to encourage the emergence of independent philosophy faculties in the early modern period. There were now professional philosophers. The only drastic way to achieve institutional control over such tendencies was to purge theology itself of an essential metaphysical detour through a vision of the participatory reflection of the divine essence in the cosmos, and to insist that it is rather a purely positive discourse founded upon the divine *potentia absoluta*. In this way there can be a final court of appeal against wayward reason, a court whose procedures are not so much guaranteed by partial illuminatory intuition and dialectical discursiveness, but rather by recourse to positive sources and to methods for discriminating among and ordering those sources.

What is important to grasp here is the (to us) counterintuitive link between a new autonomy for philosophy and yet at the same time an increased censoring (or aspiration to censor) of philosophy by theology. This, I think, remains crucial for understanding our situation even today. But as Jean-Yves Lacoste has well described, this had well-nigh ludicrous consequences. Granted autonomy to explore pure nature, philosophers quickly did not find what they were supposed to find—soon they were announcing materialisms, pantheisms, idealisms and so forth. A little later they were disconnecting natural beatitude from any contemplation of the divine whatsoever. This meant that the only "true" philosophy was mostly done with their left hand by theologians. Philosophy was supposed to be able to reach natural truth solely by reason; however, as faith knew that the higher truth of revelation overrides apparently sound reasoning, every philosophy conflicting with faith must be denied twice over: once on positive grounds of faith, secondly in terms of a better reasoning, which then had to be sought out.

Such convolutions surely have helped to bring Christianity into disrepute, yet they are entirely remote from the real outlook of the high Middle Ages. What is more, the "bad" philosophers of modernity have always been more truly theological than the "sound" ones. They refused to conclude to God from uninflected objective reason, and thereby have inadvertently, and in some measure, avoided idolatry.[8]

In the face of this situation, one natural reaction is a fideistic one. This reaction tells a story: once upon a time, it seemed as if the church could rely upon metaphysical cosmology; then it seemed as if it could rely upon a metaphysical ethics; but now it must learn to cling to the Cross alone—perhaps construing even this as the tragic presence of God in his secular absence. It is the story told by Bonhoeffer, and also the story told in large measure by von Balthasar, especially in *Love Alone: The Way of Revelation*.[9] My noting this must make it sound as if I favor a Barthian critique of von Balthasar, and a purely fideistic recourse. But such is not the case in any way.

The profundity of the fideistic grand narrative turns out to be only adolescent in character. What has been outgrown is not a natural childhood, but a noninnocent childhood of error which need never have happened—which is not *at all* to say that we should have remained forever in the culture of the twelfth and thirteenth centuries. No, it is an *unknown* future that we have missed and must seek to rejoin. Historical research done since the 1960s make it abundantly clear that the metaphysical cosmology of the high Middle Ages was thoroughly informed by, and transformed through, the biblical legacy. When this metaphysics was lost with the nominalists, it was not on the basis of a rediscovery of a biblical God of will, law, and covenant, et cetera, but rather as the consequence of a catastrophic invasion of the West by ultimately Islamic norms—norms which we now turn back upon Islam, imagining them to be the "other." The very condemnations of 1277 by the Archbishops of Paris and Canterbury, which swept away a cultural legacy shared with Islam (as with Judaism and Byzantium), also repeated within the West a gesture of Islamic orthodoxy: banish and regulate philosophy; impose instead a positivistic order based upon literal punctilear revelation underwritten by absolute sovereignty, which is now the only trace on earth of an inscrutable deity. Caliphization of the West; the Bible now read as if it were the Koran; Calvin's *asharia* looming up on the horizon.

The cosmos of participation was never argued against in some unanswerable fashion. There was simply an epistemic switch, complexly linked with social transformations, to representation and univocity. Certain tenets of natural philosophy may have been disproved, but even here one can exaggerate. Thomas Torrance has rightly pointed out how Robert Grosseteste's Christian/neoplatonic cosmology of light, with its Cantorian sets of nested differentiated infinites, was much nearer to modern physics than that of the later Middle Ages or of Newton.[10]

The point then is not at all that we must now cling to faith in ascetic nakedness. Instead we must pass beyond the still all-too-modern fideism of neo-orthodoxy, toward a radical orthodoxy that refuses the duality of reason over against faith. What has recently passed for reason is not, as far as the Catholic faith is concerned, the work of the logos at all, or only jaggedly and intermittently so. Recent reason itself shows this negatively to be the case, since the strict rigorous upshot of its objective, representing regard is to discover the rule of unreason beyond reason, the founding of sense in nonsense. Reason's domain is nihilism; whereas the discovery of a meaningful world governed by a logos can only be made by faith. This is perhaps the nearest one can get to an apologetic gesture, but it still does not decide the issue, ineluctably.[11]

What has passed for reason is, as Lacoste suggests, a mere decision to see that which is Prometheanly within our capacity as the key to our nature and the key to unlock the secrets of the world, or else the key to a knowable world limited to the truth that arises for our purposes. This, of course, has often been seen as a pious gesture: confine reason and nature within their limits, and thereby let the gratuity of grace all the more shine out upon us in its glory. Even in the case of Kant, a true reading shows that he is trying to protect a rarefied and antiliturgical pietist faith from contamination by limited images, much more than he is trying to protect reason from contamination by religion.

This worship of limits that constructs pure reason is only a *decision,* without reasons. As Lacoste has best explained, such a decision adopts a hermeneutic of the human essence and of nature that makes that which lies within perceived capacity fundamental. But supposing the human aspiration to, or even openness to, that which lies beyond its capacity were taken as the hermeneutic key instead? Lacoste here puts in a sharper light the insistence that many twentieth-century Christians—Charles Peguy supremely—place upon the virtue of hope. Reason oriented only to a beatitude supposedly within its grasp dispenses with hope, only to end up without hope, and at best resigned to this condition. Likewise, if such a reason is taken as hermeneutically decisive, it must downgrade the promptings, urgings, and longings of the body. The supernatural in us may be intelligence as such, intelligence thinking through us, but it is also always conjoined with sensation, as Aquinas taught. Therefore intelligence begins as a bodily exercise, accompanied by desire that reaches into the unknown. Only by the exercise of an artificial abstraction can we pry reason apart from desire, which reaches beyond our capacity. This pried-apart "pure reason" is also a totally individualistic reason, whether on the level of the single person or of collective humanity. For such a logos, I cannot be completed by the other, and so others cannot mediate to me the lure of a wholly Other who is also "not other" as *intimo interior meo,* according to the creationist logic of paradoxical priority of supplementation.

What *faith* proposes as *reason,* then, is taking as hermeneutic keys to reality first *hope,* and then *charity,* which is the erotic lure of the other and our giving ourselves over to the other.

How does such a perspective impact upon the task of theology today? Primarily, it absolutely forbids us to baptize the secular desert as the realm of pure reason, pure nature, natural law, or natural rights, and so forth. For this is not at all to acknowledge this sphere in its integrity. It is rather to define it in terms of an impoverished baroque theology—even though it still defines itself in this way, as if everyone were really a headless theologian. What we see is a postmodern simultaneity of remote times, places, and cultures. It cannot be dealt with in terms of a single Western liberal narrative of pure nature, because this will only issue in bombs and destruction of the other. And none of this complex confusion is exactly outside the church. The church reads it all in terms of multiple but converging narratives of typological anticipation, unrecognized scattering of the seeds sown by the incarnate Logos, and various fallings-away and partial survivals of Christian norms.

So the answer cannot be responsibility before a uniform liberal court. This court itself is a fiction, and one moreover whose dark inner secret is constituted by a voluntarist theology securing order through the formal regulation of chaos from a single sovereign center. Such a liberal option in theology in fact remains confined within a logic constructed by extrinsicism. It reveals its essentially authoritarian character when it stamps philosophical conclusions already arrived at with a theological seal of approval derived from doctrines that extrinsically symbolize supposedly universal truths.

But nor can the answer be a fideistic one. Revelation is not in any sense a layer added to reason. It arrives as the augmentation of illumination. Faith is found only in the highly complex and tortuous course of a reason that is hopeful and charitable. It is lodged in all the complex networks of human practices, and its boundaries are as messy as those of the church itself. De Lubac's paradox forbids us to privilege either a human above or a human below. Rather, what has real priority in his scheme is the supernatural, which so exceeds our human hierarchies that it includes every degree of them in equality and is as near to the below as to the above. Although the lure of the supernatural takes precedence over nature that is drawn toward it, this lure is only acknowledged by aspiring nature in all her lowly variety. Theological truth first of all abides in the body of the faithful—yet where are their bodies, especially today? Not neatly gathered in, that is for sure. Rather the faithful are disseminated outward into complex minglings and associations. A faith obedient to the church is protected from solipsism precisely at the point where one recognizes that the church always has been itself the taking up and intermingling of many human traditions. It even consists from the outset in seeing how the diverse might cohere, and continues to enact this analogical mingling.

Therefore I do not find the plural space of the academy, as perhaps *best* symbolized by religious studies departments, wherein alone *alternative* traditions of reason are sometimes recognized, to be totally other to the space of the church that is also pluralistic and also construes its truth. The difference is that the church has a project of integration, to which the theologian is bound. As a matter of personal biography, I have found it much easier to operate as an orthodox Christian theologian within this kind of department than in a traditional theology department, wherein Christian liberals always seem to bring to a high point of refinement the paradox of liberal intolerance and manipulation. Within both the academy and the church, the task of theology is to foreground the Christian difference and nondifference—to think through the Christian logos as something entirely exceptional that also continues and elevates what is most usual to humanity.

How, exactly, though, does theology relate to church authority? This is the question we must turn to next, under the heading *corpus mysticum*.

■ Corpus Mysticum

How are we to understand the nature of ecclesial authority and its bearing upon theology? Jean-Luc Marion has said in *Dieu Sans L'Etre* that the key is to realize that the bishop is the true theologian.[12] I think that he is precisely right, but that his point has usually been misunderstood, especially in the U.S.

Marion is invoking a vital link between theology and the Eucharist. The bishop is the original president at the Eucharist; he is also the prime preacher of the Word, a function that he performs only in conjunction with his representing of the body and blood of Christ. The idea that all theologians must subderive their authority as theologians from the bishop is only authoritarian under an erroneous understanding of the relationship of the bishop to the Eucharist, to the Word of God, and to his *cathedra,* which is at once his teaching office and also literally the place where he sits and presides, usually a city of long standing.

Such an erroneous understanding was already encouraged by shifts in the conception of the church and its relation to the Eucharist in the late medieval and early modern period. As de Lubac described these transformations, the term *corpus verum* ceased, roughly after the mid-twelfth century to be applied to the church, and was transferred to the body of Christ in the Eucharist. Inversely, the term *corpus mysticum* migrated from the Eucharist to the church.[13] Gradually, the latter was drained of physical solidity, which was transferred to the transubstantiated elements. "Mystical" slowly ceased to mean "to do with the liturgical mysteries of initiatory passage, participation and ascent" and came to denote secrecy, absence, and symbolism. A change in the relation of both bodies to the historical body of Christ accompanied this transformation. Earlier, the sacramental and ecclesial bodies stood near each other, and both re-presented the historical body. But in the new scheme, the historical and sacramental bodies start to stand near each other as alien sources of authority over against the church, which, as Michel de Certeau stresses in his brilliant commentary on de Lubac's *Corpus Mysticum* and *Exégèse Médiévale,* increasingly comes to be seen as an ideal space to be constructed in order to realize the dicta of authority, or else to make manifest a new inner "mystical" experience that is the residue of liturgical ascent that finds no place in a more legal and less liturgical construal of the public sphere.[14] As long as an essential relation between the three bodies remained, however, strong traces of the older view persisted—for example in the thought of Bonaventure or of Thomas Aquinas. It remained the case that the sacramental body mediated the historical body to the ecclesial body, the church. The Eucharist still "gave" the church, in such a fashion that, as Catherine Pickstock puts it, the church was not a closed self-governing entity like most political bodies, but rather received its very social embodiment from outside itself.[15] At every Eucharist, it had, as it were, to begin again, to receive itself anew from outside, from the past and from the angelic church above. Inversely, the transubstantiation of the bread and wine into the body and blood of Christ was seen as a dynamic action of divine self-giving inseparable from the bringing about and consolidating of the body of the faithful.

The really drastic change came when, as de Certeau following de Lubac stresses, the sacramental body ceased to operate this mediating function. Instead of three bodies, one had alternating dyads: a direct relation of either the absent historical body, as testified to by Scripture, to the church, or else of the sacramental body to the church, now taken as a source of authority *independent* of Scripture, deriving from a hierarchic transmission of ecclesial orders. As de Certeau concludes, this eventually brings about a total shift from a priority of the diachronic to a priority of the synchronic and functional. Previously, the past had really been made present again through the Eucharist. The church had reemerged through its sustaining of a bond to the past and projection forward to the future by reoffering of the sacraments and reinterpreting the *sacra scriptura*. Now, the past started to seem like a remote lost source of authority, which historical detective work must flesh out. As remote, the past stood apart from and over against the church, which no longer re-presented it. Its relationship to the other sacramental source of authority was bound now to be disputed, since the sacramental body was no longer seen as an essential way in which the lost historical body as traced out by the Scriptures was "performed" again in the present. Either sacraments as validated by tradition were seen as an essential supplement to the now remote Scriptures, as in the late medieval and Tridentine views, or else the need for this supplement was rejected, and one was left with the Protestant *sola scriptura*. But de Certeau's drastic conclusion here is both rigorous and undeniable: the crucial shift was certainly not the Reformation. Protestantism and Tridentine Catholicism represented two alternative versions of "reformation," which should be defined as the switch from the triadic to the dyadic account of the relation of the various bodies of Christ. It is this sort of realization that could be the ground for a more honest and self-critical ecumenism. Not to beat about the bush, it means that Protestants need to see that the Reformation was mostly a perpetuation of error, while Catholics need to see that much of what they have taken to be Catholic is not authentically so.

Under the new perspective, the power of clerical authority was necessarily increased. For when the historical body was again made present in the Eucharist, and the eucharistic body was only fully realized in the congregation, primary authority was both symbolic and collective, and initially bypassed vertical hierarchy. Only by a sort of reflex was episcopal authority constituted. The bishop was first of all powerful as identified with a particular *cathedra*, a specific intersection of time and place that recorded a particular Christian fulfillment of a particular local legacy. Thus nearly all churches were built on earlier sacred sites. This was not at all primarily a matter of propaganda, but of vital continuity. As president at the Eucharist and teacher from his chair, the bishop enacted once again the essence of a certain place and perpetuated the stream of glory refracted through it in a specific way. The bishop held authority, from Ignatius of Antioch onward, as symbolizing in his singleness the unity of the church in a single *civitas*. Of course the bishop was also the guardian and guarantor of correct transmission, and of course his exercise of these powers might often in reality overstep the mark of his representational and dramatic function. Nevertheless, it remained the case up until the mid-thirteenth century or so that clerical sacramental and preaching authority was much more mingled with lay participation than it later became—although at first in the later Middle Ages the laity defended itself with the increased activity of semi-independent lay fraternities.[16] But during this period the techniques of remote, secret, and invasive clerical control as deployed through auricular confession, exorcism, and staged miracles, first mooted in the twelfth century and promulgated through the Lateran Councils, were vastly extended. The "gothic" realm of complex overlapping spaces and social participations, started to give way to the "gothick" realm of systematic terror through *surveillance*.[17]

This increased clerical control was inseparable from loss of the economy of the three bodies. No longer was authority transmitted in a superhuman angelic fashion by the liturgical action. No longer did the historical body pass via the bishop into the mouths of communicants or (more often) the eyes of witnesses, who then performed what the liturgical script suggested. Instead, the historical and sacramental bodies were now more like inert objects in need of human subjective assistance. For the magisterial Reformation, the ordained clergy were the privileged interpreters of the Word, who quickly established orthodox parameters within which it could be read, so neutralizing its supposedly self-interpreting authority, as Catholic critics swiftly pointed out. For Tridentine Catholicism, the ordained hierarchy was the guarantee of a eucharistic miracle now seen as a spectacle quite apart from its dynamic action of "giving" the body of the church.

So we cannot possibly talk of an increased lay influence in Protestantism over against a Catholic clericalist reaction. Rather, in either case there is a substantial loss of medieval lay participation (as the British Catholic historians John Bossy, John Scarisbrick, and Eamon Duffy have all argued),[18] while in either case also there is a significant rise in compensating lay pieties and mysticisms that try to colonize the no-man's land that had now arisen in the gap between a closed humanism on the one hand, and an extrinsicist system of dogma on the other. As de Certeau argues, a mystic discourse arises with a redoubling of the sense of the absence of a true ecclesial body, although it is often itself recruited into the machinations of ecclesiastical discipline and the attempts to verify abstractions with experience and build a new future on the basis of formal method.

It would seem, then, that the earlier, high medieval model offers us a much better understanding of the relation of the bishop to teaching and so to theological reflection. Theology is answerable to the bishop as the occupant of the *cathedra* and as president at the Eucharist. But this means that the theologian is primarily answerable not so much to a church hierarchy in its synchronic spatiality—this is all too modern—but rather to a hierarchical, educative *manuductio* of the faith down the ages. Equally he is answerable to a specific locality or very often multiple specific localities, such that his sense of perpetuating a history must be combined with his sense of carrying out an archaeology and mapping a geography. Finally he is also answerable to the mode of the reception of sacrament and word by the congregation, even if now, in the early twenty-first century, this is often impossible and the theologian must exercise an excessively critical function by ideal standards.

Theology, therefore, is answerable to reason precisely insofar as it is answerable to the church. And in the latter domain it is first of all answerable to the Triune God, since theology is a participation in the mind of God before it is obedience to any authority, whether scriptural or hierarchical. But as such it is equally a participation in the whole deified church as the heavenly Jerusalem. The latter is only encountered through earthly mediation, and here theology is first answerable to the whole church militant, but this involves a certain answerability to the bishop in the way that we have seen.

◼ Scripture and Tradition

But in what way is theology also answerable to Scripture? Here, once again, we can only see clearly when we refuse post-1300 dualities. As we saw, Protestantism privileged the historical body of Christ; Trent the sacramental body. Equally, this meant a preference either for Scripture or tradition, respectively. But prior to Henry of Ghent, there had been no such juxtaposition. He for the first time asked which had priority, thereby revealing that something had already been altered.[19] Now it seemed that it was already the case that Scripture was a closed book in the past that needed supplementing by a separate oral command. Basil had spoken of written and unwritten traditions, but the latter were seen by him and by later theologians as consisting in the "performance" of the text itself. *Traditio* was the handing over of the text into practice. Thus Thomas Aquinas speaks of *sacra scriptura* as the sole authority for *sacra doctrina,* in a way that sounds Protestant by later Tridentine standards.

But Thomas was not speaking of the Protestant Bible. There was, as yet, no single bound printed book, but many manuscripts of different books of the Bible—usually surrounded by patristic commentary. Gregory the Great had said that when he read and commented on the Bible, the text itself expanded.[20] It was up to the commentator to go on trying to achieve the Bible as the infinite Borgesian library spoken of at the end of St. John's Gospel, as it was equally up to the painter and stager of miracle plays. Such a Novalis-like or Mallarmean perspective was also presupposed by the entire practice of allegorical exegesis. This rendered theology possible by showing how christological and ecclesial restoration of the world depended upon the assumption of a divine "rhetoric of things." Things referred to in the Old Testament were already redeemed, since they pointed forward allegorically to Christ. In the "time being" after Christ, we could be redeemed, because his deeds indicated and made possible our anagogic performances.

As de Certeau says, all this depended upon a sense that there were "essential" shared universal meanings between things. In consequence, nominalism ensured the collapse of allegory as the real divine rhetoric and so of the true inner basis of Christian theology. Without real intrinsic aesthetic connections, the ways of God in history became indecipherable. One was left instead with a series of positive institutions, only linked as logically possible manifestations of the divine absolute power. Logical reflection upon this situation was now divorced from ontology. The rhetorical dimension of Scripture and preaching was from henceforward somewhat confined to mere human words. The "treatise on sacred rhetoric" emerged within both a Reformation and a Counter-Reformation ambience.

It is nevertheless true that in various ways de Certeau exaggerates. He exaggerates the negativity of the "time being." The church is not just, as he says, a mystical substitute for the lost real Israel and living body of Christ. It also truly is in all its physicality and placement in *cathedrae* still exactly both these things. It only lost this positivity through the processes traced by de Lubac and de Certeau himself. Moreover, are we to perceive the work of the univocalist/nominalist Antichrist within the church only negatively? Without lapsing into Hegelian dialectic, one can acknowledge that catastrophe may help one to see more clearly. The nominalist critique exposes certain faults to view. In the face of nominalism and univocity, Nicholas of Cusa realized that both realism about universals and analogical participation requires one to see the limited scope of the law of identity. Ockham says with some truth that both a common essence would be in the same respect both particular and universal.

Likewise, he says that an analogous *essentia* would be in the same respect both shared and proper.[21] Nicholas also realized that universals are indeed constructed through language, but that fictionalized universals may still exhibit something that holds in reality, albeit in a more conjectural fashion than acknowledged hitherto. In this way Cusa opened out a new space for rhetoric and poetics and the human fabricatedness of history.[22] And in certain composers of sacred rhetorics, for example the work of the Lutheran Mathias Flaccius Illyricus, rhetoric is not reduced to ornament and propagandistic manipulation, nor is traditional fourfold exegesis totally abandoned. Instead one finds here a fusion of a human rhetoric which sustains a Longinian interest in the ways words can both reveal and enact through performance of the real, with a continued acknowledgement of the divine real rhetoric in allegory.[23] The anagogic here continues to "pro-duce" the past in the older sense of "lead forth," but this production includes now also a moment of the creative "production" of truth in words. Through a blending of Longinus with Augustine's rhetorical writings oft repeated by both Protestant and Catholic writers, the indwelling of the Spirit is re-thought in terms of a doctrine of poetic inspiration. The biblical writings themselves are considered by Flaccius Illyricus in terms of a human rhetorical construction as well as a divine allegory of the real. This was possible in terms of a Longinian perspective that saw the style with the most sublimely persuasive "coiled force" to be a brief, albeit figurative-style, full of *res* and a minimum of *verba*. Such a fusion of human and divine rhetoric carries right through to the Anglicans John Dennis and Robert Lowth in the seventeenth and eighteenth centuries, and thence to Hamann, and many in the nineteenth century, both Catholic and Protestant, influenced by him.[24]

All such people indicate how, in times of diminution, our task is not *only* to recover the pre-1300 vision, but also to acknowledge human consensus, cooperation, and varied free poetic power in a way this vision did not fully envisage. High medievalism needs to be supplemented by a Christian social-ism, conceived in the widest sense.

Theologians who may be the last of the last still have a task before them.

Notes

1. Henri de Lubac, *Surnatural* (Paris: Abier, 1946); *The Mystery of the Supernatural*, trans. Rosemary Sheed (London: Geoffrey Chapman, 1967). See also Jean-Ivres Lacoste, 'Le Desir et L'Inexigible: Préambules à une Lecture' in *Les Etudes Philosophiques*, no. 2 (1995): 223–246 and Olivier Boulnois, 'Les Deux Fin de L'Homme' in the same issue, pp. 205–22.

2. See John Milbank and Catherine Pickstock, *Truth in Aquinas* (London: Routledge, 2001), chapter 2: Truth and Vision, pp. 19–59.

3. See John Montag, SJ, "Revelation: The False Legacy of Suarez," in J. Milbank, C. Pickstock, and G. Ward, eds., *Radical Orthodoxy: A New Theology*, (London: Routledge, 1999), pp. 38–64.

4. See Michel de Certeau, *The Mystic Fable*, trans. Michael B. Smith (Chicago University Press, 1992).

5. Boulnois, "Deux Fin."

6 See Olivier Boulnois, *Être et Représentation: Une Généalogie de la Metaphysique Moderne à L'Époque de Duns Scot (xii–xiv siècle)* (Paris: Presses Universitaires France, 1999), pp. 463ff.

7. Boulnois, *Être et Représentation, passim.*

8. Michael Buckley, *At the Origen of Modern Atheism* (New Haven: Yale University Press, 1987); Jean-Luc Marion, *L'Idole et le Distance* (Paris: Grasset et Fasquelle, 1977).

9. Hans Urs von Balthasar, *Love Alone: the Way of Revelation*, ed. Alexander Dru (London: Sheed and Ward, 1977).

10. Thomas Torrance, "Creation and Science," in *The Ground and Grammar of Theology* (Charlottesville: University of Virginia Press, 1980), pp. 144-75; "The Theology of Light," in *Christian Theology and Scientific Culture* (New York: Oxford University Press, 1981). This is a decisive essay for the theology of the future. But one must, of course, unlike Torrance, admit fully Grosseteste's neoplatonism and escape his neoplatonism and escape his straining at the limits of Calvinism.

11. See John Milbank, "Knowledge: the Theological Critique of Philosophy in Jacobi and Hamann," in *Radical Orthodoxy*, pp. 21–38.

12. Jean-Luc Marion, *God without Being*, trans. Thomas A. Carlson (Chicago: University of Chicago Press, 1991), pp. 139–61.

13. Henri de Lubac, *Corpus Mysticum: L'Eucharistie et L'Eglise au Moyen Age* (Paris: Aubier-Montaigne, 1949). See also Catherine Pickstock, *After Writing: On the Liturgical Consummation of Philosophy* (Oxford: Blackwell, 1998), pp. 121–67.

14. De Certeau, *The Mystic Fable*, pp. 79–113.

15. Pickstock, pp. 158–66.

16. This is how I am inclined to interpret some of Eamon Duffy's evidence. It seems to me that Duffy takes less account than Bossy and Scarisbrick of a late medieval decadence itself inaugurating tendencies that early modernity will intensify, because he wishes mainly to argue that Catholicism was in good shape upon the eve of the Reformation. In this respect, his position is less complex than that of the two other writers. See Eamon Duffy, *The Stripping of the Altars: Traditional Religion in England 1400–1580* (New Haven: Yale University Press, 1992); John Bossy, *Christianity in the West 1400–1700* (Oxford: Oxford University Press, 1985); J. J. Scarisbrick, *The Reformation and the English People* (Oxford: Blackwell, 1984).

17. It is no accident that one of the great "gothick" novels of the eighteenth century, the Irish Protestant Charles Maturin's *Melmoth the Wanderer*, deploys a critique of the Spanish Inquisition also as a critique of Calvinist predestinationism and of modernity as such. I am indebted to discussions with Alison Milbank about this topic.

18. For a summary and synthesis of their views, see Catherine Pickstock, *After Writing.*

19. I am indebted here to the unpublished work of Peter Candler, of Duke University.

20. See de Certeau, *The Mystic Fable*, p. 222, citing the work of Pier Cesari Bori on Gregory the Great's reading of Ezekiel's vision.

21. William of Ockham, *Quodlibetal Questions* 5.12 and 14. Cusa's interest in human participation in divine creative power can be related to Scotus and Ockham. Given univocity they tend to say, unlike Aquinas, that creatures can fully bring about being. Hence Ockham says that human beings in a sense create (QQ 2.9). Nicholas says this too, but he restores the bringing about of being in a finite thing to the context of participation and mediation that still sees being as really the effect of God alone. However, he still talks explicitly of human creation in a way Aquinas and Bonaventure did not.

22. Alain de Libera, *Introduction à la Mysticque Rhenane* (Paris: Presses Universitaires France, 1984).

23. See Debora Shuger, *Sacred Rhetoric: The Christian Grand Style in the English Renaissance* (Princeton, N.J.: Princeton University Press, 1988), pp. 73–6 *passim.*

24. See John Milbank, "Pleonasm, Speech and Writing," in *The Word Made Strange* (Oxford: Blackwell, 1997), pp. 55–84.

14

Assessing What Doesn't Exist

Reflections on the Impact of an Ecclesially Based University

Michael L. Budde

The preceding chapters stand as contributions to a thought experiment aimed at stimulating innovation and imagination concerning higher education and the Christian churches. While a few contributors used this as an opportunity to reflect on ways to reform existing Christian educational institutions, most took up the invitation to outline afresh what an ecclesially based institution of higher education could be, both in general and with respect to the specifics of their assignment (e.g., various academic disciplines and curricular concerns, student life, university chaplaincy).

This chapter focuses primarily on the attempt to envision a new sort of institution. Whether and how one might construct a new sort of ecclesially based college or university (called an EBU here as an umbrella term) will be affected by the anticipated political, economic, and social impact such an innovation might reasonably make. Certainly the contributors to this volume share a conviction that the measure of an EBU will depend on no small measure on its interactions with other communities, constituencies, and actors.

Being able to assess the future impact or witness of an ecclesially based university—an entity that does not exist, and whose particulars remain undefined—inoculates one against both success and failure. There is no way to be right, and no culpability in being wrong. Still, it remains necessary to stipulate for the sake of discussion some of the traits such a new institution would likely embody if it be worth constructing in the first place; these I derive largely from the reflections of my fellow contributors to this volume as well as from my sense of the essentials that such a new institution ought to incorporate. I make no claim that my fellow contributors would agree wholeheartedly with the picture I assemble from their specific sections; different assumptions would likely generate a different assessment of future impacts.

The heart of an EBU, it seems to me, rests in the commitment of its students, faculty, and staff to a transformative vision of the ends or purposes of education. That is, the point of higher education is not credentialing, not job training, not turning out a "well-rounded person," not the development of the participant's human capital. The purpose of ecclesially based higher education is to make participants more fully into disciples shaped by the priorities and practices of Jesus Christ; to help them discern their vocation as members of the transnational body of Christ; and to contribute to the mission of the church—to help the church serve more fully and faithfully as a foretaste of the promised kingdom of God, on earth as it is in heaven.

One of the problems all of us encounter, I suspect, in trying to imagine a new sort of church-centered higher education is the degree to which we are bound by the straitjacket of received assumptions about what higher education is or should be. These run deeper than most of us can admit or discern. Too often we think we know what a college or university is—with the usual range of departments, majors, programs, services, and students—and that the object of the exercise is in trying to establish a Christian knock-off of the same. Much of value can be developed in such a fashion, but such approaches remain a prisoner of received notions that oblige would-be innovators to replicate the institutional wherewithal of "good" colleges and universities as defined by non-Christian norms, structures, and ends.

In this volume, Robert Brimlow's chapter engages this dilemma most directly. Does one have to have professional schools—in law, business, social work—in order to be a "real" university? By answering no to the question, Brimlow forces us to contemplate the prospect of constructing a new sort of educational environment that may or may not pass muster as a "real" university or college—that we will abjure one or more areas of instruction or inquiry as being incompatible with our notion of training for discipleship, or as being a lesser priority than other areas of teaching and research. For persons schooled in the dominant historical narrative of

Catholic higher education in the U.S.—given forceful expression by John Tracy Ellis in the 1950s—such a move looks like a return to what Ellis condemned as second-class educational institutions, a tendency Catholic administrators have tried to overcome for nearly fifty years by imitating élite secular colleges and universities.

Similarly, in our discussions about the natural sciences and an ecclesially centered university, Therese Lysaught expressed doubt that such fields could be taught without the considerable investment of money and personnel required to establish laboratories, provide continually updated equipment, and apprentice students in the labor-intensive ways typical of science education in nearly all American universities. The role of the natural sciences in many schools can best be described as imperialistic, at least regarding their structuring of student educational processes (a point made also by Jonathan Wilson in his contribution). At my institution, for example, science majors are required to begin their major and allied-field courses as soon as possible, with most of the university's liberal studies core curriculum—presumably intended to provide students with opportunities for exploration, values formation, and a humanistic foundation prior to the rest of their educational experience—put off until the last year or two of a student's undergraduate course. The message is clear: the formative discipline of the disciplines—biology, chemistry, physics, and the rest—is more important than the would-be formative encounters with the humanities and social sciences. The latter are written off as irrelevant to the training of junior scientists, as an annoyance that can be put off without injury until one's later years.

Whether one could reduce the hegemony of the natural sciences in an institution of church-centered higher education remains an open question. Whether an ecclesially based university should offer a natural sciences curriculum at all is a more uncomfortable one (one could always subcontract science curricula via an arrangement with another institution). Given the cost of required facilities (especially for the long hours of laboratory apprenticeship required by professional accrediting agencies) and related expenses, a science curriculum just like the "real schools'" might be a millstone around the neck of a fledgling ecclesially based university, devouring all its resources and starving curricular and communal endeavors more important—or at least requiring priority of place—for the distinctive purposes of such a new institution.

Questions such as these point to the so-very-preliminary nature of the kinds of relationships this book explores. Still, they do point to the inevitable conflicts and strains that will attend to any experimental efforts to move beyond the existing sorts of Christian colleges and universities in search of educational and formative processes oriented toward discipleship and the church rather than toward career and the requisites of liberal democracy.

To say that an ecclesially based university is concerned primarily with forming its students, faculty, and staff in determinate directions invites conflict with the dominant assumptions regarding education and formation in the U.S. A new sort of educational institution that defies these assumptions invites ridicule, opposition, and condemnation from the guardians of the status quo. Grasping these assumptions requires one to distinguish the functions of childhood and adolescent education (from preschool through high school) from those attached to postsecondary schooling. While there are broad areas of continuity between them, some notions of education-as-formation are more germane to one level than the other.

■ Elementary and Secondary Schools and Patriotic Formation

Trying to anticipate the social and political impact of one or more ecclesially based universities requires one to acknowledge that most people's ideas about the purposes of education distinguish imperfectly, if at all, between K–12 and higher education. Many of the most important cultural notions about the proper role of education in a liberal democracy are formed more deeply, I suggest, by understandings and ideas associated with preschool, primary, and secondary schools. The programs and graduates of an ecclesially based university will be received in largely such a context; that context must be explored in order to gauge the likely public response to an ecclesially based university that puts Christian formation at the heart of its mission and operations.

While there are many potentially interesting points of interaction between an EBU and norms of proper schooling typical of the U.S. and other advanced industrial countries, I want to focus on a few that highlight what elsewhere I have called "the contested politics of formation."[1]

The use of compulsory mass education to diminish and dilute the integrity of particularistic communities like the church has been a constant of the modern state for so long that few notice it anymore. Under the rubric of individual freedom (of impressionable children indoctrinated by parents and churches), personal autonomy, and progress, child and adolescent education has functioned to undercut those religious loyalties, practices, and affections it could not co-opt, transform, or subordinate.

Among the formative objectives of state education is the development of patriotic citizens. As noted by historian Cecelia O'Leary:

Rituals of patriotism were first institutionalized in the United States between the Civil War and World War I . . . In fact, many of the patriotic symbols and rituals that we now take for granted or think of as timeless emerged not from a harmonious, national consensus, but out of fiercely contested debates, even over the wording of the Pledge. Confronted by the dilemma that Americans are made, not born, educators and organizations, such as the Grand Army of the Republic, Women's Relief Corps, and Daughters of the American Republic, campaigned to transform schools, in George Balch's words, into a "mighty engine for the inculcation of patriotism."[2]

In the U.S., school-based practices of civic formation have become increasingly systematized and standardized over the past century—from the creation of ninth- and twelfth-grade civics courses nationwide after a 1916 initiative of the National Education Association, to a pair of influential programs in the mid-1990s aimed at suffusing the entire curriculum from grades K–12 with cross-disciplinary exercises in patriotism and civic engagement. Across the many changes in American society and politics, the assumption has remained strong that

> for democracy to survive, it requires the education of each generation to the ways of knowledge and active participation in the preservation of a way of life. These are not innate behaviors, they are learned. Thus the role of the school becomes paramount in preserving the Republic.[3]

For persons committed to the primacy of the state in matters of allegiance and ideology, school-centered civic formation has always fallen short of the needs of the Republic. In our day, increased ethnic and cultural diversity stands as the most recent threat to American nationalism, and once again mainstream policymakers and pundits have turned to schooling as the place to inculcate a proper measure of national allegiance. The perceived need to cultivate a sense of national unity across the divisions of American society—racial, economic, ethnic, regional, and more—in our day plays itself out against a backdrop of open-ended military mobilization and propaganda fighting a global war against "terrorism." Contemporary approaches to schools and patriotic formation aim to combine a privileging of national identity over all others with a compulsory norm of tolerance and generic public discourse imposed on students and parents alike—a regime that corrodes the capacity of any particularistic communities and loyalties to sustain an alternative to the American way of life. Liberals and conservative alike agree that

> states have the authority to see that children are educated in a way that prepares them for citizenship so as to assure the stability of the constitutional scheme of government.[4]

More significantly, a movement of liberal educators and scholars concerned with the divisiveness of nonliberal religious, ethnic, and familial groups now advocate for

> a belief in the conception of core liberal values, and the use of the coercive power of the state to enforce these values throughout the schools. Deliberative democrats [one name for such advocates] deny, in other words, that parents and children have a right to avoid instruction in their version of core liberal values.[5]

Some forms of compulsory liberal formation (an oxymoron with a surprisingly long pedigree) may run afoul of First Amendment problems; the U.S. Supreme Court has prohibited forcing individuals to salute the flag in public schools, although it upholds the right of states and school districts to require that teachers begin each day with the Pledge of Allegiance or some similar patriotic exercise. Many other types of patriotic indoctrination, however, have already passed constitutional muster. As Tyll Van Geel observes, the U.S. Supreme Court has no objections to

> a history course designed to promote patriotism. . . . by teaching only history that would tend to inspire patriotism. As long as naked compulsion is not used, government schools may seek to invade the sphere of intellect and spirit.[6]

Whether or not "deliberative democrats" like Eamon Callan, Amy Guttman, and John Rawls are able to revitalize state efforts to instill a "liberal patriotism" of autonomy, critical reason, and reciprocal justice—even if such has to be done via coercive state action—their work has more continuity than discontinuity with the long-term use of schools by the government in the U.S.. Indeed, even without the robust sort of compulsory curriculum in individualism and social conformity such liberal patriots seek, it remains true that nearly all children and adolescents in advanced industrial countries are already the objects of programs aimed to socialize them into a powerful set of political assumptions, affections, and practices.

The American context is one in which the formative processes of schools benefit from the interaction of market imperatives and government policy— even when the government entity in question cannot claim to represent the entire country even in the largely fictive sense common in national civics and political discourse. Consider the national impact of the Texas State Board of Education, the agency charged with approving textbooks used by school districts across the state. With Texas state law requiring that textbooks promote democracy, patriotism, and the free enterprise system, the Texas board routinely rejects books it deems antitechnology, insufficiently patriotic, or anti-Christian—while approving environmental science books financed by the petrochemical industry, for example. The board is now routinely lobbied by a range of right-wing watchdog organizations concerned with patriotic and capitalistic values, and the board has entered into cooperative arrangements with some of these organizations.

Given its status as the second-largest school textbook market in the United States (second only to California), the Texas process affects textbook publishing for the rest of the nation. With nearly ten percent of the national textbook market under the control of the Texas board, publishers now seek prepublication feedback from the Texas officials and conservative advocacy groups. Doing so allows publishers to avoid problems that might translate into millions of dollars in lost sales; the economics of textbook publishing preclude most firms from customizing a volume just for the Texas market, so the patriotic norms of Texas, and the self-censorship it engenders, shape much of the educational process across the country in matters of patriotic formation and indoctrination.

Higher Education and Civic Formation

There are two primary narratives situating colleges and universities in the dynamics of citizen formation and patriotism in the United States. The conservative story is of reclaiming higher education from persons and movements inimical to patriotic faith—from campus activism of the 1960s through the so-called culture wars of the 1990s, higher education has been destructive of the handiwork of patriotic formation and love of country.

The liberal variant, while it decries the campus-as-subversive argument as exaggerated, sounds its own alarm bells. The liberal assessment looks to higher education as the remedy for rising political apathy, nonparticipation, and the rise of "bowling alone"—Robert Putnam's phrase describing the decline in civic association in favor of individualistic pursuits.[7]

However they differ, both conservative and liberal renderings of higher education and civic formation occur under the umbrella of the corporate transformation of higher education. This manifests itself variously—via the enhanced role of corporations in university research and funding, the dominance of management ideologies that see students as consumers and schools as vendors, and the elevation of career enhancement and credentialing for the job market as the primary purpose of higher education. Some scholars refer to the rise to dominance of "academic capitalism," in which professors are being increasingly "disciplined by supply-side higher education focused on economic competitiveness."[8]

The commercialization of higher education shapes various expectations and strategies concerning the college or university as a site for civic formation. Conservative advocates elevate the "student (and parent) as consumer" role in order to demand an educational experience supportive of patriotism, nationalism, and capitalism (rather than hostile to them). Liberal activists look to higher education as a site to encourage political commitment and civic engagement. One of the latter's favorite initiatives, "service-learning" programs, stand as an important aid in enhancing American democracy,[9] while perhaps providing students with another experience of value on the job market subsequently. Liberal strategies of patriotic formation often attempt to avoid what they perceive as the embarrassing language of conservative nationalism, but their objectives often seem like a more genteel form of the same—the secular public realm is the primary focus of allegiance and participation, with the good of the body politic the aim to be advanced and enhanced.

Depending on the time frame in question, one or another version of these accounts have been more significant. What has remained constant across eras of change in American history is the degree to which scholarly inquiry and teaching have been surveilled by public and private enforcers of patriotism and the established order. With the McCarthy-era blacklisting and purge of higher education nearly fifty years behind us (see for example Chomsky et al., 1997),[10] it is easy to overlook the powerful but presently submerged pressures on educational institutions to produce loyal functionaries and ideologies committed to national power and prestige.

Events after September 11, 2001, have helped surface some of the disciplinary mechanisms that subordinate higher education to purposes of patriotic formation and support for capitalism. While the most visible of such mechanisms are often among the less important, nonetheless they help illuminate some politically significant scenarios facing an EBU in the future.

Directing its attention to primary and secondary schools, the Bush administration in October 2002 implemented a number of directives "aimed at prescribing patriotism among the nation's 52 million schoolchildren."[11] These included recommended programs of mass recitation of the Pledge of Allegiance, the use of military veterans to teach "Lessons for Liberty," and similar measures. The state of Nebraska revived a fifty-two-year-old law requiring schools to create curricula to promote "a love of liberty, justice, democracy and America . . . in the hearts and minds of the youth."[12]

As for higher education, a conservative organization known as the American Council of Trustees and Alumni issued a report in November 2001[13] condemning American colleges and universities for insufficient patriotism and support for the U.S. military campaign in Afghanistan and elsewhere. Among the sins it cataloged were reports of professors that "invoked tolerance and diversity as antidotes to evil." Even worse, according to the report, "the message of much of academe was clear: BLAME AMERICA FIRST."

At the root of such a moral failure, according to the organization, is a "pervasive moral relativism [which is] a staple of academic life in this country and an apparent symptom of an educational system that has increasingly suggested that Western civilization is the primary source of the world's ills." The cure for such an atmosphere, "increasingly unfriendly to the free exchange of ideas," is the recommendation of the group's founding chair, Lynne Cheney: to teach students at all levels "the ideas and ideals on which our nation has been built. . . . If there were one aspect of schooling from kindergarten through college to which I would give added emphasis today, it would be American history." The ideological vetting of American history practiced in a decentralized fashion by the Texas Board of Education would become more systematic and universal if Cheney's recommendations are adopted.

The anti-American and antipatriotic specifics cited by this conservative group would be laughable in another time and place. They include signs at campus events such as: "Hate breeds hate" (University of Maryland); "An eye for an eye makes the world blind" (University of North Carolina); the decision at the University of North Carolina to sponsor a talk by the grandson of Mohandas Gandhi; and a Stanford University professor quoted as saying that "If Osama bin Laden is confirmed to be behind the attacks, the United States should bring him before an international tribunal on charges of crimes against humanity."

In our time and place, however, matters are not so funny. One national columnist decries pacifism as "inescapably, and profoundly, immoral . . . . pacifism is on the side of the murderers."[14] Another calls for "a unified, unifying, Pearl Harbor sort of purple fury," in which America relearns the virtues of hatred.[15] Still more direct is conservative columnist Ann Coulter, whose advice is that "we should invade their countries, kill their leaders, and convert them to Christianity."[16]

■ Ecclesially Based Universities and Contested Formation

One can imagine the reactions outside opinion leaders will have to an ecclesially based university in which pacifism is a constitutive aspect of Christian discipleship. While such a university might not be branded as a "terrorist training camp" (assuming the university lacked a physical education program or an accomplished football team), it would likely be branded a center of subversion and treason during times of war and aggression. The ability of an EBU to withstand the calumny and pressures brought to bear by persons and groups offended by Christian nonviolence and insufficient nationalist zeal would be tested on a regular basis over the years.

Were an EBU to become established and viable, it would clash with both conservative and liberal projects of formation via higher education. The former would see the pacifism of the EBU as tantamount to treason during times of permanent war like our own. By not endorsing and extending the sort of patriotic formation expected of primary and secondary schools, an EBU would be seen as destructive of years of prior social investment. Not only would nationalist ideologues inveigh against such a school for being a corrosive force in social life, they would likely aim to denigrate its standing as a Christian institution—after generations of Christianity loyally subservient to state and market, the notion of a potentially "disloyal" church could not help but incite outrage and reaction in the precincts of Christianity.

Liberal enthusiasts for higher education as producers of civic engagement and participation would be similarly offended by the 'sectarian' nature of an EBU. By operating on the assumption that membership in the body of Christ (rather than the nation, the community, or even the global community) is the primary allegiance and starting point for Christians, an EBU strikes at the heart of liberal civic formation via higher education. Not only does the existence of an EBU question the legitimacy of civic upbuilding as an unambiguous goal, it also confronts the pretensions of liberal ideology with its own narrowness and sectarianism—the church, after all, is a larger community worldwide than any nation, state, or people.

Similarly offensive to educational nationalists inside and outside of governmental structures would be the transnationalist orientation of an EBU. With the worldwide body of Christ, and the local churches that comprise it, as the primary point of reference and identification for an EBU, one could expect an ecumenical variant on a time-tested anti-Catholic charge: insufficient loyalty to the American state (where Catholics were thought to be subservient to the Vatican state, an EBU might be seen as part of a cosmopolitan, anti-American orientation and movement). Such a fifth column might invite investigation and surveillance during peacetime, and more vigorous suppression, through a variety of mechanisms, during times of national emergency. Whether and how this sort of university would choose to comply with recent laws like those intended to force universities to serve as arms of the Immigration and Naturalization Service concerning the visa status of international students would remain to be seen. While such a scenario might have seemed far-fetched before September 11, it seems less paranoid as one contemplates the future prospects of an institution committed to pacifism and transnational ecclesial solidarity.

■ Economics: Choices and Questions

Who would pay for such an institution? How would it finance itself? The ability of an EBU to be something better than the forms of Christian higher education now on offer will depend in no small measure on how it manages the difficult matter of money.

Federal and state funds play an important role in most existing church-affiliated colleges and universities in the U.S. (and are even more important in many other countries). From construction grants to research support and student financial aid, government funding is thoroughly embedded in the business model of nearly all Christian colleges and universities. Even for schools that have distanced themselves from most forms of institutional support from tax sources, public money provides the major source of financial aid transferred directly to students (Pell Grants, subsidized federal loan programs, etc.). Schools completely free of public funding, including direct assistance to students, are rare—Grove City College in Pennsylvania is the best-known of a mostly obscure lot.

Were an ecclesially based university to entertain the prospects of public financing or student assistance, it could expect to enter a tangle of regulatory and reporting requirements, First Amendment issues and pressures, and the prospect of litigation at regular intervals. The present judicial climate is one in which religiously affiliated colleges and universities may receive public funds so long as such institutions do not practice "indoctrination," and are not "pervasively sectarian." The court cases establishing these criteria leave such terms vaguely defined and open to multiple interpretations. While we are now under a more open and "accommodationist" period of constitutional interpretation regarding the Establishment Clause, such a climate can change rapidly as judicial appointments reconfigure the federal judiciary (the anticipated retirement of William Rehnquist from the Supreme Court may in itself be enough to inaugurate a more constricted notion of "pervasively sectarian" practices and institutions).

Hence, part of the political and social impact of an ecclesially based university will depend on whether such an institution pursues federal support—even if only at the level of student financial aid. Such decisions, in turn, depend upon the sorts of relations—institutional and financial—between an EBU and congregations, church agencies, and individual Christian donors. Whether even an EBU can completely bypass involvement with state financing depends on the degree to which the churches support this new sort of educational venture, and whether such an institution can self-provision in nontrivial ways (e.g., some small colleges rely upon student labor for much of the upkeep and maintenance of their physical plant). Given an

EBU's interest in formation and transnational ecclesial solidarity, it would likely fail some or all tests of the "pervasively sectarian" standard—and its opponents would probably press challenges to any EBU that might seek state support of any sort. Unless one is willing to abandon the distinctive features of an EBU, government funding ought not figure into assessments of institutional support.

As mentioned previously, the existence of an EBU presupposes mutually enriching relations with at least some Christian congregations, groups, donors, or constituencies. The economic impact and significance of an EBU will be determined by how questions like the following are answered:

- Will the instrumentalist and cost-benefit assumptions about higher education held by most parents, students, and employers shape an EBU? How can churches help congregations to interrogate their own assumptions about the purposes of education—citizenship training, job and career credentialing, social advancement, etc.?

- Will graduates from an EBU find opportunities to use and develop their convictions and abilities in church-centered activities after graduation? How will secular employers view graduates of an EBU? How heavy a debt load will EBU graduates carry into their postgraduation years (should the institution commit to student support sufficient to ensure debt-free graduates)?

- How do economic pressures and assumptions shift if one serves traditional-age college students (ages eighteen to twenty-four), compared to concentrating on older adult learners? If one focuses on the latter, does an EBU function like a graduate school for the church universal, as a purveyor of enrichment courses and experiences, or in some other capacity?

- Might an EBU encourage experiments in ecclesially centered economic practices, analogous to the economic functions of state land grant institutions established by the Morrill Act of 1862? Possibilities might include experiments in producer and consumer co-ops based in congregations and networks of Christians; they might also include variants on business incubators for and from church communities and priorities (e.g. providing decommodified access to basic needs, meaningful work, ecclesially common goods and services). Can an EBU become an economic producer in its own right, either as a producer of some of its own subsistence or as a producer supplying necessities for congregations and nonecclesial purchasers?

- Given the economics of an EBU, does such an enterprise require a new sort of religious order to run and staff it? Such an organization might be ecumenically catholic like Taize; an integration of faith, formation, learning, and service with the poor such as the Catholic Worker and San Egidio communities; and self-provisioning and communal like the Benedictines. Without some sort of common economic life among faculty and staff, considerably more money will be needed to pay salaries and labor costs.

In all of this, the economic impact, viability, and witness of an EBU will depend on whether churches or other donors help finance such an experiment. Can churches provide worthwhile ways for EBU graduates to use their skills and passions? Will churches encourage their own young people to enroll in such an institution? Can churches empower mature adults in their congregations to matriculate?

Beyond Conflict: The Promise of an Ecclesially Based University

An EBU is both consequence of and contributor to the wide-ranging renewal of Christianity now underway across North America and elsewhere. Much of the significance of the EBU model will depend on the nature of relations between the churches and this new sort of educational institution.

An EBU might help churches to examine, articulate, and perhaps transform their mission and vocation (intra- and extra-ecclesial) in contemporary circumstances. An ongoing process of discernment and assessment might enable churches to prioritize their aspirations and needs while the EBU adjusts its initiatives and agenda to better serve the body of Christ. Certainly the plethora of consultancies, foundation-sponsored initiatives, and parachurch organizations devoted to helping congregations understand their vocations and priorities attests to the felt need for assistance in these matters. With curricular and extracurricular offerings designed in part with ecclesial aspirations in mind, an EBU could become in practice what previous attempts at Christian education hoped to be: a place where the church "does its thinking."

Similarly, an EBU could become a locus for church-centered social and scientific analysis, for cultural production and investigation. It could generate books, journals, symposia, and public events of many sorts aimed at aiding and supporting the activities of believing communities. In its commitment to intellectual work at the service of the church, it might model the kinds of conversations that congregations might want to establish in their own common life.

By making Christian formation an intrinsic part of the educational process, an EBU could play a crucial role in restructuring sections of the Christian laity, and perhaps even the clergy. New possibilities and pastoral experiments might emerge from a more theologically and spiritually equipped laity able to entertain multiple analytic and practical possibilities (e.g., conventional understandings of poverty alleviation compared to those from a more ecclesiocentric perspective).

The formation objectives of an EBU might also help reconfigure the often unhelpful divides between curricular activities, matters of "student life" (e.g., campus ministry), and community engagement. One could imagine sustained attention to matters of communal and individual spiritual discipline explored simultaneously in courses in theology, politics, and psychology, joined by campus and community tutorials/retreats on various traditions and practices of such disciplines (e.g. liturgy of the hours, ascetic disciplines, scripture-based prayer practices). These sorts of endeavors would also join campus and congregations in new and creative ways without concerns on either side about lost autonomy or purpose.

An EBU could also serve as an artistic and creative patron and center, encouraging everything from music and dance to drama, painting, and much more. An EBU could function as a crucial patronal buffer between creative Christians and the whims of the marketplace, the dictates of which have reduced much contemporary Christian artistic production to piety-glossed knockoffs of commodified cultural products (e.g., Christian rap music, Christian romance novels). Although there are a few places where Christianity and the arts join in a lively concern (one thinks of journals like *Image,* for example), places for creative Christians to find enrichment, challenge, and hospitality are few indeed. An EBU could be such a place, with beneficial consequences for students, congregations, and Christian artists, musicians, and cultural producers.

Part of the social and cultural impact of an EBU will likely depend on the specifics of its curriculum. For example, one could envision an EBU responding to the service-learning movement in higher education by constructing its own variant. An EBU service-learning curriculum might include "downward mobility" internships and work, tied to the ministries and initiatives of churches working with the poorest and most marginalized populations (more important, beginning to equip students with the dispositions and desires to work in such settings for the long haul on a full-time basis). An EBU approach to service learning might also involve a "house of hospitality" on campus as part of the institutional vocation of the school, supported by the labor and resources of the university, its students, faculty, and staff.

One could also imagine an EBU witnessing to society and the church by developing a variant on study abroad programs that inculcate among students an appreciation for the transnational nature of the church and the importance of cross-national ecclesial solidarity.

Additionally, the social impact of an EBU would be shaped by whether and to what extent the institution acted as a free space for transracial Christian unity, solidarity, and reconciliation. An EBU ought to have racial justice and reconciliation as an essential part of its vision; to the extent that an EBU can engage the creativity and longings of Christian congregations across racial and ethnic divides, to that extent it not only helps itself but also contributes to healing the racial lacerations in the church universal. More than just another interracial program of Christian friendliness, an EBU might unleash new energies bonded by a common purpose and project.

Conclusion

An experiment like this one—imaging the particulars of an ecclesially centered institution of higher learning—involves not only the scholars assembled here but also Christian pastors, leaders, and institutions committed to comparable ecclesiologies. Given favorable circumstances and generous participation by the Holy Spirit, a book like this one might help engender one or more of the following:

- a new standpoint from which to assess existing Christian colleges and universities;

- new sorts of programs or innovations within existing Christian institutions of higher learning;

- the willingness to launch new initiatives in Christian institution-building. These might range from fairly modest efforts (a summer institute built around discipleship-centered learning, teaching, and transformation) to somewhat more ambitious efforts (for example, creating new colleges or centers within existing ecclesial or educational structures), and perhaps to comprehensive projects (setting up an ecclesially based university from the ground up).

Whatever does or does not follow from this volume, at a minimum we hope to shift the terms of discussion onto different and—one hopes—more productive terrain. We see no need to argue further that, in most cases, the Christian component of Christian higher education is too diluted and marginal to ignite conversion of lives and communities in church or academy. We hope this volume opens up possibilities beyond the counsel that Christian scholarship should be indistinguishable from its secular counterparts, leaving one's faith simply to frame one's choice of research topics and interpersonal dealings. And by outlining what an ecclesially based university might be like, we hope to move some people beyond the sense of resignation and futility that concludes the best one can hope for is a vestigial Christian presence that finds expression in service learning and peace-and-justice programs devoid of Christian particularity or ecclesial practices.

In times like ours, sometimes the most pragmatic path is to refuse the straitjacket of being realistic, if that realism presupposes abandoning the ends to which one is committed as the price of entry. For those of us who yet maintain that discipleship and higher learning need one another in ways existing arrangements are unable or unwilling to accommodate, the most pragmatic choice is clearly to change the existing arrangements or create new institutional space for innovation and prototypes. There may yet be a road from here if we are willing to make one.

∎ Notes

1. Michael Budde and Robert Brimlow, *Christianity Incorporated* (Grand Rapids: Brazos, 2002).

2. Cecelia O'Leary and Tony Pratt, "Pledging Allegiance: The Revival of Prescriptive Patriotism," *Social Justice* 28, no. 3 (2001): 41.

3. John Cogan, "Civic Education in the United States: A Brief History," *International Journal of Social Education* 14, no. 1 (1999).

4. Tyll Van Geel, "Citizenship Education and the Free Exercise of Religion," *Akron Law Review* 34, no.1 (2000).

5. Ibid.

6. Ibid.

7. Robert Putnam, *Bowling Alone: The Collapse and Revival of American Community* (New York: Simon and Schuster, 2001).

8. Gary Rhoades and Sheila Slaughter, "Academic Capitalism, Managed Professionals, and Supply-Side Higher Education," in Randy Martin, ed., *Chalk Lines: The Politics of Work in the Managed University* (Durham, N.C.: Duke University Press, 1998), p. 33.

9. See Cogan, "Civic Education."

10. Noam Chomsky et al., *The Cold War and the University* (New York: The New Press, 1997).

11. O'Leary and Platt, "Pledging Allegiance," p. 41.

12. Ibid.

13. American Council of Trustees and Alumni, "Defending Civilization: How Our Universities Are Failing America and What Can Be Done About It," 2001. Available at www.goacta.org. See also Paul Street, "Defending Civilization and the Myth of Radical Academia," *ZNet,* July 15, 2002. Available at www.zmag.org.

14. Michael Kelly, "Pacifist Claptrap," *Washington Post,* September 26, 2001, A-25.

15. Lance Morrow, "The Case for Rage and Retribution," *Time,* September 12, 2001.

16. Anne Coulter, "This Is War: We Should Invade Their Countries," *Universal Press Syndicate,* September 13, 2001.

Contributors

Wes Avram
*Stephen Merrell Clement-E. William
Muehl Professor of Communication*
Yale University Divinity School

Robert W. Brimlow
Associate Professor of Philosophy
St. John Fisher College

Michael Budde
*Professor, Department
of Political Science*
DePaul University

Michael G. Cartwright
*Dean of Ecumenical and Interfaith
Programs and Associate Professor
of Philosophy and Religion*
University of Indianapolis

William T. Cavanaugh
Associate Professor of Theology
University of St.Thomas

Stephen E. Fowl
*Professor and Chair
of the Department of Theology*
Loyola College in Maryland

Amy Laura Hall
*Assistant Professor
of Theological Ethics*
Duke University Divinity School

Barry Harvey
Associate Professor of Theology
Baylor University

M. Therese Lysaught
*Associate Professor, Department
of Religious Studies*
University of Dayton

John Milbank
*Research Professor in Religion,
Politics and Ethics*
University of Nottingham

Scott H. Moore
*Associate Professor of Philosophy
and Director, Great Texts Program*
Baylor University

Elizabeth Newman
Professor of Theology and Ethics
Baptist Theological Seminary at
Richmond

Jonathan R. Wilson
Professor of Theology and Ethics
Acadia Divinity College
Wolfville, Novia Scotia

John W. Wright
*Professor, Department
of Philosophy and Religion*
Point Loma Nazarene University